God of Nature and of Grace

God of Nature and of Grace

Reading the World in a Wesleyan Way

Michael Lodahl

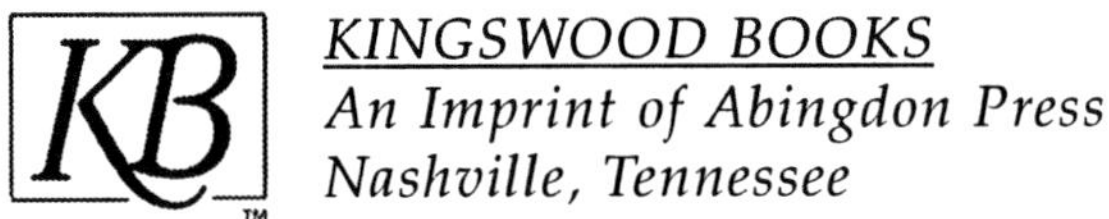

KINGSWOOD BOOKS

An Imprint of Abingdon Press

Nashville, Tennessee

GOD OF NATURE AND OF GRACE:
READING THE WORLD IN A WESLEYAN WAY

This book is printed on acid-free, elemental-chlorine–free paper.

Library of Congress Cataloging-in-Publication Data

Lodahl, Michael E., 1955-
God of nature and of grace : reading the world in a Wesleyan way / Michael Lodahl.
p. cm.
Includes bibliographical references and index.
ISBN 0-687-06666-2 (adhesive binding : alk. paper)
1. Nature—Religious aspects—Methodist Church. 2. Methodist Church—Docrines. 3. Wesley, John, 1703-1791. I. Title.
BX8349.N38L63 2004
231.7—dc22 2003012845

03 04 05 06 07 08 09 10 11 12—10 9 8 7 6 5 4 3 2 1

MANUFACTURED IN THE UNITED STATES OF AMERICA

For
Christian Lodahl (1901–2002)
and
Kenneth Lodahl (1936–)
laborers of the land

CONTENTS

Note on Titles

The title of this book and the titles of most chapters come either directly from lines of hymns penned by one or both of the brothers John and Charles Wesley, or are at least allusions to such poetic lines. Indeed, nearly all of the titles come from one hymn, No. 28 of Charles Wesley's *Hymns of Petition and Thanksgiving for the Promise of the Father,* written in 1746. One might wish that Methodists of all stripes would still sing at least some of its verses!

Author of every work divine / Who dost through both Creations shine.
The God of nature and of grace.
Thy glorious steps in all we see / And wisdom attribute to Thee,
And power and majesty, and praise.

Thou didst Thy mighty Wings outspread, / And brooding o'er the Chaos, shed
Thy Life into th' impregn'd Abyss;
The Vital Principle infuse, / And out of Nothing's womb produce
The Earth and Heaven, and all that is.

That All-informing Breath Thou art / Who dost Continued Life impart,
And bidst the World persist to be:
Garnished by Thee yon azure Sky / And all those beauteous Orbs on high
Depend in Golden Chains from Thee.

Thou dost create the Earth anew, / Its Maker and Preserver too,
By thine Almighty Arm sustain;

Nature perceives Thy secret Force, / And still holds on her even Course,
And owns Thy Providential Reign.

Thou art the Universal Soul, / The Plastick Power that fills the whole,
And governs Earth, Air, Sea, and Sky,
The Creatures all Thy Breath receive, / And who by Thy Inspiring live,
Without Thy Inspiration die.

Spirit Immense, Eternal Mind, / Thou on the Souls of lost Mankind
Dost with benignest Influence move,
Pleased to restore the ruined Race, / And new-create a World of Grace
In all the Image of Thy Love.

Abbreviations for Wesley's Writings

Letters (Telford)	*The Letters of the Rev. John Wesley, A.M.* Edited by John Telford. 8 volumes. London: Epworth, 1931.
NT Notes	*Explanatory Notes Upon the New Testament.* 3rd corrected edition. Bristol: Graham and Pine, 1760–62 (many later reprints).
OT Notes	*Explanatory Notes Upon the Old Testament.* 3 volumes. Bristol: W. Pine, 1765; reprinted Salem, Oh.: Schmul, 1975.
Works	*The Bicentennial Edition of the Works of John Wesley.* Editor in Chief, Frank Baker. Nashville: Abingdon, 1984– (Volumes 7, 11, 25, and 26 originally appeared as the *Oxford Edition of The Works of John Wesley.* Oxford: Clarendon, 1975–83). 16 of 35 vols. published to date.
Works (Jackson)	*The Works of John Wesley.* 14 volumes. Edited by Thomas Jackson. London, 1872; reprint, Grand Rapids: Zondervan, 1958.

INTRODUCTION

This is a book on the doctrine of creation. It seems appropriate, then, that it should have a distinct and specific genesis! It all began like this:

Nearly a decade ago now, while attending the annual national meeting of the American Academy of Religion, I decided to drop in on a panel discussion on religion and ecology. This was a topic whose importance had already begun to impress itself upon me, and I expected to be further informed, stimulated, and challenged to take ever more seriously, as a theological issue, the human role in protecting and sustaining the living systems of our planet. I could not have expected the personal apocalypse awaiting me.

One of the panelists was Catherine Keller, a young theologian teaching at Drew University. During her presentation she recounted being at home one day, occupied with trying to pick up a clear signal from her favorite jazz station on the radio dial. Apparently the station had little potency or else was too distant, for it was being overtaken repeatedly by a Christian radio station's signal. To her chagrin, Keller's preferred jazz was losing the battle of the airwaves to a call-in program in which a preacher, styling himself an expert on matters pertaining to the afterlife, was fielding listeners' questions. While engaged in her fine-tuning efforts—unsuccessfully—Keller heard a woman's question that got her attention: "Will there be animals in heaven?"

The radio preacher's reply was swift, short, authoritative, and mildly derisive. *Of course not*. There will be no animals in heaven, because they are here only in this life for human use and advantage. We will have no need of them in the world to come! Further, heaven and hell have to do with the destinies of immortal souls, which animals most assuredly do not possess. Finally, he pronounced, anyone who would ask such a question clearly has not reached the level of spirituality that recognizes how utterly beneath us all animals are!

Keller commented, "It is my guess that, while the woman asked a general question, she had a particular pet, perhaps a dog or a cat, in mind." Keller had been put off by the tone of the preacher's reply, to say nothing of its content. "Further," she then added, "he would have had a different answer if he'd read some of John Wesley."

At the mention of Wesley's name my ears opened wide; I had not at all expected to hear Wesley invoked in an academic discussion of the ecological implications of religious teaching and practice! What could Wesley, the great evangelist and founder of the Methodist movement in eighteenth-century England, possibly contribute to this topic? Further, who would have expected Keller, a young and obviously brilliant feminist philosopher and theologian, to bring him up? And what was it of Wesley's works that she had in mind?

For me to have asked that question, of course, immediately makes it clear that I was no expert in Wesley. But I had been raised and nurtured in the Church of the Nazarene, a denomination that identifies itself as Wesleyan, and had been educated, at both the undergraduate and seminary levels, in schools sponsored by my home denomination. I had heard of Wesley before college, read about him in college, and then read a fair amount of his material—and heard a good many lectures thereupon!—in seminary, but I still had no idea what it was of Wesley that Keller had in mind. Ruminating on her radio story, I wondered if my theology teachers had sent out a weak signal—or if, on the other hand, I simply had not been tuned in to the right frequency to hear them! Perhaps I simply had not had ears to hear?

When the AAR session ended, my curiosity got the best of me and I slowly sidled up to the podium to ask Keller about her passing reference to Wesley. She simply replied, "A sermon, the one called 'The General Deliverance.'"[1] I made a mental note of it and soon afterward read the sermon for what I am sure was the very first time. I was blown away. It marked for me the beginning of a whole new way of reading John Wesley.

"The General Deliverance," penned in 1781—when Wesley was 78 years old!—is a bold proclamation of Paul's Romans 8 text about the groans of creation and a divine promise of liberation and redemption for this material world (8:18-23). The Romans passage, and this sermon of Wesley's that is now being widely cited in the circles of ecological theology,[2] will assuredly receive abundant attention in this book. Important as that sermon is to the overall tack of this book, it hardly functions alone. In fact, my reading of that sermon encouraged me to begin to look at Wesley with different eyes, to seek out sermons and themes in Wesley's ministry that placed an unexpectedly vibrant emphasis upon God's always creative, intimately sustaining, and ultimately saving relationship to creation as a whole. To explore those often unrecognized themes in Wesley, and to argue for their contemporary relevance to Christians of the Wesleyan tradition and beyond, has been a compelling agenda for me in the ensuing years. This book represents the culmination of that agenda.

This project actually received a further, equally unexpected jolt a couple of years after hearing Keller's comment. I was part of a conference on Wesley Studies in which Claremont theologian Marjorie Hewitt Suchocki was the keynote speaker. Our assignment was to wrestle with the question, "What is missing in our Methodist and Wesleyan churches?" In her plenary address Suchocki answered the question simply, "John Wesley is!" She then proceeded with a compelling, rapturous retelling of Wesley's little classic, *A Plain Account of Christian Perfection*, arguing that the book deserved careful study in Methodist churches everywhere. What was so

---

1. That is the experience, and the conversation with Keller, as best I remember it. It is a particular pleasure, and a fitting end to this vignette, for me to mention that Keller has recently published a marvelously insightful, typically creative, and eminently imaginative book on chaos and creation, *Face of the Deep* (New York and London: Routledge, 2002).

2. Just a few of the recent books that cite Wesley's "The General Deliverance" include Andrew Linzey's *Animal Theology* (Urbana: University of Illinois Press, 1995), Jay B. McDaniel's *Of God and Pelicans: A Theology of Reverence for Life* (Louisville: Westminster/ John Knox, 1989), and James A. Nash's *Loving Nature: Ecological Integrity and Christian Responsibility* (Nashville: Abingdon, 1991).

memorable about her address was that she really made Wesley *alive* by reading him through a new lens—an overtly feminist, process-relational lens. And it was good, very good.[3]

Through the delightful influence of these two theologians—who share, despite their differences, a committed feminist perspective and a generally Whiteheadian, process-relational metaphysic—I was becoming increasingly convinced that Wesley's vision of divine salvation was far wider than the individualism and personalism I had imbibed during my nurture and education in the Wesleyan-holiness movement of Christianity. There was something much bigger here! I was finding a Wesley who understood salvation as *salve*-ation, as God's *present* salving and healing of human lives and relationships through Jesus Christ in the power of the Holy Spirit *in this world*. Further, it appeared that in Wesley's mature years, this salvation was increasingly understood to be a salving not only *in* this world but *of* this world, this creation.[4]

Hence, this book. I am the first to admit that the reflections that follow bear the influence, the *in-flowing* into my life and thinking, of process-relational thought.[5] In fact, one of the subthemes of this work is its exploration of the ways in which, and the extent to which, Wesley's sermons are amenable to a process theological reading. I am not pretending that Wesley was a proto-process thinker, but I would be far from the first to note the interesting resonances between Wesley and the followers of Whitehead. It is a resonance explored by Suchocki in an early article, by John B. Cobb Jr. in his 1995 work *Grace and Responsibility: A Wesleyan Theology for Today*, and most recently in an edited volume exploring the

3. It would be difficult for Suchocki to match in print the swirling, virtually dancing portrayal she offered of Wesley's *Plain Account* that day, but a reasonable approximation is found in "Holiness and a Renewed Church," her chapter contribution to *The Church with AIDS*, ed. Letty Russell (Louisville: Westminster/John Knox, 1990), 109-21.

4. For a concise treatment of the developing importance in Wesley's own thinking of this theme of creation's ultimate salving, see Randy L. Maddox, *Responsible Grace: John Wesley's Practical Theology* (Nashville: Kingswood Books, 1994), 235-40.

5. The best technical introduction to process theology remains *Process Theology: An Introductory Exposition*, coauthored by John B. Cobb Jr. and David Griffin (Philadelphia: Westminster, 1976). For a more accessible, readily digestible introduction, see Marjorie Suchocki, *In God's Presence: Theological Reflections on Prayer* (St. Louis: Chalice, 1996). The reader who finds that book helpful might proceed to her earlier and more challenging, but deeply rewarding, *God—Christ—Church: A Practical Guide to Process Theology* (New York: Crossroad, 1984).

(dis)relationships between Wesley and the ideas of contemporary process theologians.[6] In many ways, I offer this book as a continuation of the conversation already underway.

There is one other theologian who merits mention when it comes to considering the possibilities of wedding Wesley and Whitehead: the broadly processive, proto-feminist Nazarene theologian Mildred Bangs Wynkoop (1905–97). Wynkoop's influence upon a generation of Wesleyan students—Methodists, Nazarenes, and many others—is indisputable. What sometimes goes unnoticed is Wynkoop's debt to process theology, a debt that she somewhat tentatively admitted in the preface of her classic in twentieth-century Wesleyan reflection, *A Theology of Love: The Dynamic of Wesleyanism.* Citing the considerable influence of Daniel Day Williams's *The Spirit and the Forms of Love* upon her theological development, Wynkoop wrote,

> "Process Theology" makes a much needed correction to the dualisms of a former day. It is my considered opinion that, though the metaphysical foundation of process thought is not the only solution to theological problems, its insights are inescapable in a biblical theology. The *dynamic* emphasis in relation to God, man, love, grace, nature, and salvation and interpersonal relations is crucial to the Christian faith.[7]

Given Wynkoop's admission of process influence within her, it is no great surprise that Cobb, the leading Christian process theologian of the twentieth century, should have written that he is "in substantial agreement . . . with [Wynkoop's] understanding of Wesley."[8]

Nonetheless, despite her championing of process theology's "correction [of] the dualisms of a former day," there is a dualism

6. See Suchocki, "Coming Home: Wesley, Whitehead and Women," *Drew Gateway* 57.3 (Fall 1987): 31-43; see also John B. Cobb Jr., *Grace and Responsibility: A Wesleyan for Theology Today* (Nashville: Abingdon, 1995); and the collection of essays edited by Brian P. Stone and Thomas Jay Oord, *Thy Nature and Thy Name Is Love: Wesleyan and Process Theologies in Dialogue* (Nashville: Kingswood Books, 2001), in which the aforementioned Suchocki article has been reprinted.

7. Mildred Bangs Wynkoop, *A Theology of Love: The Dynamic of Wesleyanism* (Kansas City, Mo.: Beacon Hill, 1972), 11.

8. Cobb, *Grace and Responsibility*, 168.

that Wynkoop's work did not overcome. To put it simply, her theology and anthropology lacked a cosmology. Though influenced by process thought, she tended strongly to fixate on God, human beings, and the various possible relations among them. Missing, for the most part, was any richer sense of creation as the setting in which and whereby such relations occur—indeed, of creation as itself an infinitely complex process of becoming through its vast and dense network of relations.[9] What was missing in Wynkoop's thinking three decades ago was *the world.*

* * *

It is this world of ours, in all of its own rich interrelations as well as its thoroughly graced relation to God, that I hope to consider deeply in the nine chapters that compose this book. The chapters are gathered into three sections entitled *Making, Molding,* and *Mending*. Beyond whatever alliterative value this triple rubric might possess, my intent is to use terms that evoke God as Creator, Sustainer, and Fulfillment of all things—and yet to do so with verbs that bespeak an earthy, "hands-on" ambience. Further, I hope that the use of the gerund form might evoke a sense of the continuing, ongoing, ever-creative hands of God laboring to bring forth a truly good and radically renewed creation. The psalmist declared that God knit each of us together in our mother's wombs, and virtually in the same breath that we were all "intricately woven in the depths of the earth" (Ps. 139:13, 15). God the Weaver reaches deeply into our mothers, indeed into our great mother Earth, to knit us together with great care. It would be wrongheaded to assume that the knitting process is ever completed! God is ever making, molding, and mending us—and, indeed, all of creation—toward the divine image of love embodied in Jesus Christ. We are written on God's hands (Isa. 49:16), and the burden of this book is to demonstrate that, for John Wesley, it was increasingly the case that *all of creation and all of its creatures* are inscribed into the bruised and bloodied hands of God in Jesus Christ, the Living One.

---

9. I have explored these themes in greater detail in "The Whiteheadian Wesley and the Evangelical Wesley: Can They Give Each Other Their Hands?" (Unpublished manuscript of a lecture presented in February 1998 at the Center for Process Students at Claremont School of Theology, Claremont, CA; available on-line at www.ctr4process.org).

Under *Making,* then, I attempt to explore the theme of God as Creator from a Wesleyan perspective. Chapter 1 provides a theological exegesis of Psalm 104, a creation psalm that sheds light on the cosmology and theology of ancient Middle Eastern peoples. This in turn provides a helpful lens for reading the opening chapters of the Bible in a Wesleyan way, which is the subject of chapter 2. In chapter 3, I wrestle with the most obvious point of contention between process theology and traditional orthodoxy in regard to the doctrine of creation—the idea of *creatio ex nihilo.* I hope to show how some of the distinctive hues in Wesley's theology help bridge the differences between process thought and Christian tradition on this point.

In the second section, *Molding,* I turn to the theological ideas that cluster around the proposition that God is the Sustainer of all creation. In chapter 4 I argue that Wesley's doctrine of salvation was deeply rooted in his understanding of God as the intimately present Sustainer, probably best encapsulated in that allusive line of Acts 17:28, "In [God] we live and move and have our being." Throughout the book I will name that sustaining presence of God *creative grace.* In chapter 5, then, I reflect upon this notion of creative grace in relation to the radical newness announced and embodied in the gospel of Christ. If the good God who calls creation "good" from the beginning is also sustaining the entirety of creation by intimate presence, then we are challenged to think about what new possibilities are provided for the world through the coming of Jesus Christ. This leads naturally into chapter 6, which provides a close textual-theological reading of one of the table graces penned by the Wesley brothers. The entire poem of eight stanzas offers a profound meditation upon the goodness of creation, the human fall into idolatrous relations with our fellow creatures, the coming of the Second Adam to redeem and restore us and all creation, and thus finally the possibilities of living in God's glorious creation by the powers of divine grace in Christ.

The last section, *Mending,* invites us to reflection upon eschatology. In chapter 7 I argue that Wesley's understanding of grace as cooperative or, in Randy Maddox's term, "responsible," mitigates against an overly simplistic eschatology that simply anticipates a divine foreclosure on the world. Instead, I shall propose that a truly Wesleyan eschatology envisions God's end for the world in terms of the *telos* of ever-deepening love for God and all neighbors. In chapter 8, I take my cues primarily from Wesley's sermon "The General Deliverance" in order to suggest that there are certain theological emphases in Wesley's theology—most notably his ideas on prevenient grace, God as holy love, entire sanctification, and the witness of the Holy Spirit—that can offer important resources to ecotheology. Finally, in chapter 9, I explore Christian eschatology in light of the presently dominant cosmological models that project our universe's eventual demise. I draw again on "The General Deliverance," this time to highlight the theological implications of the Christian hope for the resurrection of the body in the world to come.

* * *

Since I intend in the chapters that follow to reflect upon the act of *reading the world in a Wesleyan way,* it may be helpful to suggest what "a Wesleyan way" might entail. I have in mind three basic elements in this particular way of reading Scripture, tradition, life, indeed the world itself.

First, this way of reading the world involves the notion of "responsible grace," already alluded to above, that Maddox has so ably championed as the "orienting concern" of Wesley's ministry and theology. Maddox has described this concern as Wesley's enduring attempt "to preserve the vital tension between two truths . . . : without God's grace, we *cannot* be saved; while without our (grace-empowered, but uncoerced) participation, God's grace *will not* save."[10] Though Wesley certainly demonstrated growing concern to broaden his vision of God's saving work to include all of creation, he did not (and could not, in his time, have been expected to) extend his ideas about God's grace toward human beings as having applicability to nonhuman creatures or to creation as a whole. With other-than-human creation, Wesley assumed, God could and did work irresistibly. However, we live now in an era where the natural sciences discourage such a bifurcation between human beings and the rest of the creaturely realm. Further, it

10. Maddox, *Responsible Grace,* 19.

makes theological sense to assume that God works with all of creation, and with every creature, in ways that bear a true analogy to the ways in which God works with us human beings. We may not know what "responsible grace" might mean in relation to a rock or a tree, but a working assumption throughout this book is that every element of creation exercises some measure of power that bears an analogy to human agency, and that God is pleased to work in such a way as to respect and to cherish those creaturely powers. Again, in this book I shall call this divine labor in and with all the world *creative grace.*

A second vital component in reading the world in a Wesleyan way has to do with God's purpose in creating a world with such powers as ours. As Theodore Runyon has argued in *The New Creation: John Wesley's Theology Today,* for Wesley divine purpose is ultimately reducible to *love.* It is the *perfection of love* that motivated and drove Wesley's ministry. As Runyon typifies Wesley's thinking, "Of course God's love is real whether it is responded to or not, yet its obvious intention is to be received and to create that bond which the reception and reciprocation of love make possible."[11] A fundamental assumption throughout this book, accordingly, is that God creates a world (and perhaps worlds) such as ours *in order that love might flourish.* But love has a possibility to flourish only where there is agency, where creaturely response is real and creaturely powers truly count for something. The sobering side of that, of course, is that agency, the power of one creature vis-à-vis another, can be harmful, even destructive. Thus, even as reading the world in a Wesleyan way encourages us to great hope for the possibilities of love in God's creation, that hope is tempered by the realism of radically contrary possibilities.

Finally, I submit that reading the world in a Wesleyan way always involves us in "practical divinity." Thomas Langford, in his book by that title, wrote that for Wesley "theology is important as it serves the interest of Christian formation. Theology is never an end, but is always a means for understanding and developing transformed living. . . . He consistently turned theological reflection

11. Theodore Runyon, *The New Creation: John Wesley's Theology Today* (Nashville: Abingdon, 1998), 26.

to practical service."[12] Divinity, or theology, that is *practical* always and inevitably involves us in *practices*—practices that "make perfect," over time, our love for God and all neighbors. The practices, or habitual activities, of our lives as Christian disciples are of crucial importance precisely because our agency—what we actually do moment by moment, day by day—arises out of our divinely intended response-ability. We have a role to play in God's presence! And even if that role boils down to a heart and life filled with love for God and neighbor, Wesley was never shy about suggesting ways, or particular practices and habits, whereby we contribute our energies toward God's project of "renewing us in love." So also in the book, I intend to stay close to our real, material lives and habits in this social, physical, graced environment in which we live.

* * *

Much of the material of these nine chapters has been tried out on a variety of listening and reading audiences over this past decade or so. I owe my greatest debt in this process to the Wesleyan Center for Twenty-First Century Studies of Point Loma Nazarene University in San Diego, California, where it is my joy to serve as a professor. The Center, under the expert direction of Maxine Walker, helped to fund the final stages of my writing with a Wesley Center Fellow research and writing grant during the summer of 2001. During the previous academic year of 2000-01, the Center commissioned me to present a four-part lecture series on "Why the World Matters to Wesleyans." Those lectures provided the initial versions of what became chapters 1, 4, and 6 of this book.

Another important institution contributing to the evolution of this work has been the Center for Theology and the Natural Sciences, a part of the Graduate Theological Union in Berkeley, California. I spent the summer and autumn of 1997 on sabbatical at CTNS, and was rewarded with many rich and stimulating conversations with some of the leading voices in the science / theology conversation—people such as Ted Peters, Robert John Russell, Mark Richardson, and Richard Randolph. They were all

12. Thomas A. Langford, *Practical Divinity: Theology in the Wesleyan Tradition* (Nashville: Abingdon, 1983), 20-21.

enthusiastically supportive of my attempts to usher Wesley into the conversation, particularly as it turned to the human role and responsibility for caring for the earth and for all of God's creation. During the sabbatical I had opportunity to present a CTNS public lecture on eschatology and contemporary cosmologies, which eventually became chapter 9 of this book. Along the way, an earlier, less developed version of chapter 8 was published in the *CTNS Bulletin*.[13] Further, CTNS bestowed a generous grant upon Point Loma Nazarene University to help fund a conference on our breathtakingly beautiful campus during the 2001-02 school year. That conference, not coincidentally called "God of Nature and of Grace: Wesleyan Perspectives on Creation," provided a context in which I could test in a public forum the ideas that were to jell as chapter 2 of this book. Thanks once again to the pioneers of the science / theology dialogue at CTNS and to wonderful friends and colleagues at Point Loma who continue that dialogue. Thanks, too, to those whose careful and critical reading of much (if not all) of this book, in various stages of its development, has been of tremendous help to me in this process. In this vein, deep gratitude goes especially to my biologist friend and colleague Rebecca Flietstra, and to two who were once my students but now, much better, are only my friends, Eric Severson and Andrew Yoder.

Chapters 5 and 7 appeared in earlier incarnations as articles in the *Wesleyan Theological Journal*,[14] and a previous version of chapter 3 was published in the volume I have already mentioned, *Thy Nature and Thy Name Is Love*.[15]

* * *

Many of my growing up years were lived on farmland and among farmers. There I learned a little of what it means to live close to the earth: to feel its dust cake on hands and face, to refresh the arid land

13. " 'The Whole Creation Groans': Is There a Distinctively Wesleyan Contribution to an Environmental Ethic?" *CTNS Bulletin* 18.2 (1998): 10-19. Material from that article is used in chapter 8 with permission.

14. Chapter 5 contains material from "The Cosmological Basis for John Wesley's 'Gradualism,' " *Wesleyan Theological Journal* 32:1 (1997): 17-32. Chapter 7 contains material from "Wesleyan Reservations about Eschatological 'Enthusiasm,' " *Wesleyan Theological Journal* 29:1-2 (1994): 50-63. The latter has been reprinted in *Heart of the Heritage: Core Themes of the Wesleyan/Holiness Tradition as Highlighted by the Wesleyan Theological Society 1965–2000*, edited by B. L. Callen and W. C. Kostlevy (Salem, Oh.: Schmul Publishing Company, 2001), 345-56. These are used with permission.

15. See footnote 6.

and one's own thirst with cooling waters, to behold the wonder of green plants growing, to ride a horse and drive a tractor. I learned these things first of all from my dad, who labored hard in the sun-baked lands of eastern Washington. He, in turn, learned them from his dad, who had come on a boat all the way from Denmark in 1926 to do in the new world what he had done in the old: to grow food for his family and for others. It is to these two choice men that I dedicate this book about dirt and water, plants and air, people and other animals—and God.

PART I
MAKING

CHAPTER 1

"THE CREATURES ALL THY BREATH RECEIVE"

The Celebration of Creation in Psalm 104

These all look to you
to give them their food in due season;
when you give to them, they gather it up;
when you open your hand, they are filled with good things.
When you hide your face, they are dismayed;
when you take away their breath, they die
and return to their dust.
When you send forth your spirit, they are created;
and you renew the face of the ground.

Psalm 104:27-30

The Creatures all Thy Breath receive,
And who by Thy Inspiring live,
Without Thy Inspiration die.

Charles Wesley, *Hymns of Petition and Thanksgiving for the Promise of the Father*, #28

To read the world in a Wesleyan way means, first of all, to read it—to interpret it, even to *feel* it—as the world God is creating in love and continues to this very moment to *love perfectly*. God's love can be described as perfect for several reasons, but certainly one of those reasons is that this love embraces and enfolds all creatures and excludes absolutely none. Wesleyans, after all, still love the

Charles Wesley hymn that praises the Maker of all things as "Love Divine, all loves excelling." Accordingly, John Wesley loved to cite Psalm 145:9 (ESV), "[The Lord's] mercy is over *all* of his works"—and just as he interpreted the "all" of God's works as inclusively as he possibly could, so shall we in this book.

So, we are encouraged by the Wesley brothers to read the world as God's beloved creation, enfolded in God's everlasting love in its most minute details. But perhaps we should ask, *What does it mean to "read" the world?* Broadly speaking, human beings—and a great many other sorts of earthlings as well—are readers of their world. In every moment of experience, we all engage in the act of "reading": we sift through a host of sensory (and often nonsensory) data, sorting for meaningful signs among a vast confusion of signifiers, interpreting them in light of experiences of the past, expectations of the present, and anticipations of the future, trying to make a little sense of it all. Usually we do this without giving the processes involved much attention. But it is nonetheless true that we *interpret our way* through life, attempting ever and again to navigate its sometimes strange waters, to find our way, to arrive at satisfactory readings of life's intricacies and mysteries. We read not only newspapers, books, and magazines—not only printed words. Perhaps, in fact, if we exert too much of our energies in reading texts (if we become overly "bookish"!) we dull the edge of our abilities to read the rest of the world.[1] It is apparent, for example, that human life is fitted to "read" the weather and other phenomena of nature, as well as other people's moods, vocal tones, and body language. We try to read "the signs of the times." We read our pet animals' behaviors, and we also read stop signs, yield signs, perhaps even occasionally speed limit signs! Sometimes at least some of us seem able to read other people's minds, especially people whom we love and with whom we have long shared together in life. We are interpreters, reading our way through the bustling morass of sounds, sights, smells, words, lights, and relations that intersect and intersplice our lives. In an important sense, it is precisely our *reading of the world* in all of its buzzing complexities of bundles of experience

1. See David Abram, *The Spell of the Sensuous: Perception and Language in a More-Than-Human World* (New York: Pantheon, 1996).

that gives to us a world in the first place—a world of often fragile and tenuous meanings, a world that we try to shape into relatively predictable and manageable patterns.

It is impossible for anyone to read the world without some set of spectacles: the language we first learn, the stories our tribes tell, the traditions of life and practice that shape our becoming, the commonsense wisdom that our mother culture bequeaths to us. We learn to read the world by *being taught how* to read the world as our families, our cultures, our peoples have read it. Obviously, not all persons read the world in the same way. The world does not simply present itself in obvious clarity and precise meanings—it is, after all, the world's ambiguities, mysteries, and elusive signs that make interpretation a necessity to begin with! And the burden of interpretation inevitably gives birth to a variety of readings, a host of ways to navigate existence, an overwhelmingly vast panoply of avenues of meaning.

People of faith, of course, are not exempt from this burden of interpretation. We too have been taught to read the world in particular ways. For instance, we learn to confess with the psalmist that "the heavens are telling the glory of God,/ and the firmament proclaims his handiwork" (Ps. 19:1), and in so doing we affirm creation's capacity for bearing witness to its Creator. But we should remember that it is a written psalm, a text, that instructs and encourages us to read the world in that way! The psalm continues, "Day to day pours forth speech,/ and night to night declares knowledge" (v. 2), suggesting yet again that the world speaks on its own terms, and *in* its own terms, about God. And perhaps the world does! Yet the ambiguity of the world's speech is underscored in the very next lines:

> There is no speech, nor are there words;
> their voice is not heard;
> yet their voice goes out through all the earth,
> and their words to the end of the world. (vv. 3, 4)

No words, no voice—*and yet* these (non)words and this (non)voice reverberate throughout creation! Further, it is not long before the psalmist moves entirely from a consideration of the world's strangely silent yet eloquent testimony to a different testimony, one a little less elusive: the Torah, God's word of precepts, commandments, and ordinances (vv. 7-11). The reader of the psalm perhaps even begins to suspect that, for the psalmist, it is in and through reading the *word* of the Torah that our eyes are better enabled to read the *world* as a testimony to the God of Israel.

All Christians read the world in certain and particular ways because they read, or at the least hear, *Scripture*. This means that we read the world with particular spectacles, the clarifying lens of Holy Writ. Like John Calvin before him, John Wesley was certain that we need divine aid in discerning the nature of God's presence and labor in the world. We cannot simply "read God" off the many faces and the myriad experiences that the world of nature presents to us. In fact, the possible meanings of such terms as "world" and "nature" vary widely and are far from self-evident. We look to our traditions to help us bear this burden of interpretation—while, to be sure, the burden must still be borne as we then attempt to interpret our texts and traditions.

How ought Christians of the Wesleyan tradition read the world? That is the primary question of this book as a whole. In this opening chapter I suggest that we begin by reading the world through the lens we are given in a wondrous but often-neglected psalm—the 104th.

I grew up memorizing Psalm 23, as have most church children. Many of the church folk of my home congregation also liked Psalm 37 a great deal. As I grew older I gravitated toward Psalm 139 and in fact preached my first, fledgling sermon on that beautiful text. But no one ever taught me to read, to ponder, to appreciate one of the most eloquent celebrations of the natural world to be found anywhere, anytime. Why did no pastor preach on Psalm 104, and why were no Sunday school sessions devoted to memorizing its lines? Is it not sufficiently "spiritual"? Is it entirely too "natural"? And what do bifurcations such as spiritual/natural tell us about how we are reading the world? Further, what was my home religious community teaching me about how to read the world?

As it turns out, *not much*. The silence of Psalm 104 in many churches, and certainly most evangelical ones, is a testimony to the reticence of many Christians to truly engage the world as beautiful, as good, as nature, as bodies. It is likely, then, that Psalm 104 is a good place to begin our quest for reading the world in a Wesleyan way; after all, Wesley did often cite many of its lines and phrases in his own writings. More important, Psalm 104 offers us a lens for beholding the world as a vast web of life continually created and renewed by the Spirit of God. It is a psalm that suggests that the world, in all of its wildness and wonder, is graced in every moment by "Love divine, all loves excelling." What follows in this chapter, then, is a handful of proposals for a Wesleyan theology of nature, all of which flow from a reading of this lovely ancient hymn—and all of which will figure significantly through the remainder of this book.

MEDITERRANEAN COSMOLOGY

The compellingly poetic imagery of Psalm 104 should help us, first of all, to appreciate the nature of the reigning cosmology among Israelites and other Mediterranean peoples of the era during which the Hebrew Bible was coming into existence. It is difficult, for example, to miss the importance of water, or "the waters," in this psalm. God is said to have laid the beams of the divine dwelling place "on the waters " (v. 3), and it should be obvious that these waters are the same as the waters of Genesis 1:7. There we read that God separated "the waters from the waters" (1:6) by an "expanse" or "dome"—essentially, a sky-ceiling. "And God said, 'Let the waters under the sky be gathered together into one place, and let the dry land appear'" (1:9).

It is crucial that we understand that Genesis 1 assumes, more or less intact, the cosmology or picture of the world that most other Mediterranean peoples assumed. It is not, to be sure, what we today would properly describe as a scientific account of the world's structure. Nonetheless, it is an extremely commonsensical picture based upon observation.

Pretend for a moment that you live by the Mediterranean Sea. You are grateful for good old solid land, because you know that people can drown in too much water. And those waters can look somewhat intimidating at times, and there is so much of it! You see the blue-green waters come rolling in, wave upon wave, ever threatening to engulf the shoreline, and you have to wonder why those waves come up to the shore and no farther. You are also grateful for the power that must be holding back those dark, churning, sometimes threatening waters.

You peer upward and see the same color above you as that of the seas. That *must* be water up there, too, with *something* holding those waters from cascading down in destructive power. While you are grateful for the "dome" above that keeps the waters from engulfing the earth below, you are grateful also that there are openings in that dome, for it is through them that some of the waters fall to nourish the earth and its fruits. You have to hope, however, that the openings do not become too large! Floods in all their destructive power are a real possibility, occurring whenever God the Creator opens the floodgates, those "windows of the heavens" (Gen. 7:11).

This cosmology, by the way, was far from unique to Israelites; in Bernhard Anderson's words, "the poet [in Psalm 104] has made use of the myth of the Creator's subduing the powers of chaos which was known in Mesopotamia and particularly in the Canaanite (Ugaritic) literature from the fourteenth century B.C."[2] What we find, then, is that Israel's priestly writers and editors found it possible to use, indeed probably to assume, the reigning "science" of their day and thereby to proclaim that their Deliverer, their Exodus God, is the Creator of all things. In the words of Wolfhart Pannenberg, "The theological doctrine of creation should take the biblical narrative as a model in that it uses the best available knowledge of nature in its own time in order to describe the creative activity of God."[3]

Despite this proclamation of God's creative power, when we begin to understand the implicit uncertainty underlying such a cosmology—"water, water everywhere!"—we begin also to appreciate just how tenuous the world could feel to Mediterranean peoples. In this cosmology, we are utterly surrounded by water, and there is only the command of God keeping all that water at bay. It is crucial to the hymnic quality of this psalm that the Creator "set the earth on its foundations, so that it shall never be shaken" (Ps. 104:5), for this is assurance in the face of the deep waters. Meanwhile, the Creator dwells even higher than the waters above

2. Bernhard W. Anderson, *Out of the Depths: The Psalms Speak for Us Today*, revised and expanded edition (Philadelphia: Westminster, 1983), 156.

3. Wolfhart Pannenberg, *Toward a Theology of Nature: Essays on Science and Faith*, edited by Ted Peters (Louisville: Westminster/John Knox, 1993), 45.

the dome (v. 3), implying that this sovereign God is well able to keep those waters in check. In verses 6-11, God is described as having appointed a place for the waters and marked a boundary they are not to cross—thanks to God, the world is stable, safe, and relatively dry! In fact, because God can channel those powerful, churning, chaotic waters there is life and sustenance for God's creatures (vv. 9-10). "In Israelite thought," writes commentator A. A. Anderson, "springs had their origin in the waters of the great abyss, so that the destructive Chaos was utilized for furthering life."[4]

In a great deal of Mesopotamia's mythic literature this taming of chaos assumes much more militant hues, such that the reigning deity has destroyed a serpent or sea monster who symbolizes or embodies the threatening, chaotic seas.[5] There are hints of this in Genesis 1 and in Psalm 104, though such hints have been considerably subdued. In the Bible's opening chapter, for example, the "great sea monsters" have been reduced from mythic stature to simple creatures of God and nothing more; our psalm even does Genesis one better and says that the sea monster ("Leviathan") has been made for divine amusement, almost like a bathtub toy (v. 26)!

Nonetheless, as Jon Levenson has demonstrated in his provocative study *Creation and the Persistence of Evil*, the element of struggle against the monsters of the chaotic deep is not entirely dispensed with in the Hebraic tradition.[6] Psalm 89:9-10 can offer up confident praise, "You rule the raging of the sea;/ when its waves rise, you still them./ You crushed Rahab like a carcass." But Psalm 74, which celebrates the same victorious theme, is a lament that begins with the cry, "O God, why do you cast us off forever?" (v. 1). Later on this outcrying to God becomes a reminder (for God *and* for the people?) of victorious divine power: "You divided the sea by your might;/ you broke the heads of the dragons in the waters./ You crushed the heads of Leviathan;/ you gave him as food for the creatures of the wilderness" (vv. 13-14). This theme becomes even more obvious in a text like Isaiah 51:9-10:

---

4. A. A. Anderson, *The New Century Bible Commentary: Psalms (73–150)* (Grand Rapids: Eerdmans, 1972), 721.

5. See Norman Cohn, *Cosmos, Chaos and the World to Come: The Ancient Roots of Apocalyptic Faith* (New Haven: Yale University Press, 1993).

6. Jon D. Levenson, *Creation and the Persistence of Evil: The Jewish Drama of Divine Omnipotence* (HarperSanFrancisco, 1988).

Awake, awake, put on strength,
  O arm of the LORD!
Awake, as in days of old,
  the generations of long ago!
Was it not you who cut Rahab in pieces,
  who pierced the dragon?
Was it not you who dried up the sea,
  the waters of the great deep;
who made the depths of the sea a way
  for the redeemed to cross over?

It is clear that in texts such as these, the people are reminding God of former victories over the chaotic and destructive powers threatening their world, and essentially are begging God to "Do it again!" Ronald Simkins writes in his book *Creator and Creation: Nature in the Worldview of Ancient Israel*:

> In God's battle against chaos, whatever form it might take, God defeats but does not annihilate chaos. God merely confines or restricts chaos to fixed bounds. Chaos remains a latent element within the creation, ready to break its fetters and wreak havoc on the creation. . . . Consequently, the Israelites, or their ancient Near Eastern neighbors for that matter, did not perceive the world as a static creation—created once at the beginning of time. This creation is repeatedly being threatened by chaotic forces, and so God, as its creator, must repeatedly fight in new cosmogonic battles.[7]

Whatever else we might say, we must say that this is not the cosmology that we assume today—not exactly the way we read the world. We do not assume that there are waters abundant above a sky-ceiling suspended overhead. Nor should it be claimed that this once was a scientifically accurate cosmology in the earliest, pre-Flood world, as so-called "creation scientists" claim, as though after the Flood all of those waters above got emptied onto the earth. Psalm 104, after all, is still assuming a "waters above, waters below" cosmology long after the supposed time of the Flood. For that matter, there is no reason to assume that Genesis 1 purports to offer a

7. Ronald A. Simkins, *Creator and Creation: Nature in the Worldview of Ancient Israel* (Peabody, Mass.: Hendrickson, 1994), 109.

picture of the world that would very soon be undergoing radical structural change. In other words, Genesis 1 is not an attempt to describe how the world was in the very beginning; it is an attempt to portray how the world *is*. The Hebrew people believed, like other Mediterranean peoples, that the world was a large hunk of land with waters "separated" to the side, waters above the firmament or sky-ceiling, and waters below the land. That was how they read the evidence that the world's appearances offered them at the time—or, more precisely, that was how their cultures, their languages, their peoples taught each succeeding generation to read the world.

A careful look at the cosmology operative in both Genesis 1 and Psalm 104 (and in most of the Hebrew Bible, for that matter), if read straightforwardly and plainly, makes it clear that we are dealing with a typically ancient Mediterranean way of understanding the world. Given the nature of this ancient picture of the world, those who today attempt to read Genesis 1 as a strictly scientific or literal description of our world's beginnings are doing severe injustice to the biblical text as well as to the contemporary scientific enterprise. If we can see that the biblical writers assumed the prevailing cosmology of Mediterranean peoples as they proclaimed the God of Israel, we should also see that Pannenberg is correct to indicate that we would not be following the biblical precedent if we "simply stuck to a standard of information about the world that became obsolete long ago by further progress of experience and methodical knowledge."[8] The poetic nature of the Psalms and the Prophets may help us to see the Bible's creation theology far less in terms of historical-literal description and far more in terms of lyrical praise to God. Thus it must be said: any attempt to read this ancient cosmology as a legitimate scientific alternative to contemporary scientific observation and theory is misguided at best and ludicrous at worst. This ancient cosmology is beautiful, but it is not science. It very well may encourage us toward profound theological convictions, but it is not offering us a literal description of the world's beginning or its continued existence. This is a fundamental assumption throughout the book in your hands, and in chapter 2 we will explore a Wesleyan rationale for its importance.

8. Pannenberg, *Toward a Theology of Nature*, 45.

PREVENIENT GRACE—THE SPIRIT IN ANCIENT EGYPT

In addition to its typical Mesopotamian cosmology, many scholars point out that Psalm 104 has remarkable similarities to an Egyptian hymn to the Aton, the sun. This "Hymn to the Aton" was discovered in a tomb at Tel el-Amarna, Egypt, the capital city of the apparently radical reforming Pharaoh Akh-en-Aton (or Amenhotep IV), who ruled for about twenty years during the first half of the fourteenth century B.C.E. It appears that this pharaoh attempted to introduce a form of monotheism to Egypt, even if rather closely associated with the sun.

If indeed the psalm's origins lie in Egyptian religious poetry, then our sensitivity to the nature of God's activity in the world—outside temple, synagogue, and church—should be broadened accordingly. For we would be reading in our own Scriptures the hints and possibilities of a theology of nature that recognizes and draws upon the rich insights and experiences of extrabiblical religious and philosophical traditions. Compare, for example, this passage from the Egyptian hymn to Psalm 104:24:

> You appear beautiful on the horizon of heaven, O living Aton,
> You who were the first to live . . .
> You created the earth according to Your will, being alone . . .
> How manifold it is, what You have made, hidden from [human] view!
> O sole God, like whom there is no other! You created the earth—
> All people, cattle and wild beasts,
> Whatever is on earth, going upon [its] feet,
> And what is on high, flying with its wings.

Or this to 104:27-30:

> The world came into being by Your hand, according as You have made them.
> When You have risen they live, when You set they die.

Out come the lions; the serpents sting.
You are lifetime Your own self, for one lives [only] through You.[9]

Or compare 104:26 to the Aton hymn's mention of "ships" that "sail upstream and downstream." Roman Catholic biblical scholar Mitchell Dahood notes that Psalm 104 has numerous typically Phoenician parallelisms and forms of expression, suggesting "an indirect Egyptian influence through Canaanite mediation, more specifically through Phoenician intervention," adding that "the Phoenicians were regularly in close commercial and cultural contact with Egypt."[10]

For some of a more conservative bent, this possibility of Egyptian-Phoenician roots for Psalm 104 may seem a dangerous and threatening notion. I would argue, however, that its presence in the Bible only helps to underscore the theological conviction that God's presence and activity are not restricted to Israel and the Church. In Wesleyan circles, of course, we locate this conviction in the doctrine of prevenient grace: that the light of God, identified in John 1 with the eternal *Logos* that became flesh in Jesus Christ, is given freely to all. In Wesley's own words, "Every man has a greater or less measure of this, which waiteth not for the call of man. . . . Everyone has some measure of that light, some faint glimmering ray, which sooner or later, more or less, enlightens every man that cometh into the world."[11] Wesley was not hesitant, for example, to treat Micah 6:5-8 essentially as a fragment of pagan oracle whose existence was due to the work of God's prevenient grace in the Moabite prophet Balaam.[12] Wesley, then, offers us a promising precedent for understanding the Egyptian precursor to Psalm 104 along those same lines: God leaves no nation without witness, doing good to all by giving "rains from heaven and fruitful seasons, satisfying [human] hearts with food and gladness" (Acts 14:17 ESV). It should be no surprise if all people demonstrate

9. Cited in B. Anderson, *Out of the Depths*, 152.

10. Mitchell Dahood, S.J., *The Anchor Bible: Psalms III: 101-150* (Garden City, N.Y.: Doubleday & Co., 1970), 33.

11. Sermon 85, "On Working Out Our Own Salvation," §III.4, *Works* 3:207.

12. Sermon 105, "On Conscience," §I.6, *Works* 3:482-83.

some awareness of the divine presence, goodness, and love through the joys and blessings of living in this world.

On the other hand, the likelihood that this psalm originated in a different, pagan context before being adapted by learned Israelites may for some people be a sufficient reason to be suspicious of its usefulness as a source for a truly Christian creation theology—perhaps it represents, instead, something of a foreign import. The counterargument is, essentially, that its importation is a *fait accompli*; this psalm, whatever its origin, is now a part of Israel's and the Church's canon, Israel's and the Church's songbook. In other words, we have in essence canonized a possibly long and complex historical process that may well have begun in an ancient Egyptian's profound wonderment about his world and his worship of what he took to be the maker and preserver of that world. "This is entirely possible," writes Claus Westermann, "because in the description of creation a point of contact with other religions is entirely understandable and meaningful."[13]

While one must be alert to the possibility of overstating this point, it is nonetheless fascinating to contemplate the implications of our now reading from our Bibles in synagogues and churches a psalm attributable, at least in part, to an ancient pagan pharaoh. Such a real possibility does indeed embody, or more precisely textualize, an important aspect of what we mean when we speak of prevenient grace. Further, this consideration raises the lively possibility that one of the most potent means of prevenient grace in the world *is* the very world itself—the world as filled with beautiful and sometimes threatening living creatures, the world as radically wild *nature*. There is no denying that the human experience of our wild, beautiful, and mysterious world can and often does have deeply moving religious implications. Perhaps this helps explain why Psalm 104 often evokes a sense of Holy Mystery not entirely dissimilar to the *Tao te Ching* when that ancient Chinese document attempts to point toward the Tao, "the Way." For example:

---

13. Claus Westermann, *The Psalms: Structure, Content, and Message* (Minneapolis: Augsburg, 1980), 95.

The myriad creatures arise from it yet it claims no authority;
It gives them life yet claims no possession; . . .
It accomplishes its task yet lays claim to no merit. . . .
It is because it lays claim to no merit that its merit never deserts it. (I/2:7)

Later in this book, particularly in chapters 4 and 5, we will look more closely at the doctrine of prevenient grace as a significant factor in reading the world in a Wesleyan way. I will, in fact, argue that this doctrinal category is of sufficient importance as to merit its own distinctive name: *creative grace.*

A COMMUNITY OF LIVING CREATURES

It should be obvious that we do not and cannot read the cosmology of this psalm as literal or scientific description. We may, nonetheless, read it as a testimony to God's creative and sustaining power at work in a vast community of living beings existing in a complex web of interrelations. And what a celebration of the community of life is Psalm 104! From birds to wild asses, from badgers to green grasses, from mountains and waters to bread and wine, from storks and goats to sun and moon and lion and Leviathan: "These all look to you to give them their food in due season" (104:27). To be sure, the food by which God feeds one creature is generally another creature a little lower on the food chain, but that does not seem to trouble the psalmist. Wesley himself commented on verse 21 that "[the lions'] roaring is a kind of natural prayer to God for relief,"[14] and this psalm insists that when relief comes it is indeed because "you open your hand [and] they are filled with good things" (v. 28). God, in other words, answers the prayers of all the creatures according to their own capacity for prayer, simple though it may be.

It is noteworthy that in this psalm human beings are simply mentioned along with the rest of God's myriad creatures; no particular importance is placed upon human existence *per se.* The extravagance of God's creative labors is celebrated for its own sake,

14. *OT Notes,* Psalm 104:21.

rather than for the sake of human utility. This hymn encourages us, then, to think about the world from a new and different angle, as James Luther Mays indicates:

> We imagine ourselves autonomous, distinct from the world and different from its creatures, disposing of it and them, not accountable to any transcendent person. We are learning slowly that we damage ourselves, live in alienation from that to which we belong, and threaten the future of life. But we cannot break out of the perspective of our current identities unless we also learn to speak to God about the world. That can be done only in the language of praise.[15]

Indeed, not all of the creatures mentioned in Psalm 104 would have possessed obvious benefits for the people who sang this hymn, and some of those creatures would have been downright threatening! Thus the vantage of the psalm is not human utility and superiority, but divine creativity and compassion. The healthy mutual respect with which lions and human beings are assumed to cooperate in the world of night and day, respectively, is a marvelous example (vv. 20-23). C. S. Lewis observes, "The thought which gives these creatures a place in the Psalmist's gusto for Nature is surely obvious. They are our fellow dependents."[16]

Fellow dependents, fellow creatures—we all depend radically upon God for life, breath, and sustenance. Thus Calvin could write of this psalm that it "describes God as acting the part of . . . a foster-father towards all sorts of living creatures, by providing liberally for them [and] cherishing all the parts of the world."[17] I point out again, however, that the provision for one creature very often demands the sacrifice of another creature—whether it be pelicans dive-bombing for a fish supper, African lions seeking their gazelle luncheon from God, or we human beings sitting down tonight at the dinner table. Something must give of its life for others to live, and thus *sacrifice* abides in the very heart of existence as we know

---

15. James Luther Mays, *Psalms*, of the *Interpretation: A Bible Commentary for Teaching and Preaching* series (Louisville: John Knox, 1994), 336.

16. C. S. Lewis, *Reflections on the Psalms* (New York: Harcourt, Brace and Co., 1958), 85.

17. John Calvin, *Commentary on the Book of Psalms* (Grand Rapids: Eerdmans, 1949), 166, 160.

it. There is indeed a vast and deep beauty in this world of God's, but it is also a harsh beauty. The psalmist neither glosses over this consumptive violence, nor glorifies it, nor offers any particular reason for it; we may assume that it is an inevitable aspect of living as creatures, among creatures, in a world of such radical interdependence as ours.

Even as we recognize the extent to which this psalm teaches us of "an intricate divine ecology into which human life itself is integrated,"[18] and thus of our humble and hopefully grateful participation in God's community of creation, it is worth remembering that it is human beings who sing this song. It is a simple fact (but an important one!) that it was human beings who composed, altered, edited, adapted, and sang this song of praise to God. Lions may seek from God their prey, and may even offer a kind of natural prayer to God, as Wesley put it, but it is human beings who are created and invited to *pray*. Indeed, even as he cited Psalm 145:9 in proclaiming that God's compassion is over all creatures, Wesley equally insisted that of all God's precious creatures it is human beings who are "capable of God . . . capable of knowing and loving and enjoying the Author of their being."[19] This is precisely what it means, according to Wesley, that we are created in God's image. Thus, we human beings are not *simply* creatures amongst myriad other creatures; we are those creatures that God intends to be the image of God in the world, the divinely called caretakers of creation.[20] This important point will be picked up and explored much more thoroughly in chapter 8.

CREATIO CONTINUA—CONTINUOUS CREATION

Psalm 104 does indeed proclaim the radical dependence of all creatures upon the Creator, but not simply for their food. All creatures, says verse 29, also look to God for God's look upon them, for it is the countenance of God facing creation that empowers the creatures *to be*. It is only as God faces the creatures that the

18. Mays, Psalms, 334.
19. Sermon 60, "The General Deliverance," §I.5, *Works* 2:441.
20. See Runyon, *New Creation*, esp. chapter 1, "The Renewal of the Image of God."

creatures' faces can receive the *ruach* of God, the Spirit/Breath of the One who blew over the face of the deep chaotic waters in Creation and in Exodus. *God's Breath is the life breath, the living Breath, of all creatures.* Hence the line of Charles Wesley's hymn that provides this chapter's title:

The creatures all Thy Breath receive,
and who by Thy Inspiring live,
without Thy Inspiration die.

To "in-spire" is, of course, to breathe into; our minds naturally and appropriately hearken back to Genesis 2, wherein Yahweh bends low to breathe "the breath of life" into the *adam* (derived from the Hebrew word for dust, *adamah,* this is a dust creature or "earthling") and through this divine inspiration, this inbreathing, the formed clay becomes "a living being" (v. 7). But if human beings live by God's breath, Psalm 104 nudges us to ask about the power of breath by which all the other creatures live. Not only human beings, but all creatures are created "when you send forth your spirit" (104:30). When God sends forth the divine Spirit/Breath, all creatures *are created!* In that line the psalm offers a tantalizingly brief taste of a notion of ongoing, continuous creation by the Spirit/Breath of God, and thus of a world that ever hangs by the marvelous threads of God's freely given and eternally creative love. God breathes the Spirit, and all the creatures live in that rich and graciously bestowed breath.

This is lovely and compelling poetry, and undoubtedly one of the most powerful statements about the intimate and ongoing relation between God and all God's creatures within Scripture. We must, however, ask what it means for us now. If we have already interpreted the cosmology of the psalm as being scientifically obsolete, how shall we understand a biology that reduces creaturely life to globs of molded dirt living on the borrowed breath of God?

Again, we can understand and appreciate the commonsensical nature of such claims. Living and breathing do indeed appear to go hand in hand! And to feel someone's breath on your cheek is not at all unlike feeling a breeze caress your face; hence, the wind that blew in from the seas and whistled across the desert was readily and understandably assumed to be God's own exhaling. Jesus was drawing on centuries of Hebraic tradition when he compared the

Spirit's birthing labors in the human heart to the wind that "blows where it chooses, and you hear the sound of it, but you do not know where it comes from or where it goes" (John 3:8). We live by breathing, and we breathe of air that often *feels breathed upon us*—and that, thought the ancients, is the breathing of God that "renew[s] the face of the ground" (104:30). This phrase in verse 30, writes Pannenberg, "identifies the divine spirit with those prolific winds which renew the surface of the ground in springtime. Yahweh's spirit had taken over this function from Baal who was a god of storm as well as of fertility."[21]

Now that human beings understand better what causes winds to blow, do we dispense with the poetry of God's continually breathing life into the creatures? Now that we understand that the blue above us is not a vast reservoir of divinely dammed waters, or that tides are related to the moon's gravitational pull and shorelines have a history grounded in plate techtonics, do we dispense with a theology of creation in which we affirm that God continually restrains the threatening powers of chaos? Now that we have some comprehension of the process of photosynthesis, need we no longer praise God for "caus[ing] grass to grow for the cattle," or "bring[ing] forth food from the earth" (104:14)?

The crucial point here is that scientific explanation should not be understood as competing with theological conviction, as though one would rule out the other. We may not be able to describe how God causes grass to grow, or holds the chaotic and destructive powers at bay, or bestows life on sentient creatures. Such activity of God is not subject to scientific description, even if and though the creatures themselves are. By the same token, we cannot force theological convictions somehow to stand in the place of scientific description. We may not want simply to appeal to mystery, but the nature of God's creative labors seems to be well past finding out. Any attempt to describe finely God's activity in the world runs the dual risk of (1) becoming obsolete in the face of subsequent scientific discovery (the great abyss into which the "God of the gaps" repeatedly has fallen) and (2) reducing God to an identifiable and manageable factor in the world, an object among other objects (as Paul Tillich so often and so deeply feared) who causes effects in the world much like any other agent.

21. Pannenberg, *Toward a Theology of Nature*, 126.

Perhaps, then, we are "reduced" to poetry. To say that we live by the breath of God is indeed theological poetry and no more a scientific statement than saying that God marked a boundary the waters should not cross (v. 9), or that God planted the cedars of Lebanon (v. 16)—a beautiful image evoking a green-thumbed deity but hardly adequate in understanding the nature of a cedar! Were we to take such statements as literal scientific description, we would be squelching the very power, joy, and wonder of this and any other hymn. And yet, beyond a literalistic reading, there is what Paul Ricoeur called a "second naiveté"—a playful and imaginative reading of Scripture that frees me to stand on the Sunset Cliffs of San Diego (as I often do!) and breathe deep of "the breath of God." I inhale the salty air, savoring the mystery of God's creative hand as I watch the waves roll in, breaking on the rocks—"this far and no further!" says God!—and feel the ocean spray on my face like waters from an ancient chaotic deep. I can sit on those cliffs and rejoice in the open hand of God as dinosauric pelicans execute their awkwardly beautiful dive-bomb fishing maneuvers whereby they "gather" and "are filled" (v. 28). Psalm 104 must be read with something of this second naiveté if its poetry is to find its place in our increasingly scientifically explained world. Of course, scientific explanations do not and cannot remove all mystery, and often evoke an even greater and deeper sense of awe before the world. My primary point here is that the biblical cosmology, rooted also in a profound sense of wonder, should not be read as a competing scientific explanation for the nature and processes of our world. It is poetry, addressed to God in praise.

Such poetic sensibility can, I believe, lead us to theological conviction. Walter Brueggemann writes, for example, of the psalm under our consideration:

> The whole world is daily dependent on God's sustenance, God's face, God's presence, God's breath. The world is impressive and to be celebrated. But it has no independent existence. It is genuinely creation, i.e., always referred to the Creator. The world is well-ordered and reliable. But on its own, it has no possibility of survival or well-being. All of that is daily gift.[22]

---

22. Walter Brueggemann, *The Message of the Psalms* (Minneapolis: Augsburg, 1984), 32.

Indeed, we might press Brueggemann further to say that the world is not only "daily dependent" and "daily gift," but that it is *in every moment* and *in finest detail* utterly and intimately dependent upon God's preserving and sustaining empowerment. Again, this cannot be scientifically demonstrated, but it is a root conviction in our doctrine of God as Creator. This in turn implies a continual process of re-creation whereby God continually bestows not simply *life* but the very *being* of all things and of creation as a whole. Thus Wesley in his 1788 sermon "On the Omnipresence of God" could claim that this omnipresent One "acts everywhere . . . by sustaining all things, without which everything would in an instant sink into its primitive nothing."[23]

Whether with Wesley we call it "primitive nothing," or instead hew more closely to the Hebraic metaphor of "dust," the point remains the same: all creatures are *being given being* by their Creator, and that continually. "When you take away their breath," says verse 29, "[the creatures] die and return to their dust"—they breathe out their last, because their breathing depends upon the continual breathing of God. The doctrine of creation, then, affirms both the creature's otherness or difference from God, and at the same time the creature's utter and intimate dependence, moment by minute moment, upon God's sustaining, nurturing presence. In Calvin's words:

> [T]he world is daily *renewed*, because *God sendeth forth his spirit*. In the propogation of living creatures, we doubtless see continually a new creation of the world. In now calling *that* God's spirit, which he before represented as the spirit of living creatures, there is no contradiction. God sendeth forth that spirit . . . and as soon as he has sent it forth, all things are created. In this way, what was his own he makes to be ours.[24]

In this way, what was his own he makes to be ours! Incredible, divine generosity! God gives of God's own breath, God's own life, God's own being—and so truly and thoroughly *gives*, that we truly do *exist as other* to God! We who thoroughly and utterly depend on

23. Sermon 118, "On the Omnipresence of God," §II.1, *Works* 4:42.

24. Calvin, *Book of Psalms*, 168. Calvin is wisely observing that God's *ruach* and the creatures' *ruach* appear to be virtually indistinguishable in verses 29-30.

God for our very being in every moment exist, nonetheless, as that which is not God. We creatures are not puppets on a divine string, nor are we simply manifestations or projections of divine presence. We are not "God in disguise"! We are *not God*—and yet it is *in God* that "we live and move and have our being" (Acts 17:28). Such is the mystery at the heart of the biblical understanding of creation—a mystery we shall encounter more fully in chapter 4.

ESCHATOLOGICAL RENEWAL OF CREATION

Though its testimony has been largely absent from evangelical churches, Psalm 104 is traditionally read in liturgical churches on Pentecost Sunday "and has been from the earliest Christian history."[25] There is, to be sure, an obvious and natural connection that justifies such usage: the psalm alludes to the life-giving power of God's Spirit, and Pentecost celebrates the outpouring of the Holy Spirit upon the disciples of Jesus in Jerusalem. No wonder the Church in its Nicene Creed identified the Holy Spirit as "the Lord, the Giver of Life," or that the Church has prayed "Come, Creator Spirit, and renew the face of the earth," or that the Church in its Pentecost liturgy has confessed that "the Holy Spirit filleth the world and all things have knowledge of the Voice."[26]

On the one hand, the Church's association of this psalm with the celebration of Pentecost on the Christian calendar provokes us to ponder the ways in which creation and re-creation are related, and to wonder about the eschatological implications of God's renewing the face of the earth by the sending forth of the Spirit. On the other hand, the challenge we face is to keep Psalm 104 and Acts 2 together in the same canon without sacrificing the theological and historical integrity of either text.

Christian tradition has properly associated the Pentecostal outpouring with eschatology, if for no other reason than that Peter makes that very connection in the Acts 2 sermon. This lavish gift of the Spirit is linked with "the last days" and with such apocalyptic

25. Mays, *Psalms*, 336.
26. Norman Pittenger, *The Holy Spirit* (Philadelphia: United Church Press, 1974), 23.

wonders as "blood and fire and smoky mist," the sun turning to darkness and the moon to blood—all this "before the coming of the Lord's great and glorious day" (vv. 19, 20). It is certainly clear that the apostle Paul also understood the gift of the Spirit to be a "foretaste" or "firstfruits" of the age to come (Eph. 1:13-14; 2 Cor. 1:22; Rom. 8:23). The Spirit, in Christian faith and thought, is *the Spirit of the age to come,* the Presence of God's future already in the present.

Interestingly enough, on the few occasions when Wesley alludes to the gift of God's Spirit as described in Psalm 104:29-30, his use follows this eschatological suit. For example, in the opening paragraph of his sermon "The General Deliverance" he freely gathers from the psalm the various images of God as One who kindly and mercifully cares for all creatures; near the sermon's end, he returns to Psalm 104 but does so in order to anticipate the world to come when all creatures are liberated from the " 'bondage of corruption,' when God has 'renewed the face of the earth.' "[27] It appears that in this sermon Wesley has shifted this image of the life-giving, renewing power of the Spirit in creation away from the context of Psalm 104's celebration of God's continually vitalizing gift of Breath, moving it instead toward an expectation of God's eschatological future for the world. Similarly, in the conclusion of another sermon, "The General Spread of the Gospel," Wesley believes that this future act of God is already in the process of beginning—essentially, we should add, among the Methodists. He writes, "All unprejudiced persons may see with their eyes that he is already renewing the face of the earth."[28]

I do not want to imply that this is an either-or proposition, that is, *either* the Spirit is God's empowering, vitalizing, and renewing Presence in creation in this very moment, *or* the Spirit is essentially a Future Reality, an eschatological gift with at best tangential relation to the world in which we live. Surely we need not bifurcate on this matter. On the other hand, it seems that the natural tendency is that, once we begin to place the weight of priority and importance on a world to come, the world of this present moment is automatically devalued. Thankfully, it is difficult to read the world as devalued in Psalm 104!

---

27. Sermon 60, "The General Deliverance," §III.4, *Works* 2:447.
28. Sermon 63, "The General Spread of the Gospel," §27, *Works* 2:499.

At the same time, the psalm does not allow us to rest content with the world as it is. The final verse demands our attention: "Let sinners be consumed from the earth, and let the wicked be no more" (v. 35). After this long and glorious litany of praise for all of God's good creatures in this vast and deeply interrelated world, it almost seems rude for Psalm 104 to end with a curse on wicked people! If this psalm were *really* "the Wordsworth of the ancients,"[29] surely such intense antagonism would be out of place in this celebration of nature's wonders!

But Psalm 104 is not Wordsworth. Further, it is essential that we read that final line of judgment so that our eyes do not become blinded to the destructive effects of sin and wickedness. The world, for all its beauty and wonder, is also deeply marred and scarred by human rebellion against God. A celebration of nature's beauty and creation's goodness can sometimes blur the eyes of the privileged to the deep suffering and evil in the world. It is a fundamental biblical conviction that God's creation is good (Gen. 1; 1 Tim. 4:4), but there are in fact a great many people and creatures in God's good world that do not *experience* God's world *as* good. Their experience of God's creation is radically impoverished, in many instances, precisely because there is a minority of people on the planet—mostly the so-called "first world" and especially North Americans—who consume and waste the good earth's resources at the expense of the poor and powerless. As the contemporary Jewish commentator Herbert J. Levine writes:

> Creation was not completed once and for all but is renewed, according to this psalmist, on a daily basis. . . . If creation can be daily renewed, then surely God can complete the work begun at the start of time when chaos was banished and the land emerged as the home of life. God's ultimate work is yet to come: "May sinners disappear from the earth, and the wicked be no more."[30]

This psalm's rather jarring conclusion, in concert with the eschatological context into which it has been placed in Christian liturgy, should have the effect of shaking us from our complacency. This is an important point, indeed a characteristically Wesleyan point, to

29. As cited by A.A. Anderson, *Psalms (73–150)*, 718.

30. Herbert J. Levine, *Sing unto God a New Song: A Contemporary Reading of the Psalms* (Bloomington: Indiana University Press, 1995), 172-73.

consider at the outset of this book: a theology of nature can become a dangerous thing if it cultivates within us an awe before the world's beauty and at the same time dulls us to the harsh reality of wickedness in the world, or to the spiritual, physical, political, and economic consequences of sin.[31] If we become too comfortable to hear the yearning cries of the poor and marginalized for a new and better world, then we have also severed the vital nerve and eschatological impulse of biblical faith.

Can we honor and uphold both biblical streams—both the eschatological hope for a *new* world and a profoundly awe-inspired awareness of the wonders and beauties of the *now* world? One route that offers us some hope in this regard has been explored by contemporary American Lutheran theologian Ted Peters, who, under the acknowledged influence of Pannenberg, has traced the outline of a cosmology that is radically future-oriented. In his systematic theology *God—the World's Future* Peters suggests "a proleptic concept of creation," meaning essentially that "God creates from the future, not the past."[32]

In this understanding of creation, Peters argues that we must think beyond the common notion of causality that assigns causal power to the past—a notion he nicknames the "bowling-ball" theory of creation. In his own lively words:

> The image here is that of a divine bowler providing the power of being by hurling the creation down the alley of time. We assume we presently are rolling somewhere down that temporal alley. The hand of the divine bowler is behind us. There may be a strike yet ahead of us. Our task, to the extent that we can make a contribution to our direction, is to keep ourselves in line with God's original aim so as to avoid a gutter ball.

---

31. This danger in a theology of creation is unmasked sharply by Brueggemann: "I understand that creation theology may indeed express a bold claim for the sovereignty of Yahweh against idols and false orderings of the world. The social function of creation theology, however, is characteristically to establish, legitimate, and advocate order at the cost of transformation. It is of course reassuring to claim that God's good order of creation is a sure decree against chaos. The problem is that regularly (I believe inevitably), creation theology is allied with the king, with the royal liturgy, and therefore with reasons of state. The outcome is to coalesce the royal ordering of economic distribution and political power with the goodness and reliability of God's intended order, thereby absolutizing the present order as the very structure God has decreed in and for creation." *Israel's Praise: Doxology against Idolatry and Ideology* (Philadelphia: Fortress, 1988), 101.

32. Ted Peters, *God—the World's Future: Systematic Theology for a Postmodern Era* (Minneapolis: Fortress, 1992), 134.

> But does this image of a push from the past adequately describe how we actually experience time and the power of being? I suggest not. Although we certainly do experience some current effects due to past causes, we implicitly recognize a certain priority given to those things that have the power of creativity for the future. Without a future, things drop into nonexistence. Without a future, the present moment becomes a death trap.[33]

Peters suggests, accordingly, that "the first thing God did for the world was to give it a future . . . by opening up the possibility of its becoming something it never had been before and by supplying it with the power to change."[34] It is only logical to assume, then, that this bestowing of a future, this opening up of new possibilities for the world and all its creatures, continues to be the mode of God's creating activity. Peters elaborates:

> From our perspective today, of course, we have the sense that we are looking back upon this first divine act. It seems now to be a part of the dead past. But we need to be careful because God is continuing to bestow upon us a future, even at this very moment. . . . The bowling-ball theory of time places all power in the past, which cannot help but result in a determinism regarding the present. The power of God, however, comes to us not as a brute determination from the past but as that which counters such determinations. Each moment God exerts divine power to relieve us from past constraints so as to open up a field for free action, for responsible living.[35]

Any perceptive Wesleyan should be able to read clear indications of what we mean by prevenient grace in Peters's words. (The idea of prevenient grace, after all, is not utterly unique to Wesleyans!) And Peters may help us understand prevenient grace as a dynamic, *future-oriented* gift of God through Christ by the Spirit. He may also help us interpret the doctrine in broader, more cosmic dimensions. I have quoted Peters at length here because this idea is

---

33. Ibid., 135.

34. Ibid., 135-36.

35. Ibid., 136. See also John B. Cobb Jr.'s essay, "God and the Scientific Worldview" in a book of essays coauthored by Cobb and David Tracy, *Talking About God: Doing Theology in the Context of Modern Pluralism* (New York: Seabury, 1983).

sufficiently important that I do not want to misrepresent it, and because I do not think I could state it more clearly. If God creates "from the future," and if God is continually creating "from the future," then perhaps we may think of the Spirit as the living Presence of God's Future, the One who tantalizes with tastes of the world to come in the midst of the present world, in every moment bestowing eschatological life to all that lives—life that pushes always toward a divine future that is beckoning. And yet it is not a predetermined future! It is open to a variety of possibilities, shaped by the responses that we and all creatures make to the Spirit's overtures. Even as God gives the world a future, we must soberly understand that this future is not a given.

To put it simply, the world is not finished yet. Christian faith teaches us that its goal, its *telos*, has been decisively revealed in the person, ministry, and work of Jesus of Nazareth. We therefore who believe in Jesus hang on to hope—a "hope against hope" (Rom. 4:18)—for the healing and mending of God's world through the ministrations of Christ the Physician. (This is a theme we shall explore further in chapter 6.) Meanwhile, the Spirit who proceeds from the Father through the Son—and thus who proceeds from the One who offers the world a viable future—is continuously creating us lowly but graced creatures, and ever renewing the face of the earth.

CHAPTER 2

"THOU DIDST THY MIGHTY WINGS OUTSPREAD"

Reading Genesis in a Wesleyan Way

Thou didst Thy mighty Wings outspread,
And brooding o'er the Chaos, shed
Thy Life into th' impregn'd Abyss.

Charles Wesley, *Hymns of Petition and Thanksgiving for the Promise of the Father*, #28

Is there such a thing as a "Wesleyan" reading of the opening chapters of Genesis? We might be tempted to answer in the negative, assuming instead that any good *Wesleyan* reading would be nothing other than a good *Christian* reading. Might not the adjective "Wesleyan" be taken to imply, after all, a superiority over other Christian traditions? What would distinguish a so-called "Wesleyan" reading from any others? Why not drop the Wesleyan and simply be Christians about this?

To a certain extent, we shall attempt to do precisely that. Immediately, however, we face a new question: Is there but one "Christian" reading of Genesis? Do all Christians agree about what is important in those opening chapters? Surely we do not assume so, for experience teaches us otherwise. Many Christians insist that the opening chapters are straightforward historical recounting, and thus must be read literally as a kind of scientific document. Others argue that it is more like a parable or myth, shedding light on theological questions but hardly to be read as hard history. Even reading simply the opening sentence raises questions; while it has traditionally been read by Christians as teaching that God created the heavens and the earth *ex nihilo* ("out of nothing"), that has never been a unanimous interpretation. Moreover, scholars have tended increasingly to interpret the Hebrew text as implying a pre-existing primordial chaos—inviting an ambiguity that Augustine himself wrestled with in Book XII of his *Confessions*. Much more recently, Karen Armstrong has written that "the question of which reading is correct may prove impossible finally to resolve. Right from the start, therefore, Genesis implies that . . . we are dealing with ineffable matters, and a wholly straightforward style may not always be appropriate."[1]

Let us admit, then, that there are many different Christian (not to mention Jewish!) readings of Genesis's beginnings. It would be difficult to improve upon Augustine's sentiments as he, Jacob-like, grapples mightily with God over this issue of how to interpret the opening chapter of the Bible:

> O my God, . . . how can it harm me that it should be possible to interpret these words in several ways, all of which may yet be true? How can it harm me if I understand the writer's meaning in a different sense from that in which another understands it? . . . Provided, therefore, that each of us tries as best he can to understand in the Holy Scriptures what the writer meant by them, what harm is there if a reader believes what you, the Light of all truthful minds, show him to be the true meaning? It may not even be the meaning which the writer had in mind, and yet he too saw in them a true meaning, different though it may have been from this.[2]

This is a remarkable admission on Augustine's part, no doubt motivated at least partially by the tremendous difficulties inherent in the very beginning of the Book of Beginning. *Multiple meanings, all of them true?* Meanings in fact not intended or recognized by the writer? Meanings that differ so much from one another that it is difficult, perhaps impossible, for us to reconcile them? And all this

1. Karen Armstrong, *In the Beginning: A New Interpretation of Genesis* (New York: Alfred A. Knopf, 1996), 14.
2. Saint Augustine, *Confessions*, translated and introduced by R. S. Pine-Coffin (London: Penguin Books, 1961), 295-96.

in nothing less than the very *opening* of our Bibles? Augustine here treads on ground quite familiar to contemporary literary theorists and critics. Perhaps more important, he makes it clear that we who read this text must be willing to bear the burden of interpretation. As I suggested in chapter 1, by this term "burden" I mean that the hard, but often rewarding, work of interpretation is unavoidable. It is unavoidable in every moment of existence, in every act of reading the world; it is equally unavoidable in every attempt to read a text, and all the more unavoidable when that text is Genesis 1. "There is no doubt of these truths in the minds of those whom you have gifted with insight," continues the great North African bishop. "But from these truths each of us chooses one or another to explain the phrase 'In the beginning God made heaven and earth.'"[3]

Not only Genesis, of course, but all of Scripture spawns a vast host of interpretations and applications. Christians of the Wesleyan tradition do not assume that they alone understand the correct or proper meaning of any given biblical passage—how could they, since they themselves do not all agree! One of the things, though, that makes them "Wesleyan" is a confidence that John Wesley was, to borrow Augustine's language, one of those "whom God has gifted with insight." If this is so, what insights might Wesley share with us? What lens does he offer to help us see into the opening chapters of Genesis? In what follows, I will argue that Wesley's most distinctive contributions to the reading of Genesis are *a hermeneutic grounded in love* and *a method attentive to experience.*

A WESLEYAN HERMENEUTIC

First, it is evident that while Wesley recognized a variety of Christian readings of the Scriptures at many junctures, he clearly did value some theological emphases over others. Further, the Anglican divine offers us his most fundamental theological assumption as a working hermeneutical clue, a key to biblical interpretation. In his sermon "Free Grace," among other places,

3. Ibid., 297.

Wesley insisted that the fundamental fact about God is that "God is love" (1 John 4:8, 16). This simple proposition spurred his confidence that God loves all people (and all other creatures, for that matter), everywhere, at all times—a confidence he could not find in the Reformed doctrine of predestination. If it is the very nature of God to be love—the *self-giving* and *other-receiving* love revealed in Jesus' laying down of his life for us (1 John 3:16)—then there is no one and no thing excluded from this "Love divine, all loves excelling." Perhaps the most dramatic example of Wesley's theological and hermeneutical principle occurs in "Free Grace" when Wesley replied to fellow Christians of a Calvinist bent who insisted on a literal and straightforward reading of the biblical statement "Jacob have I loved, but Esau have I hated" (Mal. 1:2-3; Rom. 9:13 KJV). "Now," he responded, "what can possibly be a more flat contradiction than this, not only to the whole scope and tenor of Scripture, but also to all those particular texts which expressly declare, 'God is love'?"[4] The upshot is that Wesley insisted that the doctrine of divine *sovereignty* must be interpreted through the lens of suffering and sacrificial *love*. "They infer," he continued, "that God is love only to some [people], viz., the elect, and that he hath mercy for those only: flatly contrary to which is the whole tenor of Scripture."[5] He found the notion of divine predestination or selective love to be particularly contrary to one of his favorite lines from the Psalms, a line that figures prominently in this book: "The Lord is loving unto *every* man; and his mercy is over *all* his works."[6] For Wesley, this psalm teaches us to sing not only of God's love for all human beings, but for all of God's "works," that is, all creatures God has made and is making even in this moment.[7]

By taking this Wesleyan insight to heart, we are led to read the opening of Genesis as a testimony to the God who is love. Further, since the writer who testified that "God is love" also wrote in the same epistle that "we know love by this, that [Christ] laid down his

4. Sermon 110, "Free Grace," §20, *Works* 3:552.

5. Ibid.

6. Ibid.

7. Probably the most dramatic instance of Wesley's predilection for Psalm 145:9, "The Lord is loving to every man, and his mercy is over all his works," is in the opening line of Sermon 60, "The General Deliverance," *Works* 2:437. There he employs it to set the stage for his strongest argument regarding God's tender compassions for all creatures—"all that have sense, all that are capable of pleasure or pain, of happiness or misery."

life for us" (1 John 3:16), we are constrained to interpret the divine act of creating through the sacrificial love of the cross. Creation will be interpreted first of all as an act of *this cruciform, Christlike love;* this leads to the assumption that God's intention for all of creation involves the expression, purpose, and goal of such love. Indeed, a fundamental assumption throughout this book is that "Love Divine" (all loves excelling!) has created the world *in order that love might flourish.* God is creating a vast and wonderful universe in order that the generous overflow of God's great compassions might be received and shared among God's creatures, particularly (but not exclusively!) among those created in the divine image.

One of the dominating themes in Wesley's preaching, in fact, is that God's full intent for human beings is that they be "renewed in the image of God"—or, as he also put it, "renewed in love."[8] If God *is* love, then for us human beings to function as God's image strongly implies that we too will love; indeed, Wesley interpreted 1 John 4:17 to teach that as *God* is love, so are *we* called and empowered to be "love" in this world, frail and finite creatures though we are.[9] Wesley stood in a broad stream of Christian thinkers who have understood God's sanctification of human lives as entailing wholehearted love for God and love for the neighbor as oneself. Of course, in so doing Wesley and all those others were simply taking cues from the Synoptic Gospels' depiction of Jesus. Matthew's version of the dual command of love is especially pertinent to our purposes:

> When the Pharisees heard that he had silenced the Sadducees, they gathered together, and one of them, a lawyer, asked him a question to test him. "Teacher, which commandment in the law is the greatest?" He said to him, "'You shall love the Lord your God with all your heart, and with all your soul, and with all your mind.' This is the greatest and first commandment. And a second is like it: 'You shall love your neighbor as yourself.' On these two commandments hang all the law and the prophets." (Matt. 22:34-40)

On these two commandments hang all the law and the prophets! It is noteworthy that "the law," the Torah, is composed of what are

---

8. *Plain Account of Christian Perfection*, §25, Q. 26, *Works* (Jackson) 11:423-24.
9. Ibid., §17, 390-91; §26, 442.

traditionally known as the five books of Moses. The first of those books is Genesis, and our present concern is with the opening chapters of that opening book. If *all the law* hangs on these two commandments, then so must all of Genesis! It would seem, then, that the dual command of love for God and neighbor is the point and goal of even the creation stories of Genesis! On the commandments of love hang the priestly creation story of Genesis 1 and the yahwist creation story of Genesis 2. How tragic, then, that even today there are Christians virtually willing to spill blood over the issue of interpreting Genesis's creation stories! How ironic that texts whose purpose is to encourage and evoke love for God and neighbor should become an ideological battleground!

Once again, it is remarkable how precisely Augustine anticipated our own age. For a moment he considers the possible advantage of an audience with authorial immediacy; would it help if we could interview Moses? "Even if Moses were to appear to us and say, 'This is what I meant,'" writes Augustine, "we should not see his thoughts but would simply believe his word."[10] In other words, a face-to-face, spoken interpretation of the Genesis text—even one given by the author himself!—would not and cannot do away with the burden of interpretation. We would not "see his thoughts," and thus the author's subjectivity remains alien to our own. We would still need to *interpret* what Moses said he meant! Augustine responds to this apparently endless layering of interpretation:

> Let us not, therefore, "go beyond what is laid down for us," . . . "Let us love the Lord our God with our whole heart and our whole soul and our whole mind, and our neighbour as ourselves." Whatever Moses meant in his books, unless we believe that he meant it to be understood in the spirit of these two precepts of charity, we are "treating God as a liar," for we attribute to [God's] servant thoughts at variance with [God's] teaching.[11]

"God's teaching" is, for Augustine, nothing more nor less than *love*: love for God and all neighbors. This, then, is the point of Genesis and of all Scripture—*that love might flourish!* In other words: if indeed Jesus has taught us that all the Torah and the Prophets hang

10. Augustine, *Confessions*, 302.
11. Ibid., 302-3.

on the two commands of love for God and neighbor, then that dual command is the heart and essence of every Mosaic line. Once again, this principle would extend to the opening chapters of Genesis as well. Nothing else can supply the lens for a Wesleyan (and Augustinian!) reading of Genesis's opening chapters. If Genesis 1 describes human beings as created in God's image, for Wesley sin-sullied human beings are now *re*-called to be recreated and renewed in the image of God. Simply put, according to Wesley what God intends in us is a "renewal in love" that issues in "love of God and our neighbor," and for Augustine this love for God and neighbor is the very point of Genesis.

Wesley did not quote Augustine widely, and only occasionally did so approvingly. But certainly Wesley should have perceived a close ally in the African's understanding of Scripture's purpose. A little further on in his *Confessions* Augustine asks, "Do you not see how foolish it is to enter into mischievous arguments which are an offense against that very charity for the sake of which [Moses] wrote every one of the words that we are trying to explain?"[12] Once again, for our purposes here, it is worth noting that Augustine is still grappling with the opening verses of Genesis—and is suggesting that, most fundamentally, those verses were written "for the sake of . . . charity," for the sake of calling its readers and hearers to greater and deeper love for God and all neighbors. To dispute bitterly over how to understand Genesis's opening chapters—as, say, creationists and theistic evolutionists too often have done—runs the great risk of perverting this purpose of the text.

Given this Augustinian-Wesleyan hermeneutic, the teaching of Genesis 1 that human beings are created in God's image ought to be interpreted in the light of the dual command upon which all the Torah hangs: to be created in God's image is to be created *to love God and neighbor*. This is the essence of holiness, for it is the divine purpose for humanity. Thus, the creation story of Genesis 1 points well beyond itself toward a fulfillment of God's calling and image in the New Adam, straining with an eschatological trajectory toward the entire sanctification of the creatures made in God's image and, through them, the sanctification of all creation. We will explore this idea much more fully in chapter 8.

12. Ibid., 303.

THE VOICE OF EXPERIENCE

Scholars of Wesleyan thought have devoted considerable attention to the importance of *experience* as a factor in John Wesley's theological reflections.[13] Indeed, to the extent that the term "quadrilateral" can still be used by careful scholars, it is justified by Wesley's recurrent tendency to add the category of experience to his Anglican tradition's recognition of Scripture, tradition, and reason as providing the contours of Christian theology.

It has not been unusual for Wesleyan theologians to highlight the category of experience specifically in terms of *religious* experience. In this regard they certainly have not been untrue to Wesley, who, in Thomas Langford's words, "took Christian experience to be a medium of theology, for scriptural teaching is confirmed in evangelical experience."[14] But Wesley also demonstrated a remarkable willingness to learn, to grow, to change his mind—in short, to allow his *experiences of life* to shape his theological reflections. Indeed, Langford continues, "A major characteristic of Wesley's theology is that importance is placed on empirical data as well as on direct immediate experience."[15] Even if we raise appropriate questions about the notion of "empirical data" (especially if it is construed to imply the absence of an interpretive interest on the part of the observer), it is clear that this is "experience" more broadly conceived than simply as the testimony of the Spirit's saving and sanctifying work in the lives of believers.

One of the more dramatic illustrations of Wesley's commitment to learning from experience arises in *A Plain Account of Christian Perfection*. At the end of a long section of arguing for the biblical truth of the doctrine of Christian perfection, Wesley imagines (or, more likely, quotes!) an opponent's questions, "But what, if none have attained it yet? What if all who think so are deceived?" His reply is crucial:

---

13. For a rich discussion of the role of experience in Wesley's thinking and practice, see Maddox, *Responsible Grace*, 44-46, 124-31. See also Maddox's chapter on experience (chapter 5) in W. Stephen Gunter et al., *Wesley and the Quadrilateral: Renewing the Conversation* (Nashville: Abingdon, 1997).

14. Langford, *Practical Divinity*, 25-26.

15. Ibid., 26.

> Convince me of this, and I will preach it no more. But understand me right; I do not build any doctrine on this or that person. This or any other man may be deceived, and I am not moved. But, if there are none made perfect yet, God has not sent me to preach perfection. . . . If I were convinced that none in England had attained what has been so clearly and strongly preached by such a number of preachers, in so many places, and for so long a time, I should be clearly convinced that we had all mistaken the meaning of those Scriptures.[16]

Let us accentuate Wesley's point: empirical evidence is crucial to the establishing of correct interpretation of Scripture. It is not enough to be able to "prove" a point biblically if it is not borne out in real life somewhere, by someone, in the observable world. Notice, by the way, that for Wesley what is not up for dispute is the truth and reliability of the Scriptures. Perceived gaps between Scripture and observable life are not assumed to disprove the veracity of the Bible, but to raise doubts regarding the interpreter's reading thereof. Of course, raising doubts about a particular interpretation, or interpretive tradition, is often in practice (or at least in perception) inseparable from raising doubts about the Bible itself.

Take the opening chapters of Genesis, for example. There are Christians who believe that any interpretation of Genesis's opening other than the "literal" (i.e., strictly historical, and thus "scientific") is tantamount to rejecting the Bible itself. But if we attempt to read Genesis in a Wesleyan way, we will, like John Wesley, be open to having our interpretation of any given passage chastened by empirical observation. A contemporary Wesleyan reading of Genesis should be open to new experiences of the natural world, including of course the varieties of evidence the natural sciences offer us. Wesley did assume that our planet was only six thousand years old,[17] but would he today? He would have no good reason to do so. Astronomical evidence clearly teaches us that our universe is many billions of years old; geology's evidence is that our planet is at least several billion years old; biology and genetics offer abundant evidence that living things have evolved in amazingly complex and painstaking routes over many millions of years. It is

16. *Plain Account of Christian Perfection*, §19, Q. 28, *Works* (Jackson) 11:405-6.
17. See Sermon 71, "Of Good Angels," §I.3, *Works* 3:8.

obvious that Genesis teaches us nothing of this, nor need we expect that it should. But the evidences of the natural sciences provide us radically different, new ideas about the world that have become a part of our *experience of* the world. This experience of the world in which we live provides an unavoidable and critical hermeneutical context for reading Genesis in a Wesleyan way.

An intriguing example of this kind of experience at work in John Wesley's own thinking about Genesis can be found in the second of his two sermons titled "What is Man?"[18] Wesley assumed the commonplace notion of his time that there are four basic elements that compose the natural world: earth, air, fire, and water; further, "a particle of ethereal *fire* is connected with every particle of air (and a particle of water too)."[19] It is quite obvious that Wesley did not glean this concept from the Bible; rather, it was part and parcel of his experience of the world, culturally mediated, as the "popular science" of his day. In the light of such experience of the world, Wesley could confidently write that "the human body is composed of all the four elements, duly proportioned and mixed together; the last of which constitutes the vital flame, whence flows the animal heat."[20]

Wesley, then, offered this "scientific" description of the human body within the context of a sermon addressing theological anthropology, a sermon rooted in self-observation and the dominant cosmology of his time. It bears repeating that he did not get this from the biblical text! He *brought it* to his reading of Scripture—and he was not wrong to do so. His experience of the world included these notions of his own time, and he assumed that they were correct. They were not, however, the most important things Wesley had to say in that sermon! Far more weighty, he insisted, is "to know, and deeply to consider . . . the end of life," which is that we "might know, and love, and enjoy, and serve [our] great Creator to all eternity."[21] Wesley's scientific assumptions about the physical composition of the human being took a back seat to his theological convictions regarding the human relation to God.

---

18. Both sermons were written late in Wesley's life, the first in the summer of 1787 and the second in the spring of 1788. The first is a more typically Wesleyan exposition of Scripture; the second is more philosophically oriented, veering toward a speculative theological anthropology.

19. Sermon 116, "What is Man?" §2, *Works* 4:20.

20. Ibid.

21. Ibid., §13, 4:26.

It is important to note further that Wesley did not simply read Genesis in the context of the science of his day; he also interpreted those scientific notions theologically, under the conviction that the God revealed in Jesus through the power of the Holy Spirit is indeed the Maker of the heavens and the earth. Thus, Wesley surmised that the movement of air in the world (i.e., wind) is due to this "ethereal fire" that is connected with "every particle of air"—but added that this fundamental fiery element "itself is moved by the Almighty Spirit, the source of all the motion in the universe."[22] His scientific understanding of the world and its elements, then, was couched within his theological vision of a creation sustained and animated by the divine, life-giving Spirit.

Just as Wesley operated under the broad assumptions of the popular science of his day, so a Wesleyan reading of Genesis—and of the world—need not and should not shy away from the dominant ideas of the contemporary natural sciences. It is obvious that if the evolutionary story of the universe (including our own planet and all of its living inhabitants) is generally accurate, then the opening chapters of Genesis cannot be assumed to be giving a straightforwardly literal account of the creation of the world. Those who do assume that a literal description of the world's beginning is what we read in Genesis cannot, of course, subscribe to the story of the universe told by evolutionary theory. Conversely, most Christians who have a serious and sound awareness of the evidences of science do not assume that Genesis's opening chapters should be read literally. The issue before us, then, is how they *should* be read. To ask the question another way: if we take seriously as our model for theological reflection Wesley's willingness to allow his experience(s) to change his thinking, how will we read Genesis in the light of evolutionary science?

We have already suggested a fundamental hermeneutic, gleaned from Augustine: love for God and neighbor. This hermeneutic certainly must provide our key for answering the question of how we shall read the creation stories of Genesis. In the remainder of this chapter, then, we shall attempt a reading of Genesis 1 and 2 with an

22. Ibid., §8, 4:22-23.

eye toward the question: How do these texts inspire and increase love for God and neighbor?

GENESIS 1:1–2:4A: GOD'S CREATIVE WORD OF LETTING-BE

We began this chapter with the recognition that Genesis begins rather awkwardly and ambiguously. It appears likely that Genesis draws back its opening curtain to reveal a formless, watery chaos with which God begins the labor of creating. If this is correct, then Genesis does not begin with the pure omnipotence of divine fiat, but with God's evocative, alluring call to deep, unformed possibilities that swirl in the darkness.[23] Of course, even before God speaks a word there is the divine *ruach*, the breath/wind of God, that "hovers" or "broods" upon the face of the deep.[24] Here we encounter a truly pregnant image of the blowing, whispering gift of the life-giving Spirit, stirring and troubling the dark and threatening waters, brewing up a world; in the striking imagery of Charles Wesley's hymn text,

> Thou didst Thy mighty Wings outspread,
> And brooding o'er the Chaos, shed
> Thy Life into th' impregn'd Abyss.

It is toward, and into, this chaotic abyss that God outpours the life of the Spirit; it is toward these unfathomable depths that the Maker faces and speaks the creative word. And what is the nature of the word that God speaks? In Genesis 1 this divine speech repeatedly is "*Let there be*"; it is a word that allows for, makes room for—indeed "creates space" for—the creatures of sea, sky, and land. It is not so much a word of command as it is a word of hopefulness, a word that offers promise and evokes possibilities.

---

23. The issue at this point is not whether or not God created *ex nihilo*. It is more simply the recognition that the opening passage of Genesis does not make such a claim for the nature of God's act of creation. We will attempt to examine the ramifications of Genesis 1, and of the development of the doctrine of *creatio ex nihilo*, in chapter 3.

24. For a provocative and eminently creative *tour de force* on the opening verses of Genesis, see Keller's *Face of the Deep*.

It may be instructive to compare the nature of this evocative word in our Bible's opening to the divine word of the Qur'an. Is it not more than merely a difference of nuance that Muhammad's revelation repeatedly insists that God only need say "Be!—and it is" (e.g., 3:47)? While in much popular Christian imagination God's word has been understood to operate very much along those Qur'anic lines, Genesis actually tantalizes the careful reader with a very different sort of speech. The divine address of Genesis 1 is far less demanding, we might say, and far more permissive, far more inviting of creaturely integrity and agency. This becomes all the more apparent in the Hebraic wordplays lurking within the divine invitation to the earth and the waters: the earth is invited to "put forth" *(tadse)* vegetation *(dese)* and the waters are called upon to "bring forth" *(yisresu)* living creatures of the sea *(seres)*. In other words, God's creative activity is expressed precisely through the appropriate creaturely contributions; God's creating fits, and is fitted to, specific creaturely capabilities.[25]

Then there is the captivating refrain in this "Hymn of Creation," this "Poem of the Dawn": *and God saw that it was good.*[26] The fact that, in Genesis 1, God "sees" that various creatures of the world are good after they have been produced by the earth and the waters—rather than God simply pronouncing or announcing that they are good de facto—implies a real and timely interactivity between the Creator and the developing creation. God does not "already know from eternity" that the creatures are good; God sees (experiences?) their goodness, their fittedness to God's creative purposes. God, in other words, responds with approval to the world's own response to the divine invitation to *let there be.*

The inviting, interactive, and responsive nature of God's spoken word and satisfied seeing in Genesis 1 goes a long way toward softening the more popular traditional notion of unilateral divine fiat. More to the point, it corresponds nicely with Wesley's ideas about the loving, noncoercive, and responsive nature of God's interactions

---

25. See ibid., especially chapter 5, "The Sea of Heteroglossia."

26. These titles were favored descriptions of Genesis 1 employed by the dean of Nazarene theologians in the twentieth century, H. Orton Wiley. See his *Christian Theology* (Kansas City: Beacon Hill, 1940), 1:449.

with human beings. However, as John Cobb has already argued, we must go further than Wesley did in his restricting of creaturely agency to human beings.[27] It is incumbent upon us to extend and broaden Wesley's libertarian reading of God's interactions with human beings to include all of creation. It serves neither contemporary science nor the biblical doctrine of creation to espouse too wide of a difference between human beings and the rest of God's creatures. In other words, God relates to all of creation in a way that is at least analogous with God's dealings with human beings: with a respect for the difference each creature makes, with a nurturing of every creature's otherness and creativity, evoking creaturely response through the alluring presence of noncoercive love.

In Christianity this theme is given a unique and potentially revolutionary twist in the incarnational theology of the Gospel of John. Christian theologians have often followed the cues of John's prologue, identifying the creative word of Genesis 1 with the Logos that became flesh and dwelt awhile among us, that indeed was crucified by and among us. Such a Word is not a coercive omnipotence unilaterally forcing the world to conform to its demands; it is, to the contrary, a vulnerable, sacrificial, and ostensibly "weak" Word that invites and allures through the wooings of love.

Thus, while Judaism, Christianity, and Islam all have tended to place a significant emphasis upon God's spoken word as the mode of divine agency in creation, this word has assumed a variety of differing nuances for these traditions. For Islam, this word is an omnipotent, unilaterally effective command; for Judaism, this word is evocative and covenantal; for Christianity, this word even becomes flesh, entering profoundly into the creaturely realm—a vulnerable body of flesh, bone, and blood. For all of these differences, in all of these traditions creation by God's word is clearly a theological notion and not even remotely a scientific one. While science has as its purpose to illuminate and clarify empirical observations and details concerning our world, the most important of our theological claims embrace ambiguity, mystery, and human unknowing. Scripture again suggests itself: In 1 Timothy we read that "everything created by God is good" (4:4) and that God "gives life to everything" (6:13), but we are in the same Breath reminded

27. Cobb, *Grace and Responsibility*, 51-52.

that it is this Creator "alone who has immortality and dwells in unapproachable light, whom no one has ever seen or can see" (6:16). The precise nature of God's presence and activity in the world remains an insoluble mystery.

Notwithstanding the utter mystery of God, the traditions of biblical monotheism all insist on the goodness of creation as an important implication of divine speech. It is an implication rendered explicit by Genesis itself, for the God who speaks the creative word of *Let there be* is described repeatedly in the creation hymn's chorus as One who "saw that it was good" (1:4, 10, 12, 18, 21, 25), even "very good" (1:31). As we have seen, Christians supplement this confidence in the goodness of creation, grounded in the goodness of the God who speaks it into being, with the Johannine conviction that the Word whereby all things were made "became flesh and made his dwelling among us" (John 1:3, 14 NIV). In other words, if the goodness of creation is predicated upon the conviction of the goodness of God, then Christian faith presses further to say that this Word-become-flesh "laid down his life for us" (1 John 3:16), thereby revealing that *God is love*. God is the Transcendent Mystery who is outpouring, self-giving love toward the creation in and through the Word incarnate (1 John 4:8, 16). Thus Paul the apostle could write: "For God, who said, 'Let light shine out of darkness,' made his light shine in our hearts to give us the light of the knowledge of the glory of God in the face of Christ" (2 Cor. 4:6 NIV).

Christian theologians of many traditions, especially during the past few decades, have indicated that this rendering of the divine Word evokes a radical reinterpretation of divine power and, more than likely, of the nature of God's activity in creating the universe. A God whose Word shares intimately in creaturely realities and exigencies does not bespeak sheer, arbitrary power creating with the snap of a finger; instead, as suggested earlier, the idea of an incarnate Word suggests a much more *involved* and *invested* process on God's part. If the Word whereby things are called into being is a Word that humbles itself even to the point of death on a cross, outpouring divine love / human blood for our sakes and the sake of all creation, then God is love and God's Word is "love one another" (1 John 3:11). God's utterly mysterious being, then, in whom we live, move, and have our being (Acts 17:28), is opened and openly *agape* toward the other—toward the creation loved and lured into being by the everlasting Lover. "Thy nature, and thy name, is Love," the Wesleys taught the Methodists to sing it.[28]

Of course, this is far more than can be garnered from the opening chapters of Genesis alone. But a Wesleyan reading of God's activity in creation—starting as it does with the Johannine convictions that "God is love" and that we know the nature of this love through the crucified Christ (1 John 4:8, 3:16)—must necessarily begin not simply in a divinely spoken word of the Genesis hymn, but in the Word incarnate of John's Gospel, the *logos* become flesh and dwelling among us. The heart of the Christian confession is not primarily that God is Maker of heaven and earth, but that "God was reconciling the world to himself in Christ" (2 Cor. 5:19 NIV). Of course, we readily affirm that only the One who is the world's Creator can also be the world's Reconciler, so that Christian soteriology immediately implies a theological cosmology as well. No wonder then that John's prologue, as well as several passages in the Pauline corpus, explicitly draw upon the creation account of Genesis 1. Certainly we may follow suit. Thus, having staked out some crucial christological ground for our reflections upon the nature of divine activity in creation, let us now return with John and Paul to our Bible's beginning.

We might suggest that the opening creation account of Genesis (1:1–2:4*a*) is a text dominated by the logos of order, of neatness, of clean and clear boundaries. It is a text greatly concerned with separation and distinctions: light is separated from darkness (v. 4); the waters above from the waters below (v. 7); the waters below from the dry land (v. 9); each kind of vegetation from the others (v. 12); the night from the day (v. 14); and, of course, the seventh day from the six days of labor before it (2:3). Here is a priestly *logos* heavily invested in making the proper distinctions, in putting and keeping things in the right places. The narrative smacks of logical, mathematical, and—most important—religious exactitude:

---

28. Hymn #136, "Wrestling Jacob," *Works* 7:251-52. Of the twelve verses of this hymn recasting the story of Jacob's nocturnal wrestling in the light of the gospel, the last six all end with the line "Thy nature, and thy name, is Love."

Day 1: Creation of light, which is separated from the darkness. The light is called day, and the darkness night.

Day 4: Creation of "lights" to separate the day from the night—a "greater light" and a "lesser light," as well as the stars.

Day 2: Separation of the waters from the waters by an "expanse" or "firmament" or "dome"—the "heavens" or the "sky."

Day 5: The waters are commanded to "swarm" or "teem" with creatures, and birds are created to fly in the expanse of the sky.

Day 3: Separation of "the waters below" (the seas) from dry land, which permits the earth to "bring forth" vegetation and trees.

Day 6: The earth is commanded to "bring forth" land creatures—and then humanity as male and female is created in God's image in order to "have dominion" in creation. The plants are given "for food" to all the other creatures of land and sky.

Day 7:
God rested, and blessed, and sanctified the seventh day. "This is the account of the heavens and the earth when they were created" (Gen. 2:4*a*).

The order, the symmetry, the clean definitions and distinctions of Genesis 1, particularly as the account climaxes in the hallowing of the seventh day, all bespeak a priestly document whose concern is not with scientific description *per se*. Rather, this text is concerned with putting creatures in their proper places, we might say, and in so doing it denies any of them divine status. The various nature and sky deities are all assigned nothing but creaturely rank, and thus the text functions as a powerful critique of idolatrous practices of Israel's neighbors during and after the Babylonian exile. As Pannenberg has observed of one creaturely detail of Genesis 1, the reduction of the status of stars to "lamps" created on the fourth day undercuts any temptation to offer them worship as deities and "is certainly due to the struggle of Israel's faith against those gods of the ancient Orient who were connected with sun or moon or other heavenly bodies."[29]

If the text had said something like, "Lo, and by the way, the great light that rules the day is itself only a star, but considerably closer to earth than other stars," we would have a remarkable piece of scientific information in this ancient text. Or if it had said, "Behold, not all stars were made on the fourth day because they are in various stages of formation, and God continues to create stars even in this moment," we might be amazed by the text's scientific verity. But of course Genesis says neither of these things, nor should we expect it to have done so. Genesis's purpose is to "put the stars in their place" as God's creation, no longer to be worshiped as deities or followed in astrological chartings.

Further, the observance of sabbath as a day of God's rest from all of God's labors would provide a potent reminder to the Israelites of their allegiance to their Redeemer and Creator rather than to the allurement of creaturely attractions. Here is a practical outworking of the idea that this text, like all of the Torah and the prophets, has as its function to call its readers to greater and deeper love of God. In this connection, Lloyd Bailey points out that in the Hebrew text, the opening verse of Genesis has seven words, the second verse has two times seven, and "the concluding section of the unit (2:2-4, concerning the seventh day) contains 35 words (5 x 7), with three of its clauses containing seven each."[30] Further, the term *elohim* is found 35 times, while "heaven" and "earth" occur 21 times each. One begins to get the impression that the number 7, as the number of the sabbath day, is of critical importance. On the seventh day of the week, every week, the people of Israel were called to remember their God, their Creator, who is none other than *the* Creator of all things. Indeed, they were called not only to remember but to *love* this One who not only created the world but also created the people of Israel, in order that this people in particular might love God with all of their heart, soul, and might (Deut. 6:5).

If, as Bailey has cogently argued, sabbath observance provides the goal and inner logic of Genesis 1, then it is again evident that

---

29. Pannenberg, *Toward a Theology of Nature*, 45.
30. Lloyd Bailey, *Genesis, Creation, and Creationism* (Mahwah, N.J.: Paulist Press, 1993), 96.

the passage's intent is not primarily, nor even secondarily, to give scientific information. Further, its only description of the nature of divine activity in creation, as we have already explored, is that of *speech*, of the permissive and evocative "Let there be." This model bespeaks the ease, perhaps even the relative effortlessness with which God calls worlds into existence—as opposed, one might presume, to the harsh and violent deity battles that provide the basis for the cosmology of the Babylonians. Nonetheless, it is a word that addresses the world in the tones of "responsible grace," calling upon the world to contribute its own creaturely energies to the divine labor of creation: *Let the earth bring forth!* (1:11, 24).

So we detect hints of the two commands upon which all of the Torah and Prophets, and thus also Genesis 1, purportedly hang. Genesis calls Israel and the church to love for God: this God is generous in bestowing being, in calling forth creatures by the gracious invitation, *let there be*. This is love for God as the Creator of all things, in distinction from the things themselves—good as they are in God's own sight. Ideally, this love for God is rekindled with every sabbath, a time for resting in God's presence and for remembering that God is God and we are not. This is love for God as the One who is graciously willing to share in power, to create land creatures in the divine image who are called upon to "image," to reflect and to represent, the Creator. This creature, the human, as *male and female*, is called upon to exercise divine rule and divine care in and toward the rest of creation. Thus, the love of God to which Genesis 1 calls us implies also a love for the neighbor as a fellow bearer of God's image.

Genesis 2: God's Indwelling, Fashioning Presence

With the second creation account (Gen. 2:4*b*–4:26), there is no concern for days, divisions, or neatly arranged schematics that eventuate in sabbath observance; creation here occurs more diffusely and flowingly. Here we do not hear the commanding word of a transcendent *elohim*; instead, we see a much more immanent *Yahweh* at work in the clay and dirt. This God fashions an earthling *(adam)* and breathes into the dirt-creature's nostrils "the breath of life" (2:7), plants a garden, forms other living creatures out of the earth and finally works a woman up out of the rib of the *adam*. One might readily suggest that if the first creation account climaxes with the sabbath, the second account offers us its *raison d'etre* in 2:24: "Therefore a man leaves his father and his mother and clings to his wife, and they become one flesh."

If, however, the marital union of male and female is the thrust of the second account, the narrative certainly takes its time getting there. Notice that whereas Genesis 1 has *elohim* repeatedly seeing that creation at each step and stage is "good," Genesis 2 is not hesitant to report that *Yahweh* could say of creation that something is "not good." Not only was nothing of the sort said in Genesis 1, it is not too much of a stretch to suspect that nothing of the sort could have been said in Genesis 1. But Genesis 2 is a different story! "It is not good that the man should be alone," says Yahweh. "I will make him a helper as his partner" (2:18). Those who insist upon a literalistic reading of the narrative must recognize that God then is portrayed as molding all of the rest of the animals out of the ground—and bringing them to the human with apparent hopes of landing an adequate partner! But alas, "for the man there was not found a helper as his partner" (2:20). Not only is it declared "not good" for the earthling to be alone, but the Creator's first attempt to correct the problem is less than sparkling. God's creative activity as narrated in Genesis 2 seems to have something of a jerry-built quality to it!

But there is also a marvelous dialogical, open-ended character to this God's creativity. As Yahweh formed the creatures from the ground, one by one—who could really think this should be taken literally?—God "brought them to the man to see what he would call them" (2:19)! The portrait here, of course, is decidedly anthropomorphic; admitting that, it is nonetheless tantalizing to imagine a God who intends "to see" what the human will do. There is almost a hint of divine curiosity flowing as a subtext in this narrative, suggesting the open future implied in human agency. Further, remembering the critical importance of a person's or thing's name for the ancient Semitic peoples, it is all the more remarkable that Yahweh freely bestows the responsibility for naming the creatures upon the human being. Again, we need not take the narrative literally in order to appreciate the fact that human beings do indeed continue to assume this task of naming the creatures, of studying and classifying them, of attempting to make sense and order of their surrounding world. (We call such human beings "biologists.")

Further, we need not take the narrative literally in order to appreciate its implicit theology: the Creator is not simply curious about what the human will name each creature, the Creator is also willing to allow the human to carry out this task without divine interference. There are no heavenly cue-cards, no alterations or corrections: "and whatever the man called each living creature, that was its name" (2:19). There appears here to be far less concern for divinely ordered exactitude than what we encounter in Genesis 1, though the divine trust implied in allowing the human to name the creatures is not unlike the divine dictum of 1:26-28 to humanity (as male *and* female) to "have dominion" over them (1:28). Once again, it is instructive to compare Adam's naming of the creatures in Genesis 2 to the Qur'an's version of the story, in which we are told that God "taught Adam all the names" (2:31). For the Muslim tradition, such matters are not left to the risk of human error, ignorance, or even finitude. In Genesis 2, on the other hand, God is narrated as one who willingly enters into the real risks of dialogical relation to the human creature and, by implication, to the world as a whole.

If indeed Genesis 1 can be characterized as a text of order, of straight lines and sharp corners, then Genesis 2 is a bit dreamy and meandering, right-brain all the way. There are no clean categories of separation in the second creation story, but instead the earthy feel of God as an artisan whose creatures of clay live on borrowed breath. Here we read of a garden, planted by *Yahweh,* and a river flowing by naked but unashamed human bodies delighted with each other. Here is the stuff of real, down-to-earth narrative, but certainly precious little in the way of scientific information or input. And it is with such wonderfully variant creation stories as these that our Bible has its beginning!

And what of a Wesleyan reading of Genesis 2? What might we say about Genesis 2 as far as its power to call forth a greater and deeper love for God and neighbor? The God we encounter here is unafraid of creation, one who can mold mud and share life-giving breath with the creature. This rendering inspires in us a love for a God who is not afraid to get dirty, a deity who loves gardens and gardening. This God is willing to take risks, willing to entrust the task and responsibility of giving names to the creatures to human beings—and is, therefore, a God who is eminently *lovable*. And what of love for neighbor? There is no question that in Genesis 2 the foremost neighbor in question is the spouse; there is nonetheless a kinship with all the other creatures, also formed of dust, who, while not "a helper as his partner," are nonetheless our neighbors, deserving of our relationally formed capacity for naming and for caring. All of the creatures of the garden, which is entrusted to us earthlings to tend, are in fact our neighbors.

The Jewish tradition in its wonderfully intuitive, Spirit-led, and Shekhinah-indwelt wisdom found a way to conjoin these creation stories and even had the *chutzpah* to make them bat lead-off in the Hebrew Scriptures. As Armstrong keenly observes,

> By allowing these contrasting views of creation to coexist side by side, the Bible makes it clear from the very beginning that it will not give neat, tidy answers to questions that simply do not admit of a simple solution. Instead, the authors make us wrestle with the complexities of the text, . . . demonstrating the basic religious principle that no one human account can ever comprise the whole of divine truth.[31]

If Genesis does indeed force us to wrestle, then perhaps we find ourselves again in Jacob's sandals, wrestling through the night with a mysterious heavenly figure on the shores of the river Jabbok ("Jacob" turned inside out!). We shall find in such wrestling no pat or easy replies to our questions of the text, nor to the questions the text puts to us. Perhaps we feel ourselves turned inside-out, like Jacob's wrestling *in* Genesis, or like Augustine's reading *of* Genesis. But if we are willing to wrestle as Augustine did, we may wrest from those opening creation stories the same good news sung in Charles Wesley's arresting lines:

31. Armstrong, *In the Beginning*, 19-20.

Contented now upon my thigh
  I halt, till life's short journey end;
All helplessness, all weakness, I
  On thee alone for strength depend;
Nor have I power from thee to move;
Thy nature, and thy name, is LOVE.[32]

32. Hymn #136, "Wrestling Jacob," *Works* 7:251-52, verse 11.

CHAPTER 3

"OUT OF NOTHING'S WOMB PRODUCE"

Is Next-to-Nothing Enough?—or Is It Too Much?

The Vital Principle infuse,
And out of Nothing's womb produce
The Earth and Heaven, and all that is.
That All-informing Breath Thou art
Who dost Continued Life impart,
And bidst the World persist to be.

Charles Wesley, *Hymns of Petition and Thanksgiving for the Promise of the Father,* #28

If God is the Creator of all things, must we assume that there was necessarily a time when there was *nothing but* God? Since Augustine's famous reflections on time in Book XI of his *Confessions,* if not before, Christians have tended to think that time itself began with, and is an aspect of, God's act of creating. If that is a sound assumption, then in fact there never was a "time" when there was nothing but God—for time began even as all other things of creation began.

Considerations of time aside, though, can we imagine a state of being in which only God exists—God and nothing else? This, of course, would be a pre-creation state of being. This state of being presumably would be entirely outside of the bounds of time, one occupied solely and wholly by God, however God might be conceived.

That is to say, many theists have assumed such a state of being for God, whether they be trinitarian Christians, traditional Jews, or typical Muslims; in all of those cases, a dominant assumption has been that God exists necessarily and eternally, and did at one (non)time exist without the "other" that we usually call "creation" or "the world." Simply stated: for most people who believe in a creator deity, the ruling assumption is that there was some point at which this creator brought the world into being. Most Jews, Christians, and Muslims assume something along these lines when they think about God's creation of the universe. Christians traditionally have believed, in fact, that biblical faith implies (if not demands) the notion that our universe had a precise beginning point, a beginning of time at which point all things were called into existence *ex nihilo* ("out of nothing") by God. This understanding of creation was, and generally is, believed to provide the most adequate view of the sovereign power of God the Creator in relation to the world.

What is the alternative to believing in a Creator of all things? Obviously, we occupy a vast universe of which each of us is an infinitesimal and fleeting part, and it is a natural question to wonder where this universe has come from. If it did not come about as a result of divine activity, could it have come from "nothing"? Can anything come from absolutely nothing? Even as astrophysicists speculate on the possibilities that our vast universe could have had its beginnings in a quantum fluctuation—a phenomenon in which subatomic particles seem to "pop" into existence out of nowhere and nothing—we must remember that even in that case there is a quantum vacuum into which these particles do their popping. A quantum vacuum is *not* nothing. Strictly and logically speaking, no thing can come from nothing. No way.

Such considerations could lead many people who do not assume the existence of a creator deity to conclude that there has always been some world, some kind of universe or another. If there is no creator, and if the universe could not have come from utterly nothing, then it would appear to be necessary that the world has always existed in one form or another. Perhaps it was similar to the one we presently observe, but quite possibly not. In this case, the Big Bang that began our particular universe billions of years ago presumably had its origin in a preceding world, a world that (as we now understand it) would have been very small by our standards, as well as unimaginably dense and hot. Beyond and before such a point of singularity, of course, our speculations cannot go. It is not impossible that there have been innumerable universes, some more or less like the one we now inhabit. There would, however, presumably be some kind of real kinship among all possible universes; after all, if there could be plural universes with no inherent relation to one another, the problem of a beginning or source would simply be compounded! Some people speculate that our present universe is the result of only one in an infinite series of Big Bangs, each of which expands the universe outward until at some much later point, the powers of gravity begin to pull all of that matter back inward toward a moment of very hot Big Crunch. Then, according to this theory, the universe explodes back outward only later to collapse back inward upon itself, *ad infinitum*.

Whatever the scientific merits or demerits might be regarding this theory of an oscillating universe, for many of its adherents it appears to be a way to avoid the necessity of a divine creator. If the universe simply has always been, existing in infinite and eternal oscillations of expansion and contraction (or in some other arrangement), then perhaps one could simply assume no need for a deity to have created the world in the beginning—simply because there *is* no beginning. In Stephen Hawking's words from *A Brief History of Time*, "So long as the universe had a beginning, we could suppose it had a creator. But if the universe is really completely self-contained, having no boundary or edge, it would have neither beginning nor end: it would simply be. What place, then, for a creator?"[1]

Of course, the notion of a universe that simply has always been does not necessarily dismiss the possibility of a creator deity; after all, even with an eternally existing universe one might still be tantalized by the simple question of why such a universe exists at all! In fact, Hawking himself asks a much more profoundly theological question than the first when he writes later in the same book, "What is it that breathes fire into the equations and makes a universe for them to describe? . . . Why does the universe go to all

1. Stephen Hawking, *A Brief History of Time: From the Big Bang to Black Holes* (New York: Bantam Books, 1988), 140-41.

the bother of existing?"[2] Nonetheless, it is certainly not impossible to assume that the universe simply does exist, *period*, and that there is no getting around its sheer facticity. It appears that many people are not terribly bothered by the notion that the universe might be nothing other than simply there, in all of its ancient and brute facticity. Indeed, this would entail reading the world as what some philosophers have called a "brute fact."

But let us return to where we began this chapter, with the theistic conviction that the universe has its source in a creator. In the bounds of this conviction, the universe need not always have been—but neither would it simply have appeared out of nothing, or nowhere, without any "outside help." On the other hand, I believe that it is within the bounds of this conviction to hold that it is logically possible that there is a creator *and* that the world in some form or another has always been. In other words, though it has not been a popular option for faith, it is not at all impossible that a creator deity has everlastingly been the creator of worlds, perhaps even infinite worlds before (or alongside!) the so-called "big bang" onset of this present observable universe.

Could such an understanding of the God-world relation still be deemed *creatio ex nihilo*—creation out of nothing? Perhaps the more basic question is, How crucial is *creatio ex nihilo* to Christian faith? What is at stake in the traditional claim that God created the world from nothing? While most Christians probably assume the idea to be biblically and theologically sound, I mentioned already in chapter 1 that for some biblical scholars and theologians the case is not closed on the doctrine of *creatio ex nihilo*.

The theological movement best known, and regularly criticized, for its resistance to this doctrine is that associated with the process philosophy of Alfred North Whitehead (1861–1947). It would be an overstatement to say that all process theologians are in hearty harmony over their rejection of *creatio ex nihilo*, for there is a considerable amount of conversation over this issue among theologians who are at least sympathetic with process thought. Nonetheless, the rejection of this traditional Christian

2. Ibid., 174.

teaching certainly has been something of a hallmark characteristic for process theology, generally speaking. By the same token, while not all process theologians are Wesleyans, there is no doubt that the Wesleyan heritage is notably and widely represented among theologians who identify themselves, to one extent or another, with process thinking.[3] Given this fact, it seems appropriate to wonder whether there is some trend in Wesley's thinking that has lent itself to an amenability with process theology—and further, to wonder whether Wesley's theology might contribute a fresh insight into the issues inherent in the question of the nature of God's creation of the universe.

In this chapter, then, we shall explore the question of whether there is anything distinctive in Wesley's understanding of God that might cast a different hue on the issues arising from *creatio ex nihilo*. But first, we shall explore the salient issues raised by this doctrine. What does *creatio ex nihilo* mean? Why has it been deemed important? What does it imply about God and God's relations to the world? After exploring such questions, we shall be in a better position to inquire as to whether or not John Wesley's thought and practice may lend new insights.

WHY *CREATIO EX NIHILO*?

Literally, *creatio ex nihilo* simply means "creation out of nothing." The phrase may sound simple enough, but is it really? To begin with, do we understand what "nothing" means? In exploring the concept of "nothing," contemporary philosopher Peter van Inwagen has written that "to say that there is nothing is to say that there isn't *anything*, not even a vast emptiness. If there were a vast emptiness, there would be no material objects—no atoms or elementary particles or anything made of them—but there would nevertheless be something: the vast emptiness."[4] Earlier in this

3. See Stone and Oord, eds., *Thy Nature and Thy Name Is Love*, especially chapter 2, Suchocki's "Coming Home"; and Cobb, *Grace and Responsibility*.

4. Peter van Inwagen, *Metaphysics* (Boulder: Westview Press, 1993), 72.

chapter, of course, I offered the same critique for the notion of a quantum vacuum fluctuation as the possible "place" in which our world might have begun: it is not nothing.[5] To claim then that God has created the universe out of nothing appears at first glance to be at least paradoxical, if not sheer nonsense. Nothing, after all, is not some *thing* out of which other things can be generated. From "nothing," no thing can come. "And how can 'nothing' serve as the basis of an explanation?" Van Inwagen asks. "If nothing exists then nothing is going on."[6]

Such musings about nothing may help to point us in an important direction: It is likely that the doctrine of *creatio ex nihilo* has never properly been intended to be a straightforward explanation or description of God's creative activity. Certainly it is not a scientific explanation of our universe's beginnings, and it really is not much of a theological explanation either. Perhaps, instead, it is best understood only as a certain kind of *negation*, as the rejection of an unacceptable alternative. If this is the case, then its function is not so much positive as it is negative, not so much in what it affirms as in what it denies, not so much to offer a certain content of belief as to eliminate an inadequate or dangerous idea.

If this is correct, then the purpose of *creatio ex nihilo* is not really to affirm something about the initial conditions of creation (which are utterly unimaginable to us), but rather to deny the idea that there might conceivably be some element or power that is ultimately outside of God's purview—that there is some reality that exists alongside of God, not owing its very being to God, and thus that is in some regards on equal "ontological footing" with God. The positive implication of *creatio ex nihilo* would then be that God, precisely *as God*, occupies a unique ontological status as sovereign Creator and that there is no other power, reality, or material that exists alongside God apart from God's willing it to be. It is a logical necessity that God creates *ex nihilo* precisely because there is no thing that exists apart from God's creative will and power. The contemporary Lutheran theologian Philip Hefner champions this understanding of *creatio ex nihilo* when he writes that the doctrine

5. See Mark William Worthing, *God, Creation, and Contemporary Physics* (Minneapolis: Fortress Press, 1996), 98-104.

6. Van Inwagen, *Metaphysics*, 72.

exemplifies "the only relationship between the world and God that is consistent with what Christians and Jews believe about God," wherein "the universe and our planet within it are totally dependent upon God for its origin and perseverance."[7]

There are, however, those who find Hefner's claim debatable. It certainly is no longer simply assumed by scholars that creation from nothing is a straightforward biblical teaching. Process theologians are not the only ones who raise questions about the biblical support for the idea. In chapter 2 we touched on the fact that the Hebrew construction in the opening phrase of Genesis 1 has become well known for its ambiguity. It seems likely that the opening of our Bible is saying something like, "When God began creating heaven and earth, the earth was without form and void, with darkness over the face of the deep [waters] and a wind from God sweeping over the surface of the waters." Jon Levenson has argued that the dominant and recurring image for creation in the Hebraic tradition is not *ex nihilo,* but is the more humble claim that God has sufficiently overcome the powers of the abyss to provide for a relatively ordered cosmos. In Levenson's words,

> Two and a half millennia of Western theology have made it easy to forget that throughout the ancient Near Eastern world, including Israel, the point of creation is not the production of matter out of nothing, but rather the emergence of a stable community in a benevolent and life-sustaining order. The defeat by YHWH of the forces that have interrupted that order is intrinsically an act of creation. The fact that order is being restored rather than instituted was not a difference of great consequence in ancient Hebrew culture. To call upon the arm of YHWH to awake as in "days of old" is to acknowledge that those adversarial forces were not annihilated in perpetuity in primordial times. Rising anew, they have escaped their appointed bounds and thus flung a challenge at their divine vanquisher.[8]

Levenson's argument cannot and should not be denied. There is in ancient Hebrew thinking about God and the world something of

7. Philip Hefner, "The Evolution of the Created Co-Creator," in *Cosmos as Creation: Theology and Science in Consonance.* Ted Peters, ed. (Nashville: Abingdon, 1989), 226.
8. Levenson, *Creation and the Persistence of Evil,* 12.

an unfinished struggle between the Creator and the chaotic powers that continues to threaten the stabilities of natural, communal, and individual existence. The mythological elements of that struggle may be muted considerably in Genesis 1, but they are less hidden in many other passages (e.g., Ps. 74:12-17, Isa. 51:9-11, Isa. 27:1). Levenson admits that subsequent developments in Jewish religious thought, particularly in Second Isaiah, appear to be deeply critical of the notion of God having to struggle with resistant chaotic powers, offering instead "a confession that moves dramatically toward the doctrine of *creatio ex nihilo*."[9] On the whole, however, this observation simply underscores the fact that there are uncertainties, ambiguities, and tensions in the history of Israel's thinking about creation.

If the Hebrew Bible is, at best, ambiguous on the issue of *ex nihilo*, the New Testament's testimony is equally indistinct, even if one argues that the evidence is implicitly present. A traditionally favored text is Romans 4:17, where Paul describes God as the One "who gives life to the dead and calls into being that which does not exist" (NASB). This is obviously a creation passage, but it is not particularly obvious that the creative activity described is *ex nihilo*. In fact, since Paul in this passage offers Jesus' resurrection from the dead as the decisive exemplification of God's creative activity, a creation from nothing is precisely *not* what is suggested. God does not "create" the resurrected Christ *ex nihilo*, but raises the crucified Jesus, "a Lamb standing as if it had been slaughtered" (Rev. 5:6), who indeed bears his wounds even in the state of resurrection. Even less does another text traditionally used to support *ex nihilo*, Hebrews 11:3, actually deliver the doctrinal goods. "By faith we understand that the worlds were prepared by the word of God, so that what is seen was not made out of things which are visible" (NASB). Of course we do not want to force texts into dealing with metaphysical issues that were presumably very far removed from their authors' minds, but "things which are [not] visible" is a far cry from "nothing." Wesley in his *Explanatory Notes* in fact assumes that the Hebrews text is referring to "the dark, unapparent chaos" of Genesis 1:2—but then proceeds to protect *ex nihilo* by stating that "this very chaos was created by the divine power, for before it was

9. Ibid., 127.

thus created it had no existence in nature."[10] Nonetheless, many contemporary scholars admit that the only unambiguous textual support for *creatio ex nihilo* may be in the Apocrypha (2 Macc. 7:28), if even there.

The fact of the matter is that the doctrine of *creatio ex nihilo* is not grounded primarily in Scripture but in a certain theological and religious necessity. For example, contemporary Lutheran theologian Ted Peters offers what might be styled an "evangelical" argument for the doctrine that is not dependent upon specific Bible passages per se but on what he sees to be the overall portrait of God and God's saving activity in the gospel of Christ. Peters argues that the seeds of *ex nihilo* lie in the biblical concepts of "historical time, the unrepeatability of events, the eschatological power of creating new things, and the gospel of salvation."[11] It was in the Church's early struggles with dualism and pantheism, Peters and many others maintain, that these seeds sprouted. Conceding the ambiguities in the opening of Genesis, Peters insists that "such textual ambiguity is insufficient grounds for returning to an affirmation of some sort of eternal material chaos and abandoning *ex nihilo*."[12] For Peters, the doctrine of *creatio ex nihilo* is ultimately grounded in soteriology: the only Power that can ultimately deliver us, and indeed the world, is the Power that has created the world. He writes, "If the God of salvation is truly the Lord of all, then this God must also be the source of all."[13] If, on the other hand, there is some element or aspect of our universe that exists not because God calls it into being but *just because*, then there is something of which God is not truly God. This idea is theologically suspect because it implies a dualism of "God and something else" and thus severely compromises the divine uniqueness and sovereignty; similarly, it is religiously repugnant because it means that our worship of God is directed toward a power that is less than ultimate.

On the other hand, there is a somewhat insidious implication of *creatio ex nihilo* that should be brought to light and expunged: the doctrine often seems to imply that God works like a magician who pronounces "Presto!" and pulls a rabbit (i.e., the world) out of a top

10. *NT Notes*, Hebrews 11:3.
11. Peters, *God—the World's Future*, 129.
12. Ibid., 131.
13. Ibid., 129.

hat (i.e., nothing). In this scenario, the creation of the universe appears perfunctory and arbitrary with little if any real investment or care on the Creator's part—a picture that lends itself to a devaluing of the world and our lives in it. We must insist that this is not, and cannot be, what Christians (or Jews or Muslims) mean by creation out of nothing. The particularly Christian conviction that God has created by the Word—the Word that became flesh in the person of Jesus of Nazareth—belies any hint of arbitrariness or caprice in God's act of creation, suggesting instead that creation is the deliberate expression of divine love revealed at Gethsemane and Golgotha. In this light, *creatio ex nihilo* might be well complemented by *creatio ex amore*, the notion that God creates out of—and as an expression of—self-giving, creative love. Mark William Worthing seems to be suggesting as much when he writes:

> A creation out of *absolute* nothingness is an impossibility; [on the other hand,] a creation out of God's own "substance" leads to a pantheistic deification of the physical world. *Creatio ex nihilo*, therefore, signifies the theological recognition that God created a universe distinct from the divine being, not out of any preexisting matter or principle, but out of nothing other than the fullness of God's own being.[14]

Worthing is clearly not espousing pantheism. He is, however, correctly indicating that if creation is not a matter of arbitrary finger-snapping but rather an activity that is *true of*, and *true to*, who and what God is, then it must truly *proceed from* (or "out of") God. If "the fullness of God's own being" (to employ Worthing's phrase) is indeed the love revealed in the ministry of Jesus Christ (1 John 4:8; 3:16), then *creatio ex nihilo* must be complemented (if not challenged, or even corrected) by *creatio ex amore*. Worthing writes further, "Nothing comes out of nothing—but out of nothing other than the fullness of God's own being was created a life-producing universe that is contingent on God in each moment and each aspect of its existence."[15] Indeed, later in this chapter we shall see that such an observation is germane to the Wesleyan theological tradition's understanding of God, a God who is *love, all loves excelling*.

---

14. Worthing, *God, Creation and Contemporary Physics*, 75.
15. Ibid., 110.

PROCESS THOUGHT'S ALTERNATIVE TO *CREATIO EX NIHILO*

In Whitehead's 1927–28 Gifford Lectures at Edinburgh, the grand patron of process thought put it straightforwardly: "It is as true to say that God creates the World, as that the World creates God."[16] Of course he had much more to say on the subject, but this simple statement not only gets to the heart of the process cosmology, it also provides a clear signpost for traditional theological suspicions. What, after all, does it mean to say that "the World creates God"? Even if we were to agree that the world makes its own contributions to God's growing wealth of experience and therefore in some way to God's *being God*, would we be thereby constrained to say that "the World creates God"? Need we say that the God-world relationship is as thoroughly reciprocal as Whitehead implied in his aphorism?

For Whitehead, and for most process theologians after him, to say that "the World creates God" means that there is *necessarily* a world *of some kind* that exists apart from God and independently of God's will or desire. Further, this world is understood to be, in every moment and every event, contributing its rich and multifarious experiences to the vast ocean of divine experience. Both God and the world, Whitehead continued, "are in the grip of the ultimate metaphysical ground, the creative advance into novelty."[17] This "creative advance into novelty" is the ultimate reality, the final word about the God-world reality. No matter how Whitehead's language might be soft-pedaled, even the most sympathetic reading cannot ease the jolt that most Christians would feel if they tried to imagine God "in the grip" of anything else—especially when that grip allegedly belongs to "the ultimate metaphysical ground"! Is not "the ultimate metaphysical ground" one of the things that we have traditionally meant by *God*? What could be more ultimate than God? Two of his early theological interpreters, Henry Nelson Wieman and Bernard Meland, cogently described Whitehead's position in this way:

16. Alfred North Whitehead, *Process and Reality: An Essay in Cosmology*, corrected edition, edited by David Ray Griffin and Donald W. Sherburne (New York: Macmillan, 1978), 348.

17. Ibid., 349.

> God clings to this process of creativity. He is to be found as an order in this process. He does not make this process go. He is not the power back of it. Why does this process keep going on and on and on without end? For no reason at all. It keeps on going and always will go because it is the ultimate nature of things to go and go and go. Whatever meaning and value is brought forth out of this process is due to God, but the process itself is not due to God. Rather, if one is to speak in such terms, God is due to it.[18]

Despite the initially shocking implications of notions such as these, one of the most attractive aspects of this cosmology for process theists is well known: it appears to offer a solution to the problem of evil. In the process view, God is doing the best that God can do to lure the elements of the world toward greater beauty and richer harmony, but since those elements are ultimately not God's creation, God cannot be blamed if they do not behave as God would like. God does the best that God can do, given what God is given to work with from one moment to the next. Yes, God has throughout our aeon called and lured the world into greater levels of complexity and thus of beauty; hence, God is responsible, in an important sense, for the sort of world in which we live. God *could* have left the elements of our universe at the level of the barest puffs of existence, perhaps something roughly comparable to what we now call subatomic particles.[19] (It is evident, however, that at even that "level" we are dealing with a considerable degree of organization and complexity.) If God had done that, of course, there would certainly be nothing of the pain and struggle of our world—but neither would there be creatures such as we who undergo those pains or, contrarily, who enjoy love, beauty, goodness, art, and so on. God apparently deems a world of such richness of experience to be worth the cost; such a world is deemed better than one left in utter triviality and chaos.

What God *could not* have, according to the Whiteheadian position, is no world of any kind, for whether or not there is something other than God is not up to God. We might say, then, that the dominant process notion about God's relation to the world is that God

---

18. Henry Nelson Wieman and Bernard Eugene Meland, *American Philosophies of Religion* (Chicago: Willett, Clark & Co., 1936), 231.
19. See David Griffin, *God, Power, and Evil* (Philadelphia: Westminster, 1976), 292-97, 308-10.

has created it out of *next to nothing*.[20] One might detect a hint of this even in Charles Wesley's poetic allusion to "Nothing's womb." It is creation "from scratch." That is, to be sure, an impressive bit of creative power, but it still leaves us with an unacceptable dualism of "God and something else." John B. Cobb Jr., in his 1965 work *A Christian Natural Theology*, wrote that "in every moment there is given to God a world that has in part determined its own form and that is free to reject in part the new possibilities of ideal realization he offers it."[21] The key point in Cobb's fascinating claim is that this is true of *every moment* precisely because there has always, and everlastingly, been such a world—and more important, the relation that obtains between God and the world is not a relation that God has called into being, or that God particularly wills, or for which God can give an account. It is a relation that simply is.

We might put it this way: process theologians tend to begin with the world of our present experience. In our experience, the world *is* one vast "given." Flowers grow, bloom, and reproduce. Trees take root, spread their leaves, take in the sun, and give back to the earth their seeds from which new trees shall come. Infants are conceived and given birth and begin to grow toward adulthood. New things and new organisms come into existence, but always by the energies and materials donated by other things and organisms. There is no chicken without the egg, no egg without the chicken (and rooster!). We see no evidence of *creatio ex nihilo* in our world, but we do see a continuing and lively creativity ever at work (and at play) to bring about the new. Such is the world in which we live and which lives in us—and process theologians make the claim, essentially, that our present experience is a fundamental clue for intuiting the way it has always been. There simply has *always* been some kind of world with which God creatively labors, some sort of "given" with which God must work, and which possesses its own integrity and powers.

---

20. Clark Williamson gives perhaps the most persuasive argument for this interpretation of God's creative activity in his *A Guest in the House of Israel: Post-Holocaust Church Theology* (Louisville: Westminster/John Knox, 1993), 220-24. See also David Ray Griffin, "Process Theology and the Christian Good News: A Response to Classical Free Will Theism," in John B. Cobb Jr.and Clark H. Pinnock, eds., *Searching for an Adequate God: A Dialogue between Process and Free Will Theists* (Grand Rapids: Eerdmans, 2000), especially 27-32.

21. John B. Cobb Jr., *A Christian Natural Theology Based on the Thought of Alfred North Whitehead* (Philadelphia: Westminster, 1965), 205.

Again, an important reason this is attractive to many process thinkers is that to relieve God of omnipotence in this way also relieves God of omni-responsibility for the pain and suffering of our world. Pain and struggle become a part of the "given" of a world possessing complexity. It may be easier to appreciate the power of this position by making a move similar to that made in the first section of this chapter: we might suggest that it is not so much what Whitehead and his followers *affirm* about God and the world that is important, as it is what they *deny*. They deny *creatio ex nihilo* because to affirm it would be, presumably, to affirm that God possesses the sort of power that could readily and immediately—"at the drop of a hat," as it were—change and re-create the world such that it would have no more pain, suffering, evil, or heartache. This is, admittedly, the gist of the eschatological hopes of virtually all theistic traditions, and it is a subject to which we shall return in greater detail in chapter 7. If indeed God is able to exercise such power, it seems that we are at a loss to know why God has not exercised it more effectively to this point.

The book of Revelation is traditionally and popularly thought to describe this kind of unilateral divine power, a power bringing the present age to a cataclysmic end and ushering in a new world. Yet that text begins with the claim that its divine denouement "must soon take place" (1:1). Should it not matter to theological reflection that two millenia later it has yet to take place? What is God waiting for? What are *we* waiting for God to do? Is God unable, or simply unwilling, to create "a new heaven and a new earth" (Rev. 21:1)? Are process theologians correct in their suspicions about traditional affirmations of divine omnipotence?

This is a dilemma upon whose horns it is not difficult to become impaled. A God who is, like the world, "in the grip" of certain metaphysical constraints but nonetheless labors ceaselessly to call that world forward into harmony, beauty, and zest plays the role of a tragic hero, perhaps a tragic lover. Such a God is essentially unable to bring about a perfect world; such a God is also not the sort of God that we have traditionally imagined God to be—or to *have to be* in order to be what we have meant by "God." Perhaps, however, we should be open to the possibility that we have not always imagined the right things when we have said "God." But what alternative does Whitehead's imagination offer us for our term "God"? Shall we worship and serve a maker who, along with the world, is "in the grip of the ultimate metaphysical ground, the creative advance into novelty"?

The traditional critique is that, even if one might be moved to admire such a deity, one would not likely bow one's knee in awe or worship. Yes, such an understanding of deity can exonerate God of the charge of cruelty, for in this scenario God cannot help the hard and brute fact that both the deity and the world are exemplifications of creative advance, Whitehead's "ultimate metaphysical ground." But the flip side of that consolation is that God is no longer thought to be truly the Creator of the world, but in fact a part of the world. We find ourselves in a world where the one that we call God is also a member, a being among other beings in a larger ontological environment. Which horn of this dilemma is less pointed?

Perhaps it is a function of Western religious conditioning, but the idea of God many of us bear seems unavoidably linked to what philosophers sometimes call "the cosmological questions." Why is there a cosmos? Where did the world come from? Why is there something, rather than nothing at all? These are questions that Whitehead was apparently neither prepared nor willing to answer. Thomas Aquinas (1225–74) in his arguments for God would seem to have said it well for the bulk of Western theists over the centuries when he wrote, "[It] is necessary to arrive at a first mover, moved by no other; . . . it is necessary to admit a first efficient cause. . . . We cannot but admit the existence of some being having of itself its own necessity, and not receiving it from another, but rather causing in others their necessity. This all men speak of as God."[22] To paraphrase the Angelic Doctor: *This is what we mean by God*. But it is evident that this is not what Whitehead meant by God. Whitehead's vision of the God-world relation does not intend at all to address the cosmological question. This may indeed help somewhat with the problem of evil by exonerating God, but one must wonder if, in the long run, it is a bit of cold comfort. For the

22. Thomas Aquinas, *Summa Theologica*, as cited by Anton C. Pegis, *Introduction to St. Thomas Aquinas* (New York: Modern Library, 1945), 25, 26.

same cosmology that would exonerate God of evil in our world also offers us a God who cannot truly bring about an ultimate deliverance for creation. As Cobb put it, in every moment there is given to God a world with which God works, calling each moment, each event of that world toward a greater good—but it is a good that God finally cannot guarantee.

Similarly, the metaphysical issue of unitary explanation is also at stake in this discussion. Put simply, can we accept a religious cosmology that imagines God to be one instance of creative advance, albeit a very important one, among other countless instances? Does not the mind—at least the Western, theistic mind!—earnestly yearn for the beauty and simplicity of some unitary and unifying source? If so, then Whitehead's vision of deity is indeed insufficient. As Wieman and Meland observed over sixty years ago, "Perhaps it makes more sense [in Whitehead's system] to say there are three kinds of ultimate reality—this process [of creativity], God and the eternal forms or possibilities which come into existence and pass out of existence."[23] *Three* kinds? One "kind of ultimate reality" is just the right amount for most human minds! Even only *two*—God and "next to nothing"—is one too many. Thus, "next to nothing" itself is too much when it comes to an adequate doctrine of creation. Wesley himself preached that "it is impossible there should be two Gods, or two Eternals" and drew the conclusion that "anything [that] had existed from eternity . . . must be God. Yea, it must be the one God."[24]

Earlier in this chapter, I mentioned that philosophers occasionally use a category they identify as "brute fact." For example, the prominent philosopher of religion John Hick has suggested that people who refuse to take the cosmological question ("Why is there a world?" or "Why is there anything at all?") seriously appear to be willing to consider the world to be "a mere unintelligible brute fact," that is, *it just is, period*. As Hick has written, "Apart from the emotional coloring suggested by the phrase ['a mere unintelligible brute fact'], this is precisely what the skeptic believes [the universe] to be; and to exclude this possibility at the outset is merely to beg

23. Wieman and Meland, *American Philosophies of Religion*, 231.
24. Sermon 54, "On Eternity," §I.7, *Works* 2:361-62.

the question at issue."[25] Admittedly, the traditional theist believes that the universe is not a "brute fact," accounting for it as the creation of God. But what is often overlooked, and indeed what Hick overlooks in this particular treatment of the issue, is that for the believer a brute fact yet remains: now the "brute fact" is none other than God. Granted, "brute fact" is not a particularly endearing or widely used label for God, but traditional theism would not reject the title's implications: there is no explanation for God; there is nothing "behind" or "before" God; *God simply is and one cannot ask why*. Hence, according to the logic of traditional theism, if there is no Creator then the universe must be a "brute fact"—and if there is a Creator who is truly God then this Creator is a "brute fact" for which we can give no account or explanation.

What makes Whitehead's cosmology so unusual is that it postulates two "brute facts," God *and* the world. This is twice as many brute facts as most people, at least of the Western mind, are able or willing to entertain. Whether it is because of intuition, the structure of human thought, religious tradition, or cultural conditioning may be difficult to say, but it seems that we seek some unitary and unifying ground of thought, existence, and experience. Process thought appears not to offer such a ground, or if it does, it is in the principle of creativity itself. For Whitehead and many of his followers, if there is such a ground, it is not in God. From the perspective of Christian tradition, such dualism is an obvious compromise of divine sovereignty and thus is equivalent to idolatry.

To be fair, it should be noted that some process theologians have occasionally offered cautious suggestions regarding the nature of God's relationship to the world that nudge the Whiteheadian tradition at least a little toward *creatio ex nihilo*. For example, over three decades ago Cobb observed that, for Whitehead, "the role of the creator is to provide form for a reality given to him." Cobb proceeded to argue, however, that "the role of the creator in Whitehead must be more drastic . . . than Whitehead recognized,"[26] and did so on the grounds of

25. John Hick, *Philosophy of Religion*, 4th edition (Englewood Cliffs, N.J.: Prentice Hall, 1990), 21.
26. Cobb, Christian Natural Theology, 220.

Whitehead's own metaphysic. It was characteristic of Whitehead to dismiss the cosmological question ("Why is there a world?"), but Cobb admirably and rightly pushes it anyway:

> Whitehead . . . was convinced that the process is everlasting. Creativity will always take new forms, but it will always continue to be unchangingly creative. My point is only that the notion of creativity provides no grounds for this faith. . . . If the question as to why things are at all is raised in the Whiteheadian context, the answer must be in terms of the decisions of actual entities. We have already seen that the decisive element in the initiation of each actual occasion is the granting to that occasion of an initial aim. Since Whitehead attributes this function to God, it seems that, to a greater degree than Whitehead intended, God must be conceived as being the reason that entities occur at all as well as determining the limits within which they can achieve their own forms.[27]

Cobb here makes a considerable stride toward a more traditional understanding of God's role as Creator of the world. Nevertheless, Cobb maintains the God-world relation as an everlasting and mutually creative dynamic. One is reminded again of Whitehead's jarring aphorism, "It is as true to say that God creates the World, as that the World creates God." Cobb proceeds in his ruminations on God's relation to the world:

> It is no objection to my mind that if that which has the power to give existence requires also that it receive existence, then we are involved in an infinite regress. I assume that we are indeed involved in an endless regress. Each divine occasion . . . must receive its being from its predecessors, and I can imagine no beginning of such a series.[28]

There are other process theologians, or theologians deeply influenced by process modes of thought, who have been even more adamant in questioning Whitehead's understanding of God's creative role. Thinkers sympathetic to the Whiteheadian project such as Robert Neville, Langdon Gilkey, Thomas Hosinski, and David

27. Ibid., 211.
28. Ibid., 212.

Tracy have nonetheless raised pointed questions regarding Whitehead's sundering of creativity from God.[29] They wonder if there is not a way to speak of God's continually interactive and persuasive presence in the world *and* of the world's own real powers and vitalities without surrendering the traditional doctrine of *creatio ex nihilo*. It is time for us to turn more explicitly to John Wesley as a potential resource in this issue.

A WESLEYAN READING OF *CREATIO EX NIHILO*

Wesley did not write extensively on the doctrine of creation per se, but when he did, it is clear that he assumed the doctrine of *creatio ex nihilo*. Further, as we shall detail in chapters 4 and 5, he understood this doctrine to imply that all of creation hangs every moment upon the continuing, sustaining, creative grace of God. He probably said it no more plainly than in his 1780 sermon "Spiritual Worship":

> He "beareth," upholdeth, sustaineth, "all" created "things by the word of his power," by the same powerful word which brought them out of nothing. As this was absolutely necessary for the beginning of their existence, it is equally so for the continuance of it: were his almighty influence withdrawn, they could not subsist a moment longer. Hold up a stone in the air; the moment you withdraw your hand, it naturally falls to the ground. In like manner, were he to withdraw his hand for a moment the creation would fall into nothing.[30]

29. See, for example, Robert Neville, *Creativity and God: A Challenge to Process Theology* (New York: Seabury, 1980); Langdon Gilkey, *Reaping the Whirlwind: A Christian Interpretation of History* (New York: Seabury, 1976); David Tracy, "Kenosis, Sunyata and Trinity" in *The Emptying God: A Buddhist-Jewish-Christian Conversation*, John B. Cobb Jr. and Christopher Ives (Maryknoll, N.Y.: Orbis, 1990), 139-140; and Thomas Hosinski, *Stubborn Fact and Creative Advance: An Introduction to the Metaphysics of Alfred North Whitehead* (Lanham, Md.: Rowman & Littlefield, 1993). Hosinski is the least known of these authors, but also the one most sympathetic to the Whiteheadian vision. All the more noteworthy, then, that on the question of Whitehead's separation of creativity from God, Hosinski writes that "Christian theology might need to revise Whitehead's philosophy"(244).

30. Sermon 77, "Spiritual Worship," §I.3, *Works* 3:91. It is noteworthy that Wesley was speaking in this passage specifically of Christ as "the true God, the only Cause, the sole Creator of all things."

Similarly, in his sermonic treatment of the doctrine of divine omnipresence Wesley wrote that, apart from God's continuously sustaining presence throughout the universe, "everything would in an instant sink into its primitive nothing."[31] Such scraps of evidence could be multiplied, but the point should be clear: if Wesley has a fresh word for the contemporary discussion over *ex nihilo*, it will not be an explicit word. Rather, it will have to be unearthed as a word-concept that resides implicitly in the "depth grammar" of Wesley's overall vision of the nature and mode of God's activity in the world.

One word that would decidedly *not* appear to hold much promise in this regard is "almighty." To be "all-mighty" literally means omnipotence, and omnipotence, strictly interpreted, implies that God exercises all power and thus that creatures exercise none. Hence, "almighty" at first glance seems to uphold a traditional reading of *creatio ex nihilo*. The term may nonetheless provide an important starting point. First, let us note that Wesley used it in the extended quotation immediately preceding, writing of the "almighty influence" that continuously sustains "all created things." Second, let us note Cobb's insightful exegesis of the term "almighty" in the Charles Wesley hymn "Love Divine, All Loves Excelling." Reading Wesley through a process lens, Cobb argues that the Wesley brothers celebrated the "centrality of divine love . . . most powerfully in the hymns of early Methodism,"[32] and that the Wesleyan understanding of God is never simply in terms of sheer sovereignty or unrestrained power. Rather, at the heart of this theological vision is not *power as such* but the *power of divine love* that can empower us to love.

Cobb illustrates this understanding of divine power as empowering love by some careful exegetical work on the hymn in question. He points out that in the Wesleys' carefully crafted lyrics, the second verse does not address God as "Almighty," as in "Come, Almighty, *to deliver*." Rather, the Wesleys prayed that "Love divine" would "Come, almighty to deliver" us from bondage to sin. Cobb writes:

31. Sermon 118, "On the Omnipresence of God," §II.1, *Works* 4:42.
32. Cobb, *Grace and Responsibility*, 58. The hymn is #374, *Works* 7:545-47.

> [A]ddressing God simply as "Almighty" would not be Wesleyan. In this context it would be asking the Omnipotent One to take one form of action, namely, deliverance, when divine power might be used in other ways. The Wesleys did not think of divine power in this abstract sense. . . . Hence, in this hymn, Divine Love is characterized as "almighty to deliver." Divine Love is the only power there is for deliverance. The focus in this hymn is on God's love of us and our dependence on that love's indwelling us.[33]

Cobb is right: there is no question that the preaching, liturgy, and theology of the Wesleys, and of the Wesleyan tradition after them, have revolved around this central Johannine conviction that "God is love" (1 John 4:8, 16). If one must choose between addressing God as "Love Divine" or as "Almighty," there should be no question, no agonizing, for a Christian believer of the Wesleyan stream. The question, of course, is whether one must choose. Let us not assume yet that we must; instead, let us pursue this term "almighty" further.

In the passage cited earlier from his sermon "Spiritual Worship," we observe that Wesley could refer to God in Christ's "almighty influence" in the sustaining of the entire universe. Might we follow Cobb's enlightening exegesis of "almighty" and suggest that God who is Love is not only "almighty to deliver" but also "almighty to influence"? This, in fact, raises a fascinating possibility: to "influence" literally means to "flow into," and Cobb himself has interpreted Wesley as believing that "with respect to living things, their capacity to move is itself due to the way in which God flows into them, thereby causing them to become agents."[34] This divine influencing, or "flowing into"—which I have named *creative grace* in this book—is not almighty in the sense that it absolutely or unilaterally determines either the nature or the activity of God's creatures. Such a notion would clearly go against the grain of Wesley's understanding of God's ways in the world, or at least of God's ways with human creatures. We may even detect a hint of Wesley interpreting Scripture in this very direction near the end of his sermon "On the Omnipresence of God." There he exhorts his readers, "Never forget [God's] comprehensive word to the great father of the faithful: 'I

33. Ibid., 59.
34. Ibid., 51.

am the Almighty' (rather, the *All-sufficient*) 'God; walk before me, and be thou perfect!'"[35] Wesley here explicitly interprets "almighty" not in terms of sheer unlimited power but instead as divine sufficiency, as God's empowering of the human to "walk perfectly" (i.e., in love) in God's presence.

The divine influence is, then, an *empowering* of the creature to "move itself," to exercise the agency appropriate to its capacities. God does not "move" the creature, but graciously and humbly *gifts* and *graces* the creature with the power of its own agency and integrity as a creature. God's in-flowing *is* almighty, however, at least in the sense that God is not limited in God's capacity to influence the world in precisely this way of self-emptying, other-empowering love. In Wesley's words, "there is no point of space, whether within or without the bounds of creation, where God is not"[36]—and thus no place, no creature, no event, where God is not the Inflowing Presence.[37]

To think of God as the Inflowing Presence is to read the doctrine of omnipotence in a more distinctly Wesleyan way. We may continue to say that God is omnipotent, recognizing that the very nature of this divine potency—this self-giving, other-empowering and other-receiving love—is to be everlastingly outpoured and flowing into "the other," into all creatures and the creation as an unimaginably vast and varied whole. Thus, the Indwelling Presence of "Love divine, all loves excelling" is omnipotent—but does not *have* all the power precisely because this Love does not *hoard* all the power. That power is by nature freely outpoured to the world as its empowering *to be*. As Cobb writes of the hymn under consideration, "the whole hymn follows from understanding God as Love that pours itself into human beings"[38]—and, we could surely add with Cobb's thorough approval, into all that exists. In this way, a Wesleyan understanding of the nature of God would move a step toward the process theological claim that God *cannot* exercise coercive power—not, however, because of an ultimate metaphysical structure of reality to which even God is necessarily

35. Sermon 118, "On the Omnipresence of God," §III.6, *Works* 4:47.

36. Ibid., §I.1, *Works* 4:42.

37. For a compelling extended meditation on this image of God as the Inflowing Presence, see Suchocki, *In God's Presence*, 4-5, 25-29.

38. Cobb, *Grace and Responsibility*, 58.

subject, for this simply compromises too much of a traditional understanding of God's role as Creator. Instead, a Wesleyan reading of creation might postulate that God *cannot* exercise coercive power precisely because it would be contrary to God's character of self-emptying, compassionate Love to do so. It is simply not in God's nature to coerce creatures—human or otherwise—but instead to create and empower them toward their own integrity and agency. Conversely, if God were to exercise coercive power in or over the world, this would be contrary to God's purpose in creating responsible agents who can respond to, and grow in, love. God cannot force us, or the world, to go the way of divine love because it would not be consistent with Love Divine to do so. "God acts . . . throughout the whole compass of his creation," Wesley preached, "by . . . strongly and sweetly influencing all, and yet without destroying the liberty of his rational creatures."[39]

Further, if this Inflowing Presence is everywhere present and active—if there is *no place*, "no point of space," as Wesley put it, where God is not—then there is equally *no time* where God is not this Inflowing Presence of "Love Divine, all loves excelling." Here, then, we find ourselves hedging toward the likelihood of an everlasting creation not entirely unlike the model espoused by process theologians. We have already submitted in chapter 2 that, for Wesley, the fundamental hermeneutical principle is that *God is love*. If God's eternal character is the self-offering love revealed in the cross of Jesus (1 John 3:16), and if God is not *incidentally* the Creator—that is, not creating arbitrarily but as the expression of divine creative and recreative love—then presumably there was no time when God was not this sort of God. The creator God did not pop out of a hat any more than the world did. The age-old conundrum about why God began to create when God did, and not sooner—or why then, and not some other time—is thus revealed for the false problem that it is.

Wesley himself betrayed an awareness of this "problem" (but not its solution) when, in his sermon "The Unity of the Divine Being," he wrote, "At that point of duration which the infinite wisdom of God saw to be most proper, for reasons which lie hid in the abyss of his own understanding, not to be fathomed by any finite mind,

39. Sermon 118, "On the Omnipresence of God," §II.1, *Works* 4:42, 43.

God 'called into being all that is', created the heavens and the earth."[40] If Wesley had understood the notion of God as Creator more consistently with his own "depth grammar" about God as the Inflowing Presence of Love Divine, then perhaps he could have understood creation less as *ex nihilo* and more as *ex amore*. If, in other words, it is the very nature of God to be the outflow of self-giving, other-receiving, empowering Love, then it makes theological sense to speculate that God is indeed everlastingly creating world upon world. As many theologians from at least as far back as Aquinas have observed, there is no inherent logical reason why *creatio ex nihilo* automatically or necessarily excludes *creatio continua*, the notion of an everlasting activity of creation by God in which God always is lovingly creating by "almighty influence," that is, laboring redemptively with "the world that is given to [God] in that moment."[41] The contemporary Presbyterian theologian Daniel Migliore helps us make this loosely "Wesleyan" point:

> In [a] sense, . . . creation may be called "necessary"—that is, in the sense that God creates in total consistency with God's nature. Creation fittingly expresses the true character of God, who is love. . . . To speak of God as the creator is to speak of a beneficent, generous God, whose love and will-to-community are freely, consistently, and fittingly displayed in the act of creation. . . . In the act of creation, God already manifests the self-communicating, other-affirming, community-forming love that defines God's eternal triune reality and that is decisively disclosed in the ministry and sacrificial death of Jesus Christ. God is love, and this eternal love of the triune God constitutes, in Jonathan Edwards' words, a "disposition to abundant communication."[42]

If God has never been other than a "disposition to abundant communication," then there has *never been when time was not*—for time is an aspect of creation, and such a God as we are here attempting to describe has "always" been a loving Creator, everlastingly creating, "always" laboring with a world by the almighty inflowing of divine love. Hence, both the nature of creation as

40. Sermon 120, "The Unity of the Divine Being," §8, *Works* 4:63.
41. John B. Cobb Jr., *God and the World* (Philadelphia: Westminster, 1969), 91.
42. Daniel Migliore, *Faith Seeking Understanding: An Introduction to Christian Theology* (Grand Rapids: Eerdmans, 1991), 85.

timeful, and more important the nature of God as creative, abundant, and fecund love, strongly imply the theological concept of an everlasting and continuing creation. While such a notion may play havoc with our sequentially ordered minds, it should also help Christians, and especially Christians of the Wesleyan theological tradition, to "create some space" of their own for appreciating the process notion that God has always had some world with which God labors—some world which "comes" to God, as it were, as a "given." We must add, however, that it is precisely at this point that the traditional safeguard of *creatio ex nihilo* is critical as a check to the Whiteheadian idea of a world for which God finally and ultimately cannot account, as though it were ultimately an alien "other" outside the divine purview.

Finally, and perhaps most important, a Wesleyan insistence upon *ex nihilo* should not grow out of a religious fascination with sheer power; it should not be a result of worshiping utter omnipotence as though that were in itself a religious value. For Wesley and Wesleyans, after all, "the heaven of heavens is love,"[43] not power. If we keep the primary accent on divine love as we remember Wesley's foremost theological concern—how it is that God *saves and sanctifies us*—then *ex nihilo* becomes important on soteriological grounds, as already suggested in the work of Ted Peters. Wesleyanism, it seems, generally would follow the soterio-logic of some of the Church's most important and influential early thinkers, such as Irenaeus and Athanasius, who taught that the only power that can truly save a fallen creation is the power of our *Creator*, Maker of heaven and earth. Thus, while Cobb is correct in arguing that in their hymn "Love Divine, All Loves Excelling" the Wesleys characterize God as "almighty to deliver," the argument of the early church theologians is that the only One sufficiently mighty to deliver is One who is almighty to *create all things*. Further, unless God creates all things *ex nihilo*, then there is an unaccountable power in reality that God in fact may not be almighty to deliver—or from which God may finally be unable to deliver us! In fact, in Whitehead's own words, such a God is "in the grip" (or at least in a serious grappling match) with that unaccountable power. For this reason the Wesleyan tradition in the

43. *Plain Account of Christian Perfection*, §25, Q. 33, *Works* (Jackson) 11:430.

main shall always, I predict, embrace *creatio ex nihilo*, and is on good ground for doing so. If the power to deliver is not also the power to create, then the ultimate healing of creation is uncertain on metaphysical grounds. Hence, the power of God's saving and sanctifying grace should be rooted theologically in God's power to create that which God redeems. This conviction reflects the Wesleyan insistence upon the *priority of grace*.

Of course, while a Wesleyan understanding of salvation must always begin with the priority of grace, it never simply ends there. Wesley consistently understood divine grace to be evocative grace, alluring grace, a grace that calls us but does not coerce us or negate our creaturely realities and vitalities. Once again, *ex amore* begins to assert itself as a counterbalance for *ex nihilo*. If God's labors to "renew us in love" through Christ by the Spirit always take seriously our cooperation with, and contribution to, sanctifying grace, then God does not recreate us into the divine image instantaneously or *ex nihilo*. Instead, the nature of God's activity is to work redemptively with real human beings as they truly exist in this world "moment by moment." In fact, as far as our Scriptures testify, and as we shall explore more deeply in the next two chapters, it would seem that new creation inevitably emerges from the "old" by the inflowing power of God. The apostle Paul in Romans 8, for example, describes the creation we inhabit as itself yearning for divine liberation and describes the eschatological "adoption" of God's children as specifically involving "the redemption of our [present] bodies." One could, accordingly, argue the other side of Ted Peters's "evangelical" exposition of *ex nihilo* along these lines: what we know, through experience, of God's creative and recreative activity is that God works with the material that is available. This understanding of grace, wherein God gently and lovingly works *with* us, not *above* or *in spite of* us, assuredly bears some consonance with a Whiteheadian cosmology, wherein the same can be said for how God works with the world. Such an ideal reflects the Wesleyan insistence upon the *responsibility of the creatures* to the initiatives of grace.

If these speculations about God's nature as everlastingly creative, in-flowing love are not entirely off the mark, then it is not impossible that God has never been without a world—that indeed God has labored everlastingly and always with *some kind* or *another* of creaturely responses to grace. In this view of the relation between divine grace and creaturely response, the world's capacities to respond in any given circumstance always depend greatly upon the responses of those creatures that have come before to set the scene. This much sounds "process." However, if there has been, and everlastingly will be, a world of creaturely response, it is not because such a world exists of its own necessity; rather, it exists because "Love Divine, all loves excelling" freely and abundantly creates *ex amore*! This much sounds Wesleyan. Perhaps in this way we do, in fact, find a Wesleyan interpretation of Creator and creation that at least is not inimical to a processive vision of the world. Such in fact will be a fundamental assumption in the chapters that follow.

PART II
MOLDING

CHAPTER 4

"THOU ART THE UNIVERSAL SOUL"

To Live, Move, and Dwell in God

Thou art the Universal Soul,
The Plastick Power that fills the whole,
And governs Earth, Air, Sea, and Sky.

Charles Wesley, *Hymns of Petition and Thanksgiving for the Promise of the Father*, #28

In a Wesleyan reading of the world, does the world really matter? Do we even actually care to *try* to read the world, or to listen to the world and its multitude of voices? Does the world in which we live have significance in, of, or for itself? Or is it instead merely a prelude to something better? Is the material world *truly* good, or is its goodness a theoretical notion we affirm because we recognize, at least vaguely, that this is a biblical teaching that distinguishes Christians from ancient gnostics and contemporary Christian Scientists? Is existence in this world a disappointment—and perhaps all the more of a disappointment, or disillusionment, the more "spiritual" we become? To be truly spiritual, are we constrained somehow to leave behind the body, the world, matter itself?

A consistent theme throughout this book is that the world does, or at least *should*, matter to Christians of the Wesleyan tradition. Further, the reasons the world matters (or should matter) to Wesleyans are in great measure the reasons the world matters (or should matter) to all Christians. The argument of this book is not that Christians of the Wesleyan tradition are on some kind of inside track when it comes to thinking about and caring for God's world. Rather, the point is to explore the extent to which the theological emphases, concerns, and practices that characterized John Wesley's ministry offer any distinctive contributions to Christian faith in relation to our living environment of land and sea, sky and stream, and fellow living creatures. In this chapter we shall explore another uniquely Wesleyan contribution to these crucial matters, though in a vein of Wesley's thought that has become largely forgotten and mostly unmined.

Before we have recourse to Wesley, however, let us briefly touch on the three cardinal biblical teachings that contribute significantly to the proposition that the world matters to all Christians, and not only to Wesleyans.

CRITICAL CHRISTIAN TEACHINGS ABOUT THE MATERIAL WORLD

First, all Christians, and for that matter Jews and Muslims, affirm that God's creation is good. Peoples of the biblical tradition insist on the goodness of creation because it has been called into being by God who is good, indeed who alone is good in the ultimate sense (Mark 10:18). Further, the testimony of the opening chapter of Genesis is that this God who alone is good deems creation "good" with each day's labor, a valuation that is never retracted and in fact is reaffirmed in the New Testament (1 Tim. 4:3-4).

If "in the beginning" the God who created the heavens and the earth pronounces it to be good, what about "in the end"? Jesus of Nazareth, Paul the apostle of Christ to the Gentiles, and the Apostles' Creed all teach us to expect and hope for the resurrection of the body. Whatever bodily resurrection might entail, it is clear that this hope is for more than simply the survival of a nonmaterial soul. Paul insists in 1 Corinthians 15 that it is the body that shall be raised to glory, even if he finally has recourse to describing it as a "spiritual body." It is clear that Paul assumes that Jesus' resurrection / body provides the pattern for our own resurrection / body yet to come, and whatever Jesus was (and is), the Gospels certainly teach that the resurrected Christ was no disembodied soul or wispy spirit. The doctrine of the resurrection of the body, to put it simply, underscores the goodness and redeemability of our physical nature. If we add the tantalizing suggestion of Paul in Romans 8 that in company with the redemption of our bodies, the presently groaning creation will itself be liberated from bondage in the age to come—a suggestion we will explore in some detail in chapter 8—then we begin to appreciate that biblical teaching calls us to recognize and celebrate the goodness and worth of material creation in the eyes of God.

The creation of a good world in the beginning, coupled with the resurrection of the body and redemption of creation in the end, are fundamental convictions about the material world's worth that are not unique to Christians but are in fact shared with many Jews and virtually all Muslims. Thus, these two reasons for why the world matters to Christians are in fact reasons embraced by all "people of the Book," to borrow the old Muslim phrase. But there is a third reason that is utterly unique to Christians, a reason that emerges in the midst of history rather than in its beginning or end—and a reason that would lead us to question whether Christians are really best described as "people of the Book"! This third reason for why the world matters to Christians is, of course, the incarnation of the Word who is God.

"In the beginning was the Word," begins John's Gospel, "and the Word was with God, and the Word was God. . . . And the Word became flesh, and lived among us . . . full of grace and truth" (John 1:1, 14). If creation and resurrection are doctrines Christians share in some respects with Jews and Muslims, the doctrine of the incarnation of the Word is absolutely and uniquely Christian. Thus, for Christians "the Word" refers not primarily to a book but to a truly human being. In the doctrine of the incarnation of God in the human person of Jesus Christ, Christians make the bold claim that the Creator of all things has truly, intimately, and decisively entered into creation as a first-century Jew of Galilee. Christian faith in God is, then, not simply the bare affirmation that God exists; it is rather, in Wesley's words, a confidence "steadily fixed . . . on God in Christ, reconciling the world unto himself"[1]—with the full understanding that Christ was, and is, truly human. No wonder,

1. Sermon 28, "Sermon on the Mount, VIII," §4, *Works* 1:614.

then, that Wesley's fellow Anglican of two centuries later, William Temple, wrote in his 1933 Gifford Lectures some of the most often quoted lines in twentieth-century Christian theology:

> It may safely be said that one ground for the hope of Christianity . . . lies in the fact that it is the most avowedly materialist of all the great religions. . . . Its own most central saying is: "The Word was made flesh," where the last term was, no doubt, chosen because of its specially materialistic associations. By the very nature of its central doctrine Christianity is committed to a belief in the ultimate significance of the historical process, and in the reality of matter and its place in the divine scheme.[2]

The good creation of a good God, the resurrection of the body within the context of a redeemed creation, the incarnation of the Word as a truly human person—all of these critical "moments" in the Christian estimation of history are understandably important in considering why the world matters to Christians, or at least why it should. And yet, can there be any denying that for many Christians the world is regarded largely as a prelude to "the real thing," to "what really counts"—eternity in a spiritual heaven? Is this not the likely reason for Temple's use of the adverb *avowedly* to modify the "materialist" commitments of Christianity? For far too many Christian people, we live in a throwaway world, and practices for the good of the environment are all-too-often ignored and even castigated as a misdirection of our energies. Putting it simply, if Jesus is returning any time now and the world is to be destroyed, then there is no need to concern ourselves with the world our descendants will inherit. Or, in the blunt sentiment once blurted at me, "When Jesus comes back, what good will all your environmental tree-hugging do you then?"

This brand of popular Christian thinking apparently ignores God's blessing of creation's goodness in Genesis 1, and thus also fails to take seriously the human calling to image or represent *(re-present)* the Creator by caring for the creation. Further, this sort of thinking also does not take very seriously the profound depths of the Johannine testimony that the Word who was and is God has

2. William Temple, *Nature, Man and God* (London: Macmillan & Co., 1964), 478.

become flesh and dwelled among us on this planet and in our history. Rather than recognizing that the logic of the incarnation is that God has entered into creation as a true human being—indeed, as creaturely *flesh*—in order to redeem and restore creation, all too often Christians yet fall prey to the gnostic heresy that a spiritual Christ has descended in order to deliver us out of a filthy, flea-ridden world of bodily suffering. Whereas the logic of the incarnation traces God's radical movement *toward* embodiment and *into* creation for the creatures' sake, the logic of a gnostically tinged Christianity pushes in the opposite direction of a disembodied soul's escape *from* material creation. I think of the lyrics in a song by the 1980s pop group Police, "We are spirits in the material world"; while I love the music, the song's blatant dualism of spirit and body, its incipiently gnostic degrading of physical existence, is enough to make me press fast-forward.

If the goodness of creation and the logic of the incarnation seem often forgotten in many Christian minds, our third and final "moment" of the resurrection of the body rarely fares better. For all too many Christian people, hope for life beyond our present temporal horizon is centered much more in the Platonic notion of the soul's immortality than in the Pauline confidence in the resurrection of the body. Again, the implications are obvious: all that really matters is the eternal soul, and salvation is about delivering that soul from the material world and its temptations and evils. All that really lasts, all that really *matters*, is *non-matter*: the nonmaterial, the spiritual, the eternal.

Obviously, these tendencies in thought and practice, which can only be characterized as gnostic, must be opposed. They have profound implications for the way we think about ecology, about the world we inhabit, about the nature of Christian ministry and evangelism, and certainly about ourselves as bodily creatures in a bodily world. Christian pastors, teachers, and leaders must insist that the goodness of bodily existence is celebrated in the narratives of creation, reaffirmed in the gospel of the Incarnation, and anticipated in the hope of the resurrection. Our two- thousand-year struggle with the heresies of gnosticism and docetism make it clear that this overspiritualization, this de-bodification, is a persistently recurring threat to Christian faith and practice.

Absolutely important as these three "moments" of creation, incarnation, and resurrection are to a properly biblical and Christian valuation of this world, they can too easily be seen as isolated "crisis" moments that dramatically puncture the world with an occasional divine intrusion: God at the beginning, God at the end, God in the middle, but God relatively absent all the rest of the time! In this case, while the three decisive "moments" of which we have spoken are given assent, they tend to come across as wholly discontinuous and inexplicable exceptions to an otherwise god-forsaken and seemingly autonomous world. For all of Christian orthodoxy's insistence upon these three cardinal convictions—each of them is, to be sure, given assent in the Apostles' Creed—they can easily come across as simply "three more things to believe." My argument is that these three "crisis moments" should not be divorced from, and cannot be adequately appreciated without, a more comprehensive and cosmological model of the ongoing processes of God's creating and sustaining presence in the world. Part of this model, of course, involves the expansion of our thinking about God's creation of the world beyond some originary moment so as to include a notion of God's *continual creating*. We have already explored this notion in previous chapters. In the present chapter let us press a little further the question of God's present, "in-this-very-moment" relation to the world. How are we to imagine or envision the nature of God's present relation to this world in which we live? To put the question very simply: *Where is God now*? Further, how might our answer to this question influence our thinking and practices regarding the world?

Considering Omnipresence

Let us begin to venture a reply to our question about the present location of the deity vis-à-vis the created universe by attending to the primary answer of Christian tradition. A favorite theological term for describing God in relation to the category of space is *omnipresence*. To be sure, omnipresence has not been interpreted by all theologians in just the same way, but the simplest definition would be that *God is everywhere*. Of course, if it is true that God is everywhere, three qualifications immediately suggest themselves.

First, since God presumably is no simple object among other objects, the proposition that God is everywhere ought not to be understood simplistically or too straightforwardly, that is, that God is invisibly extended substance. Instead, the notion that God is everywhere present must be chastened by the ready admission that all of our thinking of God proceeds by metaphors and analogies, none of which walks on all fours. Perhaps we could at least frame the proposition less directly, taking the path of negation, and suggest that there is nowhere where God is not. Second, if God is everywhere, it is obvious that God's presence does not displace or negate the real existence and integrity of finite creatures. Our range of daily experience of other persons, living creatures, and inanimate objects, and of all our relations to them, is in no way compromised or clouded by any sense of an overwhelming divine presence. Third, if God is everywhere, God is not terribly obvious about it! By all appearances, God's presence is subtle, flowing into the world sacramentally, drawing near to creation, "in, with, and under" all creaturely presences and energies.

This notion of God's presence in and throughout the universe challenges more typical ideas of God as "up there," "out there," or ruling over everything "from a distance." Instead, we are challenged to think of God as "the mystery of the obvious that is closer to me than my own I," in the words of the great Jewish philosopher Martin Buber.[3] But perhaps Buber's way of putting it, while evocative, is too anthropocentric and existentialist; not simply "closer to me," the omnipresent God is insurpassably nearer to *all creatures and all things*, precisely because their being is rooted and grounded in God's creative and recreative, life-bestowing and energizing Presence. Thus the Nicene Creed has taught Christians for over sixteen hundred years to confess that God's own Holy Spirit is "the Lord and Giver of life." This Spirit is the very divine Breath who broods over the chaotic depths of Genesis 1, blowing and stirring up new and creative possibilities for living things on our planet and, presumably, throughout this wondrously immense universe. Perhaps such imagery helps us appreciate why, as we shall see, Wesley was willing even to describe God as "the soul of the universe"!

3. Martin Buber, *I and Thou*, translated by Walter Kaufmann (New York: Charles Scribner's Sons, 1970), 127.

We shall explore the doctrine of omnipresence further in the following chapter, but this much should help to provide a theological context for reading a New Testament text that is crucial to our attempt in this chapter to address God, as Charles Wesley's lyric instructs us, as "the Universal Soul." That text is Acts 17:27-28, where Paul in his sermon to the Athenian intellectuals proclaims that God "is not far from each one of us. For 'In him we live and move and have our being.'"

THE INTIMATE PRESENCE OF GRACE

While it is a key element in what Wesley described as "divinely philosophical discourse,"[4] there is no question that the proposition that we "live and move and have our being" *in God* is elusive, provocative, and evocative of several readings. We find that earlier in Acts 17 Paul had wandered Athens's streets and become "deeply distressed to see that the city was full of idols" (17:16), but when given an opportunity to address the city's philosophers and freethinkers, he was able to present a civil front. "Athenians, I see how extremely religious you are in every way" (17:22). Paul nonetheless proceeds to offer an implicit criticism of Athenian religiosity, much in the spirit of the Hebrew prophets (and the Greek philosophers!), when he tells his listeners that God cannot be bound by temples or altars (v. 24). Further, when he proclaims that this "Unknown God" to whom they have dedicated an altar "gives to all mortals life and breath and all things" (v. 25), there is an implicit criticism of the typical Platonic distinction between the Supreme Being and the Demiurge, or fashioner of the physical universe. Paul insists that God, the ultimate reality, is also the Creator and Sustainer of all things, all life and breath, our very selves.

Here we arrive at a tantalizing contribution to our developing doctrine of God's presence in and to the world. God, Paul preaches, has created human beings within their historical, geographical, and cultural limitations *in order that* "they would search for God and perhaps grope for him and find him—though indeed he is not far from each one of us" (v. 27). The background for this theological

4. *NT Notes*, Acts 17:28.

affirmation is Hellenistic Judaism; we find, for example, a fascinating parallel in Philo's declaration that "nothing is better than to seek the true God, even if his discovery eludes [human] capacity."[5] The Athens sermon, though, may be a little (but probably not much!) more optimistic in its estimate of the human proclivity for God; while the text is difficult to interpret, it certainly can be read to say that God creates us humans in our diverse locations and limitations because in some way these "boundaries of our habitations" push and probe us to seek the Source of our being. A further implication of the text is that people seek (and sometimes find) God *precisely because God is so very near to them*. This is certainly an aspect of what Christians, especially but not exclusively Wesleyan Christians, mean by *prevenient* grace.

Paul graphically makes his point by citing pagan philosophical poetry: the evidence is strong that the "live, move, and have our being" triad is a quotation from a poet named Epemenides the Cretan, writing an ode in praise of Zeus:

> They fashioned a tomb for thee, O holy and high one,
> The Cretans, always liars, evil beasts, idle bellies!
> But thou art not dead; thou livest and abidest forever,
> For in thee we live and move and have our being.[6]

When Paul said that this God he proclaimed was so near that in God "we live and move and have our being" (v. 28), we can be certain at least that his hearers were on familiar ground, for similar pantheistically flavored reflections are not difficult to find among the Stoic writers. Paul, of course, is not identifying the God he proclaims with the Greek deity Zeus nor with the World Soul of the Stoics. Nonetheless, the text can be read as affirming that human beings can and do have intuitions of an immanent, sustaining Presence who "is not far from each one of us" (17:27). Further, since Paul readily cites lines of pagan poetry to make the point, one could also surmise that all people tend, naturally enough, to categorize this intuition or awareness in the religious terminology and theological framework culturally available to them.

---

5. Cited in Ernst Haenchen, *The Acts of the Apostles: A Commentary* (Philadelphia: Westminster, 1971), 524.
6. Cited in F. F. Bruce, *Commentary on the Book of Acts* (Grand Rapids: Eerdmans, 1980), 359.

Paul immediately follows the "live, move, and have our being" triad with another quotation, this time from "Natural Phenomena" by Aratus of Cilicia. Aratus's poetic reflections open with a passage about Zeus, not as the anthropomorphic reigning deity of the Greek pantheon (as apparently would have been the case with the Lystrans of Acts 14), but as the Supreme Being of Greek philosophy. Here is that opening passage of "Natural Phenomena":

> Let us begin with Zeus; never let us leave him
> unmentioned, O mortals.
> All the roads are full of Zeus and all men's
> meeting-places;
> the sea and the harbors are full of him.
> In all our ways we all have to do with Zeus;
> for we are also his offspring.[7]

Paul then adds that "since we are God's offspring, we ought not to think that the deity is like gold, or silver, or stone, an image formed by the art and imagination of mortals" (v. 29). But it is fascinating that Acts 17 not only presents Paul as an apologist, quoting from pagan poets with apparent approval (or at least with the intention of building bridges to his listeners), but also implies that Paul could affirm their intuitions of the divine presence.

Wesley offers his approval of the apologetic approach of the Acts passage, describing the triadic line from Epimenides as "one of the purest and finest pieces of natural religion in the whole world of pagan antiquity."[8] But it would actually be much more faithful to Wesley's own thought to apply to his use of the phrase "natural religion" what he often said in other places about the phrase "natural conscience": it is not simply "natural," as though inherent within the human's own creaturely capacities; rather, it is "supernatural,"[9] that is, a result of the intersection of the divine Spirit with the multitudinously particular "boundaries of our habitation." In other words, if Wesley could say of "natural conscience" that it is in fact a result of the dynamic interaction of God with

7. Ibid., 360.

8. *NT Notes*, Acts 17:28.

9. See, for example, Sermon 105, "On Conscience," §5, *Works* 3:482.

human beings in their actual, concrete sociocultural circumstances, then it follows to say something similar about "natural religion." This is prevenient grace understood in terms of the *sustaining nearness of God* to all human beings in their situatedness, their concretely historical environs. In fact, Wesley comments further on this "piece of natural religion," "We need not go far to seek or find [God]. He is very near us; in us. It is only perverse reason which thinks [God] is afar off."[10] It is important for our purposes to keep in mind that Wesley, staying true to the intent of the text of Acts 17, is not meaning only Christian believers, or even just religious people, when he writes that God is "very near us," even "in us." This is the God who is "not far from each one of us"—indeed, this is the deity whom Buber typified as "closer to me than my own I"!

Wesley's understanding of God's presence *in us* will not allow us to think of God as an absentee deity who occasionally makes an appearance and apart from whose presence we are able to exist. As John Cobb wrote in *Grace and Responsibility*, his 1995 study of Wesley's theology:

> Wesley is clear that grace is not a substance or entity introduced into human beings. . . . It is the Holy Spirit, which is the life of God within human beings. That means that concrete human beings are constituted in part by the presence of God within them. Human beings do not first exist in separation from God and then come into relation with God. Their very life is already God's presence within them. They exist by virtue of their inclusion of the divine life within them. . . . The relationship to God is constitutive of our being.[11]

While Cobb's interpretive spin on Wesley is obviously energized by the perspectives of process theology, I would argue that it does not at all distort the primary contours either of Wesley's anthropology or of his pneumatology. Of course, Wesley's pronounced emphasis upon God's immediate, life-empowering presence must be understood within the social and historical context of his resistance against Enlightenment deism. Wesley refused to brook any notion of a distant God, or likewise of distanced, autonomous human beings. While in many ways a child of the Enlightenment,

10. *NT Notes*, Acts 17:28.
11. Cobb, *Grace and Responsibility*, 40.

he refused to be lured by its ideal of autonomous, analytical reason grounded in the independent individual, a hallmark of modernism. His doctrine of God was much too rich in its appreciation of the classical categories of divine omnipresence and omniscience. Further, his anthropology was too profoundly rooted in the early Greek Fathers' vision of human participation in God to permit any capitulation to deism's autonomous individual.[12] Thus Wesley comments tersely on the prepositional phrase of Acts 17:28, "'In Him'—Not in ourselves."[13]

Not in ourselves! We do not exist simply in and of, and certainly not simply for, our "selves." To adapt Wesley again, we are not "merely natural," though we certainly are that—since we are embodied, material creatures living in a bodily world. But we are also created to live toward, indeed to live *in*, God. Further, the implication is that we cannot live outside of God's sustaining presence: to be outside of God's creative and recreative, life-bestowing and nurturing Spirit is to die, to "return to [our] dust" (Ps. 104:29). Wesley comments further on verse 28, "This denotes [God's] necessary, intimate, and most efficacious presence. No words can better express the continual and necessary dependence of all created beings, in their existence and their operations."[14]

Notice that Wesley wisely extended the *we* of "In God we live and move and have our being" to include *all created beings*. This is a proper, indeed necessary, implication of the notion of God's gracious (omni-)presence: if human beings are not autonomous individuals, neither is any other creature, living or nonliving. Nor is the universe as a whole an autonomous world; it does not exist "in itself."

THE WORLD IN GOD

It is noteworthy that Wesley broadened the "we" of Acts 17:28 beyond human beings at least one time other than in his brief comments in *Explanatory Notes upon the New Testament*. As we shall see

12. For a treatment of Wesley's use of the Greek motif of "participation in God," see Maddox, *Responsible Grace*, especially chapter 3. See also Runyon, *New Creation*, 26-29, 80-81.
13. *NT Notes*, Acts 17:28.
14. Ibid.

in chapter 5, Wesley deduced a tight connection between the traditional doctrines of omni-*presence* and omni-*potence*. In his 1786 sermon "On Divine Providence" he extended that connection to omni-*science*, or God's knowing of all things:

> [A]s this all-wise, all-gracious Being created all things, so he sustains all things. . . . Now it must be that he knows everything he has made, and everything he preserves from moment to moment. Otherwise he could not preserve it: he could not continue to it the being which he has given it. And it is nothing strange that he who is omnipresent, who "filleth heaven and earth," who is in every place, should see what is in every place, where he is intimately present. . . . Especially considering that nothing is distant from him, in whom we all "live and move and have our being."[15]

In this passage we detect the logical connection between God's omnipresence and God's omniscience: because God is "intimately present" in every place of creation, God is intimately aware of every event. Not only is it the case that, in the language of Acts 17 once more, God is not far from each one of us; Wesley properly deduces that "*nothing* is distant" from God! After all, *we all*—not simply humans, but all creatures and things—"live and move and have our being" *in God*! If it truly is the case that there is no place where God is not, and if it is truly the case that God is the impassioned, sacrificial Love manifested in the cross of Jesus (1 John 3:16, 4:8), then there can be no place where God is not the Lover of creation's most minute details. They all come to be *in God*. Omniscience should not be interpreted, then, to suggest that God is a Cosmic Computer with all possible data objectively stored and awaiting technologically impeccable recall; rather, omniscience should be interpreted with the implications of the Hebrew term for knowing, *yada*, in the foreground. God knowing all things, in this case, is God's sym-pathy for (God's *feeling with*) the universe in all of its inestimably diverse creatures and experiences.

If God is "intimately present," as Wesley surmised, then God knows nothing from a distance or at arm's length. Our attempt to understand the nature of God's knowing-all would instead be aided by drawing an analogy from our own bodies: we know and

15. Sermon 67, "On Divine Providence," §9, *Works* 2:538.

feel our own bodies not from a distance, but from within, in immediate sympathy. Again, Wesley adds: "Especially considering that nothing is distant from [God], in whom we all 'live and move and have our being.'" It is not just that no believer is distant from God, but that no human being is distant from God—we call this *prevenient grace*. But it is not just that no human being is distant from God, but that "nothing [no *thing*] is distant from [God]"—precisely because every*thing* has its being not in itself but "in God." When speaking of God's immediate and sustaining presence not only to humans but to all creatures and components of the world, I am suggesting that we call it *creative grace*.

This idea of all things existing "in God" brings to mind Sallie McFague's provocative suggestion that Christians ought to reflect on the thought-model of the world as "the body of God."[16] Drawing on the very language of Acts 17, she argues that this theological model could be "a lens . . . through which we might see that all of us 'live and move and have our being' in God, in the body of creation, the universe. As the embodied spirit of all that is, God would be closer to us than we are to ourselves, for God would be the very breath of our breath."[17] Admittedly, Wesley never suggested that we think of the world as God's body—but how different is that notion from one that Wesley *did* experiment with: God as the world's soul?

> God is in all things, and . . . we are to see the Creator in the glass [mirror, image] of every creature; . . . [We[should use and look upon nothing as separate from God, which indeed is a kind of practical atheism; . . . God . . . by his intimate presence holds [heaven and earth and all that is therein] in being, who pervades and actuates the whole created frame, and is in a true sense the soul of the universe.[18]

Just as the Paul of Acts 17 could quote pagan poets, so Wesley was unafraid to cite Virgil's *Aeneid* in describing God as "the all-informing soul, that fills, pervades, and actuates the whole."[19]

---

16. Sallie McFague, *The Body of God: An Ecological Theology* (Minneapolis: Fortress, 1993).
17. Ibid., 144.
18. Sermon 23, "Sermon on the Mount, III," §I.11, *Works* 1:516-17.
19. Sermon 118, "On the Omnipresence of God," §II.1, *Works* 4:43.

Indeed, the Charles Wesley hymn that provides this chapter's epigraph also includes this evocative line of praise: "Thou art the Universal Soul, the Plastick Power that fills the whole." Taken together, these theological sentiments of the brothers Wesley offer us a remarkable lens for reading our world: it is a world in which we live, and move, and have our being—in precious company with everyone and everything else—*in* God!

Do we know what is meant by this phrase "in God"? No, not really. But it does evoke a sense of the world as a sacrament, a bodying-forth of divine grace and divine presence. It does proclaim that no body or thing exists in its self, but always in and by its relations to God the Creator and Sustainer, and to all other creatures in God. It does deny the existence of an individual, solitaire, insulated own-being in anything. It does suggest that God *as God may be known to us* is also no insulated, self-enclosed monad but is instead the Mystery that embraces and enfolds all things in its inscrutable Presence. Once more, Wesley preaches in hues that probably sound alien to our ears:

> The manner of [God's] presence no [one] can explain, nor probably any angel in heaven. Perhaps what the ancient philosopher speaks of the soul in regard to its residence in the body, that it is *tota in toto, et tota in qualibet parte,* might in some sense be spoken of the omnipresent Spirit in regard to the universe—that he is not only "all in the whole, but all in every part."[20]

One need not assume a radical dualism of body and soul, as Wesley tended to, in order to appreciate the power of this image. Indeed, the less dualistically we conceive of body and soul, the more striking is the notion that God is the Soul of the universe! Of course, the phrase "all in the whole, and all in every part" itself already softens any harsh dualism: as the soul is not only in the body as an entirety but in every part of the body, so the analogy goes, the Spirit exists in the universe. For Wesley, of course, the soul is still in principle separable from the body as the animating and directing principle of the body. Such a dualism has not found, and will not find, much room to thrive in the volume in your hands! Nonetheless, the notion of God as the "soul of the world" may still

20. Sermon 67, "On Divine Providence," §10, *Works* 2:538-39.

exercise some evocative power for us. The intimacy of the relation between soul and body ("all in every part") that Wesley himself assumes in the quotation above would suggest that, by analogy, the distinction between God and world must not be overdrawn. "God is in this, and in every place," insisted Wesley—and so the universe as a whole is a "place for God," even as God "provides a place" for the universe in God's own eternally mysterious reality. Since "the omnipresent Spirit" of whom Wesley writes can be none other than the Holy Spirit, "the Lord and Giver of Life," it is clear that we cannot restrict the Spirit to individual spirituality (i.e., "our hearts"), nor even to the Church. The Spirit is creating and animating the universe!

As we have seen, Wesley's understanding of God's knowing and sustaining of creation is that God labors in and for the world by immediate presence, as "the omnipresent Spirit," and not as a distant, objectifiable "deity." If indeed we meditate on what we mean by omnipresence (God being fully and "intimately present . . . in every place") and by omniscience (God knowing thoroughly and intimately all things and events in utter clarity and unimaginable thoroughness), we are again led to *something like* McFague's model of the universe as God's body. God does not know any event "at a distance," but from within, and indeed through the experiences (conscious or not) of all creatures (sentient or not). If God truly knows all things in the Hebraic participatory sense of "knowing," then God's knowing must include a sharing in every creature's experiences—including even the strange and mysterious world of sub-atomic processes—"from the inside." The universe of events, things, and relationships can occur nowhere but *in God*, and thus God's knowing must be intimate, experiential, utterly thorough, and, at least in an analogical sense, *bodily*.

The fact that such suggestions may sound foreign to many contemporary Christians is probably a reflection of contemporary Western Christianity's drift toward the deism of a distant deity. But consider Wesley's speculations as he continues to reflect on God as the *anima mundi*, the "soul of the world":

> It cannot be doubted but [that the omnipresent Spirit] sees every atom of his creation, and that a thousand times more clearly than we see the things that are close to us: even of these we see only the surface, while he sees the inmost essence of everything. The

> omnipresent God sees and knows all the properties of all the beings that he hath made. He knows all the connections, dependencies, and relations, and all the ways wherein one of them can affect another. In particular he sees all the inanimate parts of the creation, whether in heaven above or in the earth beneath.[21]

The omnipresent Spirit, fully present not only in the whole but in every part—indeed, in every atom in all its "connections, dependencies, and relations"—knows every element and event in the universe by immediate, full, and participatory awareness. Our world in all its incalculably complex web of relations is experienced by the One who is present. It is especially fascinating that Wesley would suggest that *in particular* God "sees all the inanimate parts of the creation." Wesley here does not allow us to bifurcate between humans and the rest of the world, as though the latter is beneath God's considerations or compassions. It is possible that his intriguing insistence upon God's active knowing of creation's "inanimate parts" was another parry at the deistic tendency to read the world as a grand machine, well-oiled by God at the beginning but now whirling, turning, clicking, and churning by its own "natural laws" and on its own momentum. It appears that Wesley was insisting instead that God is the omnipresent Knower whose graciously sustaining presence pervades even the deepest and darkest reaches of creation.

It may be instructive to reread the classic story of Isaiah's vision of the Holy God in the Temple (Isa. 6). It would be tempting to categorize such an encounter as utterly unique, one in a million, a divine intrusion into an otherwise mundane plane of existence. To the contrary, the prophet describes the angels as chanting, "Holy, holy, holy is the LORD of hosts; *the whole earth is full of his glory*!" (v. 3). If indeed the whole earth is full of God's glory, then it is not only in the Temple that the Holy One is met! Indeed, it is almost as though the angelic song calls us to look for an Isaian vision to occur anywhere! Divine holiness is not restricted to the Temple or similar places of holiness; in fact, as one of my students pointed out to me recently, the Isaiah text says that the Temple was "filled" merely by "the hem of his robe" (6:1)! Is it too much to imagine that every thing, every place, every creature is likewise "filled" by the

21. Ibid., 539.

wondrous presence of the Holy One? If it is not, then Wesley was quite correct in teaching us "to see the Creator in the glass of every creature" as though the world were an unimaginably complex kaleidoscope refracting the glorious presence of God in billions upon billions of interdependent creatures. If indeed the whole earth is full of God's glory, then Wesley is also correct in teaching us that we "should use and look upon nothing as separate from God, which indeed is a kind of practical atheism." To *look* upon nothing as separate from God is to read each and every thing as filled with God, as an instantiation of divine presence, as existing only in and by the immediate presence of the Maker and Molder of all—*and yet* also to recognize the real distinctness, the embodied particularity, of each creature. To *use* nothing as separate from God is to live lightly and carefully in the world, in the conviction that no thing exists simply in itself or simply for me and my use or consumption. Instead, each and every thing exists as a mode and  means of divine presence.

God Transcending the World

In this chapter we have drawn from Wesley, particularly as his preaching was shaped by biblical texts like Acts 17:28 and traditional doctrines like omnipresence and omniscience, in order to argue for a reading of the world as not simply created and sustained by God, but in every place and every moment deeply and intimately indwelled by "the omnipresent Spirit." There is no question that I am reading Wesley as a champion of a decidedly strong version of the doctrine of divine *immanence*.

A legitimate question that could be raised is, *What difference is there between God and the world in this vision of things?* Has the distinction been collapsed? Is that distinction not a crucial one for Christians to uphold and defend? Further, in the concern to develop a model of the God-world relation that provides a cosmological context of continuity so that God's decisive works in the world are not interpreted to be interruptive intrusions, have I ironically undercut the decisive importance of, or even the need to talk about, those three crucial "moments" with which this chapter began: the goodness of creation, the decisiveness of the Incarnation, and the future hope of bodily resurrection?

Such questions as these represent important concerns that must be addressed before we can proceed to chapters 5 and 6. There are essentially two points I would like to emphasize.

First, whatever we might mean by "omnipresence," or even whatever Wesley might have meant in claiming that "all things are full of God," we must insist again that the nature of God's indwelling presence is never to displace, deny, or negate the creature. We must conceive of God's indwelling presence as actually "making room" for creaturely existence and creaturely agency. The Christian doctrine of the Holy Spirit, I believe, fundamentally has something to do with God as the divine Mystery whose nature it is to be outpoured, to give freely of itself, in order that an other-than-God might *be* and *become*. "I will pour out My Spirit upon all flesh," said the prophet Joel, and in that promise we may detect the divine generosity in outpouring toward and into the creation and, in so doing, letting there be a world. In other words, the distinction between God and world is maintained precisely because the outpoured presence of God actually makes for a world that is other than God. The God who is present in all places and the creature who occupies a particular place are not mutually exclusive. God's presence does not exclude the true agency and potency of the creature, human and otherwise, but in indescribable *kenosis* includes and empowers the creature to be itself and to exist dynamically in the world.

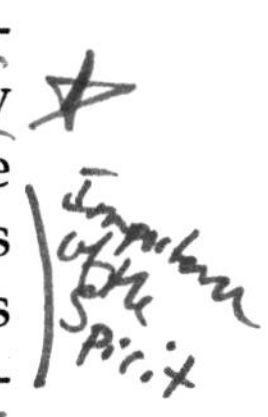

Second, whatever it might mean for us to affirm that "in God we live and move and have our being" (Acts), or that "God is in all things" (Wesley), it need not at all imply a static, full, unchanging, and fully accomplished presence. In fact, the overarching tenor of the first two chapters of this book have already placed a high premium upon the temporal dimension of the future as a distinctive category for thinking about God's creative activity in the world. We might put it this way: God's *presence* in the present age is the *present future*, so that God is not at all simply a filling-of-the-present-with-full-presence, but instead an evocative Call from an always-already inrushing *and* onleading future. Put more simply, God's presence is *eschatological*. God's indwelling presence is always also a fleeting presence because God is that One who is always leading, ever going before our incredibly dynamic, fluid, and interrelated universe.

There is certainly a strong indication of this pull of the future, this call of the age to come, in the centerpiece biblical passage of this chapter. At the conclusion of the sermon of Acts 17, Paul pulls no punches in his punchline: "While God has overlooked the times of human ignorance [the present age], now he commands all people everywhere to repent, because he has fixed a day on which he will have the world judged in righteousness by a man whom he has appointed, and of this [God] has given assurance to all by raising him from the dead" (17:30-31). The age to come *has come* in the raising of Jesus from death to life, and in the anticipation of the world's judgment in and through this Risen One. Thus, the same sermon that speaks of all people and, by logical extension, of all things as living, moving, and being in God *also* points beyond the present presence to a radically new eschatological denouement in a future already embodied in Jesus of Nazareth. We cannot settle for a settled divine Presence that simply sanctions the world as it is. The Holy One in whom we live and move and have our being is present in this very moment and in this very place—*and* is here as the Divine Call that beckons us and all the world toward new creation. Thus, for example, we might say it is precisely because Paul is filled by the Holy Spirit that he refuses to be full of the present or of the past: "Not that I have already obtained [the likeness of Christ's death and resurrection] or have already reached the goal; but I press on to make it my own, because Christ Jesus has made me his own . . . This one thing I do: forgetting what lies behind and straining forward to what lies ahead, I press on toward the goal for the prize of the heavenly call of God in Christ Jesus" (Phil. 3:12-14).

If God who calls us in Christ Jesus is also God the Maker and Molder of all things, then what Paul says of himself must necessarily be applicable, by analogy, to the world God is making and molding. To live, move, and dwell in God—as all creatures do—is not to be so filled as to be stagnant and satisfied, but to be "straining forward to what lies ahead." That forward reach, however, is not a straining to leave God's world in the dust, for God's world is in some deeply mysterious ways straining forward, too. Instead of despising or belittling or ignoring God's world, Wesley's injunction provides proper guidance for an eschatological ecology: "[We] should use and look upon nothing as separate from God, which indeed is a kind of practical atheism."[22] So may we live, pray, think, and act *toward*, and *in the hope of*, a world in which no one of us uses, or looks upon, any thing or any creature in the world "as separate from God."

22. Sermon 23, "Sermon on the Mount, III," §I.11, *Works* 1:516-17.

CHAPTER 5

"WHO DOST THROUGH BOTH CREATIONS SHINE"

New Creation and (Good) Old Creation

> *Author of every work divine,*
> *Who dost through both Creations shine:*
> *The God of nature and of grace.*
>
> Charles Wesley, *Hymns of Petition and Thanksgiving for the Promise of the Father*, #28

John and Charles Wesley believed that God "shines . . . through both creations"—not only through the *new creation* initiated in Christ, "the last Adam" (1 Cor. 15:45), but also through the *old* or *first creation* associated with the story of Adam and Eve and their descendants. Though that story of the first creation is rife with frustrations and failures (Gen. 1–11), the power of sin and alienation that characterize our world cannot finally unravel the threads of God's prevenient grace and persistent creativity; the "God of nature and of grace" labors throughout creation as the Creative Spirit who creates, enlivens, nurtures, cherishes, and seeks to redeem all creatures. It bears repeating that one of John Wesley's favorite biblical citations was Psalm 145:9, "[The Lord's] mercies are over all of his works" (KJV), and that he interpreted the *all* as widely and inclusively as the term could possibly suggest. No creature of any kind lives outside of God's immediate presence as sustaining Love.

One of this volume's most pressing concerns is that this cosmological accent in the theology of the Wesley brothers has not received adequate attention in the two centuries' worth of subsequent Wesleyan theological tradition. One might suppose that this is due largely to the tradition's characteristic emphasis upon the doctrine of *human* salvation; such attention upon the *via salutis* or "way of salvation"[1] for human beings has not left much energy for thinking about God's intentions for creation as a whole. To be sure, this is not a uniquely Wesleyan emphasis; it has been the central concern of much of Christianity. Christian faith, practice, and reflection have tended to stay closely tethered to *soteriology* (the doctrine of salvation)—and that doctrine traditionally has focused on the question of how *human beings* are saved. But the Wesleyan tradition may have outdone many other streams of Christian tradition in fixating on human salvation at the expense of attention to the larger realm of creation. As Nazarene theologian J. Kenneth Grider has noted, Wesleyans have historically majored in experiential and existential modes of reflection, betraying particular interest in issues of human freedom (mostly in contestations with Calvinists) and individual religious experience and morality.[2] This has encouraged certain idiosyncracies in Wesleyan soteriology, reflecting its anthropocentric or human-centered nature.

Clearly a soteriology that becomes fixated only upon the human is insufficient and untrue to our identity as creatures existing inextricably within this vast, mysterious, and beautiful creation. Such anthropocentrism in Christian theology has tended to create brittle distinctions between us human beings and the complex network of creaturely existence in which we live, move, and have our being by God. It has thereby fostered an unhealthy and unbiblical alienation between human and world that undercuts respect and empathy for the resilient yet vulnerable fabric of our natural environment.

This unfortunate impact is heightened by the tendency in much Christian thinking to frame the doctrine of salvation primarily in terms of the afterlife. If salvation is defined primarily as a matter of "going to heaven when I die," the importance of the present life—not to mention the biblical insistence upon the *goodness* of creation—gets slighted. A soteriology that simply teaches Christians

1. For a thorough discussion of the notion of *via salutis* or the "way of salvation" as a fitting motif for interpreting Wesley's soteriology, see Maddox, *Responsible Grace*, chapter 7.

2. J. Kenneth Grider, *A Wesleyan-Holiness Theology* (Kansas City: Beacon Hill, 1994), 28.

to anticipate a gloriously happy afterlife does little to encourage meaningful living in the present. Indeed, it tends to wrest our attention and energies away from the sufferings and groaning of God's creation.

One of the burdens of this book is to argue that the doctrine of salvation—of God's *mending* of creation—through Christ cannot properly thrive without being grounded in a more comprehensive *creaturely* and *creational* context. A truer, more adequate theology demands a greater and deeper awareness of our creaturely connections with all other living things within our world, not to mention the incalculable connections of planet Earth within its solar system and beyond—one network of interdependent relations after (and before!) another.

In this connection it is remarkable that so much of Wesley's reflection on cosmology, or the doctrine of God's creation, has gone unnoticed and undeveloped as a potential contribution to the quest for a richer Christian soteriology. Yet it is readily arguable that Wesley's famed "optimism of grace" is best and most fully understood only within the context of his assumptions about God's rich relations to the universe. He was able to preach and teach with grace-full optimism regarding God's labor of sanctifying human lives because he believed that God is intent upon salving *all of creation*. While Wesley showed little patience or sympathy for "natural theology," it is obvious that, particularly in his later years, he developed an explicit and striking theology of nature in which he explored the implications particularly of the doctrines of God's omnipresence and omniscience. In this chapter we shall explore these themes of God's *universal intimacy* with all things at all times in all of creation, particularly as they appear to exist in tension with the proclamatory nature of the gospel as a radical announcement of God's *new creation*.

GOD THE OMNIPRESENT CREATOR

Late in his life (1788) Wesley wrote "On the Omnipresence of God," one of his most philosophical sermons, with Jeremiah 23:24 as his text: "'Do not I fill heaven and earth?' saith the LORD" (KJV). The operative theme, repeated throughout the sermon, was simply that "God is in this, and every place."[3] Wesley wrote, "God acts everywhere, and therefore is everywhere; for it is an utter impossibility that any being, created or uncreated, should work where it is not. God acts in heaven, in earth, and under the earth, throughout the whole compass of his creation."[4]

To put it simply, God is no Creator from a distance. "There is no place empty of God," wrote Wesley in "The Imperfection of Human Knowledge," "[and] every point of infinite space is full of God."[5] Wesley implies that there cannot possibly be any place, indeed any microscopic point anywhere at any time, where God is not fully and actively present. Wesley's doctrine of creation assumes that where God is not—as though such a scenario were imaginable, let alone possible—no thing can be. Moreover, it is not sufficient simply to think of omnipresence as meaning that God occupies all the invisible "empty space" between perceivable objects; rather, every point, no matter how infinitesimal, is absolutely full of divine presence—and, presumably, must be so, in order to be at all.

In Wesley's day, Newtonian physics tended still to assume that a gaseous quasi-material called ether filled the space in which discrete objects moved and interacted. While eighteenth-century disciples of Newton were finding the ether hypothesis increasingly unnecessary as they developed the idea that objects exercised gravitational force at a distance, Wesley in his sermon on omnipresence reflected the still common opinion when he wrote, "And it is now generally supposed that all space is full."[6] He realized that this hypothesis was no longer unanimously accepted by his contemporaries, but could insist nonetheless on the proposition's truth simply on theological grounds. "Perhaps it cannot be proved that all space is filled with matter. But the heathen [Virgil] himself will bear witness . . . 'All things are full of God.' Yea, and whatever space exists beyond the bounds of creation . . . even that space cannot exclude him who fills the heaven and the earth."[7]

---

3. Sermon 118, "On the Omnipresence of God," §I.3, *Works* 4:41.
4. Ibid., 42.
5. Sermon 69, "The Imperfection of Human Knowledge," §I.1, *Works* 2:569.
6. Sermon 118, "On the Omnipresence of God," §II.3, *Works* 4:44.
7. Ibid.

It is obvious that Wesley operated with a remarkably strong doctrine of divine omnipresence, interpreted to mean, as he put it, that "God is in this, and in every place." If this is correct, then whatever else God may be, God is *not* nonspatial. In chapter 4 we have already examined some of the implications of the traditional doctrine of omnipresence, so there is no need to rehearse those themes. We may summarize by suggesting that, in some way that undoubtedly eludes our grasp, God indwells all of space. To take a step further, if we attempt to meditate on the utterly incomprehensible immensity of our universe as we know it—so much more immense than Wesley could ever have imagined—the notion that God dwells fully in every place, and indeed beyond every place, is a mind-blower. God, it would seem, must be "big"! Admittedly, God's "bigness" has not been touted as a traditional attribute of the divine, and it is not an idea that receives much attention nowadays, but in classical theology this is the doctrine of *divine immensity*—"immense" obviously being a more worthy term of description than "big," and meaning, more literally, *immeasurable.*

Omnipresence, at least when interpreted literally, means that God occupies all places; divine immensity, according to Thomas Oden, implies that "God is both infinitely near and infinitely far, yet in speaking this way we do not imply that God is finitely localized, but rather the cause and ground of all locales."[8] Hence, while every place has its place in relationship to other places in the universe (I live in San Diego, which is in California, which is in North America, which is on earth, etc.), the only viable theological reply to the largest question of locale—"Where is the universe?"—is, quite simply, *God.* The universe is "in God" and actually can be nowhere else. "In a word," Wesley wrote, "there is no point of space, whether within or without the bounds of creation, where God is not."[9] If this is true, then all things everywhere truly do have their being in God.

These doctrines of omnipresence and immensity become all the more unfathomable when we attempt to reflect upon them in relation to the new physics. In Wesley's era, the notion of atoms as

8. Thomas C. Oden, *Systematic Theology: The Living God* (San Francisco: Harper & Row, 1987), 60.

9. Sermon 118, "On the Omnipresence of God," §I.1, *Works* 4:42.

miniscule, rather granular "building blocks" of the universe was fairly common; now the very notion of "building blocks" appears to be disintegrating under the seemingly endless discovery of "subnuclear debris": from atoms to nuclei and electrons, from nuclei to protons and neutrons, from protons and neutrons to pions, muons, leptons, those quirky quarks, and so on—perhaps *ad infinitum*? Combine all that with the physicists' analogy that if a single atom were blown up to the size of a football stadium, those subatomic particles (if we can yet call them particles!), waltzing together in their dance of uncertainty, would be the size of grains of sand! What is left for us to imagine, then, according to British physicist Paul Davies, is a universe that is even more vastly "empty space" than we could ever conceive, no longer understood to be "a collection of separate but coupled *things*," but instead "a network of *relations*"[10] in dizzyingly infinite complexity. Davies writes, "We cannot pin down a particle and say that it is such-and-such an entity. Instead we must regard every particle as somehow made up of every other particle in an endless Strange Loop. No particle is more elementary than any other."[11] Such a strange universe this is turning out to be, where empty space overwhelmingly predominates and what is fundamental appears to be wispy, virtually *spiritual* relations!

Such considerations, however, should not be interpreted so as to contribute to the dematerializing of matter—but only so as to underscore the mysterious, but profoundly relational, nature of matter in our strange universe. Further, all of these infinitely complex relations we call the universe are occurring—are *mattering*, we might say—in this very moment *in God*, for presumably God fully indwells the "empty space" of subatomic chaotic order just as surely as God embraces the whole of the universe within God's own inestimable reality. God is indeed "our dwelling place in all generations" (Ps. 90:1).

As I mentioned briefly in chapter 4, Sallie McFague in her 1993 book *The Body of God* has argued that the metaphor of the world as God's body is a helpful theological model, among others, for encouraging Christians to take seriously the issues of bodily

10. Paul Davies, *God and the New Physics* (New York: Simon & Schuster, 1983), 112.
11. Ibid., 163.

existence within our universe. Compelling as her suggestion is, I believe my point is more bold while at the same time, ironically, more conservative in regard to traditional theological categories. This point is that when Christian theologians, including Wesley, have considered carefully the meaning of divine omnipresence, it has been difficult for them to avoid the conclusion that God truly is the "place" where the universe is happening, and thus also that the universe is *in some sense* the embodying of God. Such a conclusion is not offered simply as a useful model (as in McFague's case), but as the implication of what it means for God to be God and the world to be God's intimately sustained creation.

However, since all theological language is necessarily imprecise, limping along upon its analogies and metaphors, we are reminded that there is no simple formula for describing God's omnipresence. Like Wesley, we may affirm the *fact* (or at least the elusive notion!) of God's mysteriously immediate presence to and in all things while remaining largely ignorant of the *manner*—a distinction that Wesley employed in regard to many Christian doctrines. As he said it in "The Imperfection of Human Knowledge," "How astonishingly little do we know of God! . . . What conception can we form of his omnipresence? Who is able to comprehend how God is in this and every place? How he fills the immensity of space? . . . The fact being admitted, what is omnipresence or ubiquity?"[12]

TO LIVE, MOVE, AND DWELL IN GOD

As Cobb has pointed out, in Wesley's thinking the doctrine of God's omnipresence was directly linked with the doctrine of omnipotence, interpreted particularly as God's creative and sustaining activity in the world.[13] In Wesley's words, again from his sermon "On the Omnipresence of God," "Nay, and we cannot believe the omnipotence of God unless we believe his omnipresence. For seeing . . . [that] nothing can act where it is not, if there were any space where God was not present he would not be able to do anything there."[14] Again, here Wesley assumes that God

12. Sermon 69, "The Imperfection of Human Knowledge," §I:1, *Works* 2:569.
13. Cobb, *Grace and Responsibility*, 50-52.
14. Sermon 118, "On the Omnipresence of God," §II.6, *Works* 4:44.

creates, sustains, and redeems the world not "from a distance," but always immediately and immanently; "God acts everywhere, and therefore is everywhere."[15] God acts by continually renewing the call of Genesis 1—to *let there be* a world—

> by sustaining all things, without which everything would in an instant sink into its primitive nothing; by governing all, every moment superintending everything that he has made; strongly and sweetly influencing all, and yet without destroying the liberty of his rational creatures.[16]

While Wesleyan theologians typically have spoken much of prevenient grace as God's loving, sustaining, and convicting presence in human lives, here in Wesley we discover a broader, more cosmically oriented category for speaking of the Holy Spirit—a category we are naming *creative grace*. As we explored in the previous chapter, humans live, move, and have their being in God (Acts 17:28), but humans do so within the fabric of an entire universe that exists in God—a universe which, according to Wesley, depends "every moment" upon the One who calls it into being and sustains it in being, and without whom "everything would in an instant sink into its primitive nothing."

Where God acts, there God is present—and fully so. I believe that Wesley's instincts were correct in this matter; it would be theologically inelegant to imagine God's power to be exerted at some sort of ontological distance from God's own being. Any such notion would tend to turn God's presence into an impersonal force, an attenuated power, thereby implying that it is not in God's immediate presence that each creature exists. But in fact the doctrine of the Holy Spirit is the way in which Christians have attempted, at least from time to time, to speak about God's presence and activity in the realm of creation—and it is crucial to Christian faith to affirm that the Holy Spirit is *truly God*, intimately present and active in the world.

Christians, to be sure, have learned to think this way about the Spirit from the Jewish tradition.[17] We think, for example, of the

---

15. Ibid., §II.1, 4:42.

16. Ibid., 4:42-3.

17. I have explored the debt that Christian pneumatology owes to the history of Jewish reflection about the nature of God's presence in creation, and suggested new lessons that Christian theologians might yet learn, in *Shekhinah/Spirit: Divine Presence in Jewish and Christian Religion* (Mahwah, N.J.: Paulist Press, 1992).

powerful affirmation of the dynamic, life-giving presence of God's Breath to which Psalm 104 testifies (explored already in chapter 1). There is also the wonderful pair of questions raised by the psalmist in 139:7—"Whither shall I go from thy Spirit? or whither shall I flee from thy presence?"—which appear to indicate God's real and immediate presence first to the psalmist, and second to all of creation's places. The psalmist's wonderfully poetic dual question is obviously a Hebrew couplet or parallelism, that is, it asks the identical question in two different ways. From this we rightly suppose that God's Spirit and God's presence are perfectly interchangeable terms, and that Psalm 139:7 (and the psalm in its entirety) supports the notion of God's immediate and compassionate presence to the psalmist, to every creature, and indeed to the very finest details of creation. Further, as I suggested in the previous chapter, it is along these lines that the fragment of pagan poetry cited in Acts, "In [God] we live and move and have our being" (Acts 17:28)—a text of considerable importance to Wesley—is most naturally interpreted.

THE PROBLEM OF EVIL AND THE POSSIBILITIES OF LOVE

If all this is so, then this "old creation" is an eminently *good* creation, precisely because the One who alone is good (Mark 10:18) creates, sustains, and nurtures all things. Of course, not everything that happens to all creatures is experienced as good; indeed, far from it! Hence, Wesley in his sermon "On Divine Providence" affirmed that

> [God] knows all the hearts of the sons of men, and understands all their thoughts. He sees what any angel, any devil, any man, either thinks, or speaks, or does; yea, and all they feel. He sees all their sufferings, with every circumstance of them. And is the Creator and Preserver of the world unconcerned for what he sees therein? Does he look upon these things either with a malignant or heedless eye? Is he an Epicurean god? Does he sit at ease in the heaven, without regarding the poor inhabitants of earth? It cannot be. . . . We are his children. And can a mother forget the children of her womb? Yea, she may forget; yet will not God forget us.[18]

18. Sermon 67, "On Divine Providence," §§12-13, *Works* 2:539.

While in the passage above Wesley refers only to the thoughts and feelings of rational creatures ("any angel, any devil, any man"), the doctrines of omnipresence and omniscience must logically embrace *all* experiences of *all* creatures of *any kind*. Indeed, Wesley says as much in his sermon on "the groaning creation" of Romans 8, "The General Deliverance":

> While "the whole creation groaneth together" (whether men attend or not) their groans are not dispersed in idle air, but enter into the ears of him that made them. While his creatures "travail together in pain," he knoweth all their pain, and is bringing them nearer and nearer to the birth which shall be accomplished in its season.[19]

It is important to remember that Wesley's conviction that God's love embraces all of creation is not rooted primarily in the doctrine of omnipresence but in the Christian confession that "we know love by this, that [Jesus Christ] laid down his life for us" (1 John 3:16). The compelling beauty of a Wesleyan reading of the world is precisely this confidence that the "pure, unbounded love" revealed in the cross of Christ is in fact the omnipotent Creator Spirit who in "all his wisdom is continually employed in managing all the affairs of his creation for the good of all his creatures."[20]

Wesley admits that, given the harsh realities of misery and pain in the world, "it is hard indeed to comprehend this; nay, it is hard to believe it."[21] It is reassuring to know that Wesley admitted the difficulty involved in believing in a God of love in a world of great suffering! Yet, lest we make God out to be a liar—we are assured, after all, that not one sparrow is forgotten before God—Wesley insists that we must understand God as the compassionate Maker and Provider of every creature. Of course it should not go unnoticed that God's provision of sustenance for one creature may well demand the death of another, or of many other, of God's creatures. With so much suffering, pain, fear, and death in our world, we are left to stand in awe before the mystery of God's providential care in creation, no simplistic theodicy in our grasp.

---

19. Sermon 60, "The General Deliverance," §III.1, *Works* 2:445.
20. Sermon 67, "On Divine Providence," §14, *Works* 2:540.
21. Ibid., §13, *Works* 2:540.

Not surprisingly, the only step Wesley is willing to take toward a solution of the problem of evil is to offer the freewill defense. Wesleyan tradition has argued cogently that human agency—our wondrous capacity to do evil against ourselves and one another, as well as to do good—is consistent with the convictions that *God is love* and *God acts in love*. In order that love might have opportunity to flourish in creation, responsible agency is offered to, and nurtured in, creatures of intelligence. God's creative power "continually co-operates with" God's wisdom and goodness, laboring in a fashion expressive of a love that bestows, encourages, and evokes a response of love from the creature. Having embarked upon the divine adventure of calling forth creatures of responsible freedom, God "cannot deny himself; he cannot counteract himself, or oppose his own work"[22]—and God's work is to allow the creaturely elements "room" to *be*, to *grow*, to *exercise creaturely freedom for the sake of the possibilities of love*.

> Were it not for this [God] would destroy all sin, with its attendant pain, in a moment. He would abolish wickedness out of his whole creation, and suffer no trace of it to remain. But in so doing he would counteract himself, he would altogether overturn his own work, and undo all that he has been doing since he created man upon the earth. . . . Were human liberty taken away men would be as incapable of virtue as stones. . . . [God wills] to assist man in attaining the end of his being, in working out his own salvation—so far as it can be done without compulsion, without overruling his liberty . . . without turning man into a machine.[23]

We understand, then, that God's loving purpose in creating us is that human liberty might be persuaded toward salvation and away from wickedness and destruction. We thereby arrive at the central paradox of the doctrine of creation: God is the omnipresent, omnipotent, omniscient Creator Spirit who immediately, intimately, and continuously sustains all things as *other than God*. God "lets there be" creatures—and a great many of them!—who are not God, and who indeed may rebel against Love Divine, but who nevertheless depend immediately upon God for their continued

22. bid., §15, *Works* 2:540.
23. Ibid., 540-41.

being. Indeed, God sustains them in being not "from a distance," but profoundly "from within"!

The Proper Human Response to Divine Grace

This means that there is no one who can escape from God's Spirit, none who can flee from God's presence (Ps. 139:7; cf. Heb. 4:13). In fact, to be without God's Spirit is to be not at all, but to return to "dust" (Ps. 104:29) or, in Wesley's quaint phrase, to "primitive nothing."[24] By the same token, as we have read already in Psalm 104, "When you send forth your spirit, they [all creatures] are created; and you renew the face of the ground" (v. 30).

The fact that Wesley quotes copiously from Psalm 104 in several of his sermons provides evidence that he appreciated that text's evocative cosmology of Divine Breath. As explored in chapter 1, all creatures wait for God to give them food and sustenance; all creatures are satisfied with good from God's own open hand and indeed live by the very breath of God (vv. 27-29). This "good old creation" in and by which we live is continually made new by the life-giving Spirit who recreates and sustains all things ("renews the face of the ground") and who calls for a response from the creatures according to their capacities—and particularly from the human creatures of our planet, who are made to attain "virtue" through "liberty" (Wesley's terms).

It is precisely at this point of evoking the human response that what we have termed *creative grace* becomes the more familiar *prevenient grace*. These of course are not different kinds of grace, but different kinds and capacities of *response* to the "uncreated grace" that God the Holy Spirit is. Even as the human creature begins to respond ever so slightly to the intimations of grace, the possibility and reality of redemption is begun. Wesley thus preached:

> Salvation . . . might be extended to the entire work of God, from the first dawning of grace in the soul . . . [such that] if we take this in its utmost extent it will include all that is wrought in the soul by what is frequently termed "natural conscience," but

24. Sermon 118, "On the Omnipresence of God," §II.1, *Works* 4:42.

> more properly, "preventing grace"; . . . all the *convictions* which his Spirit from time to time works in every child of man.[25]

Though God's Spirit labors everywhere and always to call the wayward creature to repentance unto life, it is through the preaching of the gospel of Jesus Christ, Christians believe and confess, that the character, mercy, and intentions of the Infinite Spirit become most clearly revealed. This revelation in Christ, the One Anointed of the Spirit, creates the possibility of a more clearly informed response to God in terms of Christian faith, repentance, and obedience to the gospel. At the point of such a response, God's prevenient grace becomes saving (or *salving!*) grace. In the following chapter we will explore the nature of sanctifying grace, recognizing all along that it is the same grace, for it is the same God who labors at every point and every moment toward the *telos* of creation: *that love might flourish.* It is only the quality and nuance of human response to grace that creates theological distinctions. There is a continuity throughout, and within, creation of the presence of the One who makes, molds, and—we trust—mends us all.

There is, then, the possibility of new creation, or renewal, of our world. As we shall explore further in chapter 7, this renewal does not come by coercion, for that would "altogether overthrow [God's] own work," writes Wesley, "and undo all that he has been doing"[26] in the making, molding, and mending of creation. Renewal comes, instead, by human response—or, if we prefer Wesley's term, "liberty"—in relation to God's initiatives in sustaining, convicting, persuading, and liberating us to live according to the energies and vision of "Love Divine, all loves excelling." No wonder that the Wesleyan vision of Christian perfection is a call of hope toward the *telos* of Christlike lives, lives of love. In this way the "good old creation" can become "new creation" and is in fact renewable in every moment

It is noteworthy in this connection that in his comments on Jesus' promise, "Blessed are the pure in heart, for they shall see God," Wesley interprets the implicit eschatology of this beatitude by means of the cosmology of "good old creation" as explored in this

25. Sermon 43, "The Scripture Way of Salvation," §I.2, *Works* 2:156-57.
26. Sermon 67, "On Divine Providence," §14, *Works* 2:540-41.

chapter. "The pure of heart," he writes, not only shall but *already do* "see God" because they see "all things full of God."[27] But their seeing all things in this way is not simply a matter of *seeing-as*, not simply their saintly perspective being superimposed on their sense experience, not simply a model for interpreting the world: it is not simply 'reading' the world in a certain way. Rather, the "pure in heart" see "all things full of God" because all things *are* full of God (which, to be sure, is a certain kind of reading of the world), and the eyes of holy folks have been graciously salved to enable them to read the world for the "good old" creation that it truly and actually is—in every moment and place indwelled and renewed by the infinite Creator Spirit.

> [The pure in heart] see him in the firmament of heaven, in the moon walking in brightness, in the sun when he rejoiceth as a giant to run his course. They see him "making the clouds his chariots, and walking upon the wings of the wind." They see him "preparing rain for the earth," "and blessing the increase of it"; "giving grass for the cattle, and green herb for the use of man." They see the Creator of all wisely governing all, and "upholding all things by the word of his power."[28]

In Wesley's use of the Psalms, we get a glimpse of the subtle and painstaking labors of God in the world: it is the one God revealed decisively to us in Christ who is always, and everywhere, the world's Maker, Molder, and Mender. To put it simply, Wesley is careful not to overdraw the distinction between nature and grace. The pure of heart believe and perceive that God "is everywhere present, in all, and over all" and thus "as intimately present in earth as heaven."[29] Yet "in a more especial manner they see God in His ordinances"; in public or private prayer, in reading the Scriptures and hearing them proclaimed, in the Eucharist, "they find such a near approach as cannot be expressed."[30] Even so, it is the "God of nature and of grace"—or, perhaps more appropriately, the God of grace *and of nature*—who steers "a near approach" to all people, to all creatures. Blessed, then, are the pure of heart who

27. Sermon 23, "Sermon on the Mount, III," §I.6, *Works* 1:513.
28. Ibid., 513-14.
29. Ibid., §I.9, *Works* 1:515.
30. Ibid., §I.8, *Works* 1:514.

"see" the God who is always and everywhere nearer than our next breath.

Though only the "pure in heart" have received eyes to "see God" in all creatures and throughout creation, *God is there*—God is here, in this place, in this moment, in this breath. The biblical invitation is that we might live consciously in the Creator Spirit's presence. Thus, for example, while Psalm 139 opens with the declaration of God's intimate, probing knowledge of the psalmist (and, presumably, of all things), it nonetheless concludes with the invitation for God to "search me . . . and know my heart" (v. 23). To make that prayer our very own is to move closer to the Heart of "good old creation," to read and experience the world as being renewed, sustained, loved, and known in every moment and occasion by "Love Divine, all loves excelling." In order so to live in God's good creation, Wesley has counseled us to "spare no pains to preserve always a deep, a continual, a lively, and a joyful sense of his gracious presence."[31] May we heed such wise counsel!

31. Sermon 118, "On the Omnipresence of God," §III.6, *Works* 4:47.

CHAPTER 6

"AND ALL WE TASTE BE GOD"

Creation Spirituality in a Wesleyan Way

Turn the full stream of nature's tide;
Let all our actions tend
To Thee their source; thy love the guide,
Thy glory be the end.

Earth then a scale to heaven shall be,
Sense shall point out the road;
The creatures all shall lead to thee;
And all we taste be God.

John and Charles Wesley, "Grace before Meat"[1]

I am not certain how many times I had read John Wesley's little spiritual classic *A Plain Account of Christian Perfection* as a student of theology—and then as a teacher of theology with my own students—before I actually saw on its pages the remarkable stanzas from a Wesley hymn that serve as this chapter's epigraph.

Look at the concluding line of this hymnic prayer: "And all we taste be *God.*" Perhaps this sentiment was simply too foreign to my thinking to be noticed, let alone processed. What does such a

1. Hymn #104, lines 25-32, *Works* 7:211-12. This hymn was originally titled "Grace before Meat" in *Hymns and Sacred Poems* (1739). It is placed in a section titled "For Mourners convinced of Sin" in the 1780 *Collection of Hymns.*

notion as *tasting God*—and doing so in all mundane creatures and experiences!—actually entail? Of course it would go far beyond the Wesleys' intent to interpret this prayer as an ode to pantheism; on the other hand, we should not forget John's bold willingness to call God the *anima mundi* ("soul of the world") and Charles's arresting hymn lyrics, "Thou art the Universal Soul, the Plastick Power that fills the whole" (see chapter 4). Taking seriously the Wesleys' biblically informed vision of God's holy presence in the world—a world "full of [God's] glory" (Isa. 6:3), an earth "full of the steadfast love of the Lord" (Ps. 33:5)—may inspire us to read the world as thoroughly infiltrated by its Maker and Molder.

It should be no surprise, then, that particularly in the final stanza there is an unmistakable affirmation of the *sacramental* character of our creaturely relations and experiences. With this use of "sacramental" I mean to suggest that, just as several streams of Christian tradition have believed that the "real presence" of Christ is embodied and mediated in the sacrament of the Eucharist, so this Wesleyan poem intimates that *all* of God's creatures are (or at least can become) mediators of the "real presence" of their Creator. Or, to return to the Wesley brothers' striking language, we may "taste God" in our bodily and sensory interactions with the world in which we live.

Remarkable as these poetic lines are, it is even more remarkable that John Wesley deemed them sufficiently important and germane to his understanding of Christian holiness as to include them in *Plain Account*, his little *summa* on holiness. Their presence early in Wesley's slim volume drops a tantalizing hint that rich connections exist between the doctrine of entire sanctification (or "Christian perfection") and the doctrine of creation; these connections beg further exploration. To interpret Wesley's doctrine of sanctification much more explicitly within the context of the doctrine of creation and a theology of nature is one of the aims of the present chapter. This aim is undertaken with the conviction that all too often the teaching in Wesleyan circles about holiness has not been sufficiently immersed in the richer dimensions of creaturely existence and community. Earth, stars, bodies, food, beauty, tastes, textures, sexuality—all our relations with and responsibility for fellow earthlings, human and otherwise, deserve more careful attention in reflecting upon Christian spirituality and the quest for holiness.

The creatures all shall lead to Thee, and all we taste be God. Of course, this unusual declaration does not stand alone; it is merely the conclusion of a prayer composed of eight full stanzas! For the Wesleys, it was intended as a "Grace before Meat," a prayer before eating, perhaps to be sung. The purpose of this chapter is to provide a careful exegesis of this prayer as a means of exploring creation spirituality in a Wesleyan way. As we shall see, this "Grace before Meat" is no small or insignificant theological treatise! If the food on the table started out hot, it would be lukewarm at best by the time this prayer was finished. There is much more here than "God is great, God is good"; indeed, the theological deliberations of this grace before the meal serve to thoroughly re-orient those who chew on its lines, ushering them into a radically different relationship to the creaturely elements awaiting their consumption at the table.

It is certainly worth our notice that Wesley chose to place this "Grace before Meat" in his 1780 *Collection of Hymns for the People Called Methodists* in the section titled: "For Mourners Convinced of Sin." At first glance, it may appear odd to connect the traditional sentiments of gratitude for our food with the idea of bemoaning our sins under the convicting influence of the Holy Spirit. After all, people who bother to thank God before they eat their food are generally not hardened sinners! Beyond that first glance, though, it begins to make some very serious theological sense for three readily identifiable reasons.

First, while it certainly cannot be considered wrong or evil to consume other creatures in order to sustain our lives—all creatures, after all, must do so to continue living—there may well be room at the table for our mourning the lives that we have taken for our food. This is all the more evident in the case of the meat on our tables. If we eat meat, we do well to remember that sentient creatures have been slaughtered for our consumption; further, if Wesley is correct in his interpretation of creation's groanings as described by Paul in Romans 8, then the creatures' primal fears, pains, and deaths ought not to be taken lightly by us at the table.[2] I will never forget having once watched pigs being herded into a meat packing plant: a truly ugly scene in which the terrified

2. See Sermon 60, "The General Deliverance," *Works* 2:437-51, which will figure prominently in chapters 8 and 9 of this book.

creatures were first electrocuted into a daze before being summarily butchered, sliced, and packaged in the bloody and putrid nightmare of a slaughterhouse. Vegetarians rightly argue that meat is not necessary for a sustainable, healthy diet. If, however, it is a luxury that many of us continue to insist upon, the least we can do in our "grace before meat" is to mourn the mammals, fish, and fowl whose lives have been diced for our grocery store freezers.

Second, beyond our considerations for the animals themselves, our appetite for meat requires that, in the so-called Third World, food crops increasingly are replaced by feed crops for the production of beef that is exported to First World tables—and the sobering fact is that it takes seven pounds of grain, on the average, to produce a single pound of beef.[3] Thus, a prayer of mourning before meals is all the more fitting for Westerners, particularly North Americans, who generally have much, much more on their tables—meat and otherwise—than most of the rest of the world. A dominant tendency among Christians is simply to consider this a blessing and give thanks to God for all the goods we enjoy. When we pray before eating, however, it cannot simply be to thank God for our blessings in such a way that, in effect, we simply sanctify our gluttony, our hankering for more. We have all heard and read the statistics: tens of thousands of children die every day on our planet because of malnutrition and the diseases associated with it, even though "total world food production is equal to more than twice the minimum calorie and protein requirements for every man, woman, and child."[4] Surely even as we give thanks to God, our prayer honestly prayed ought also to place a divine check upon the American drive to consume. Can our prayer before meals also become a prayer of mourning our sin of injustice rooted in gluttonous consumption? Could it thereby begin to sensitize us, even as we begin to eat, to the necessity of our learning to live much more lightly in the world—indeed, to *eat less*? Ought not our prayers of thanksgiving for the food before us move us "to be rich in good works, generous, and ready to share" (1 Tim. 6:18) with the millions of fellow human beings

---

3. Ian G. Barbour, *Ethics in an Age of Technology* (HarperSanFrancisco, 1993), 102-3.
4. Ibid., 86, 88, 109.

who are famished and extinguished by our exorbitant North American and European demands for meat and other imported luxuries?

Third, it is all too evident that human beings easily tend toward idolatry; we are highly adept at "worship[ing] and serv[ing] the creature rather than the Creator" (Rom. 1:25). Creation is filled with many good and delightful sights, aromas, tastes, and textures. We human creatures, surrounded by and enmeshed in such creaturely goods, too readily seek joy and fulfillment in them quite apart from the Creator and Giver of all good gifts. Prayer before a meal is an opportunity to direct our attention and thanks to the Source of the goods we enjoy and share (1 Tim. 6:17); further, it gives us necessary pause to recognize that the creaturely goods before us are not to be lustily pursued or hoarded. In the Jewish tradition particularly, it has been emphasized that blessing God before eating is God's prescribed way for us to remember that we are not simply animals eating other creatures in order to stay alive; we are that, but we become more than that when we pause before eating to give thanks to the One who provides for our needs. In this way, perhaps we begin to approximate Wesley's instructions that we "love the creature as it leads to the Creator."[5]

Wesley's prayer, then, may serve as a critical caution against an all-too-inviting "creation spirituality" that encourages us simply to celebrate the goodness of creation—food, bodily existence, sexuality, physical beauty, and so on—but gives insufficient attention to the ever-looming danger of idolatry.[6] If, as the apostle Paul suggests in Romans 1, idolatry involves our exchanging "the glory of the immortal God" (v. 23) for the allurements of fellow creatures, then we must admit just how deeply this temptation runs in our veins. So easily we seek our ultimate joys and fulfillments in the creature—and no wonder, since the creature (whether, for examples, the sensuous curve of the human body or simply the aroma of fresh-brewed coffee) is indeed often so attractive! It would be nothing short of lying to deny the beauties that loom and bloom around

5. Sermon 17, "Circumcision of the Heart," §I.12, *Works* 1:408; reprinted in *Plain Account of Christian Perfection*, §6, *Works* (Jackson) 11:368.

6. The author most susceptible to this criticism is Matthew Fox, whose "creation spirituality" writings have been widely influential, particularly among disaffected Roman Catholics. See, for example, his *Original Blessing: A Primer in Creation Spirituality* (Santa Fe: Bear & Company, 1983).

us in so many shapes and forms! Further, we believe that the beauty of the creature is a gift of God (a gift of which God is not jealous), which in its particular attraction is capable of pointing beyond itself to its utterly generous Giver. Thus, idolatry is the underside of existence in a good and beautiful creation—an eminently understandable sin, indeed, and yet a thoroughly destructive and disintegrating power in human existence. It is this effect of dis-integration created by idolatrous relations to other creatures that the Wesleys explore in the opening three stanzas of their mourning prayer.

THE POISON OF IDOLATRY

Enslaved to sense, to pleasure prone,
Fond of created good,
Father, our helplessness we own,
And trembling taste our food.

We scoot up to the table with the Wesleys, hesitating and halting, unsure of our status before God and our relations with the creatures prepared for our consumption. Of course the Wesleys' language is strong in this opening stanza; God, after all, is the Creator of sense and of pleasure. Far be it from us nowadays to be captured by a Platonic distrust of the body or a gnostic distaste for material pleasure! The fact is, however, that Christians—at least most of us who dwell in the lavish wealth of North America—have very little danger of this. We have over the past decades overreacted so harshly against the perceived extremes of asceticism and legalism that many of us now need to hear Wesley's warning that we readily become enslaved to created good. Thus we "trembling taste our food" because when we are alienated from our Creator we are also out of right relations with fellow creatures. We have found ourselves in addictive relations with so many of the creatures around us, and addictions cannot finally satisfy.

Trembling we taste; for ah! no more
To thee the creatures lead;
Changed, they exert a baneful power,
And poison while they feed.

The implication of this stanza, obviously, is that creatures in their many and varied relations with one another are intended to point, to lead, to gesture one another toward God. This theme had been explored by earlier theologians, perhaps most notably by Thomas Aquinas (1225–74).[7] If our fellow creatures no longer lead us to God, as the Wesleys' prayer teaches us to mourn, it is precisely because we have fallen into relating to them as ends in themselves, seeking our joy and ultimate fulfillment in them. In this case, we are expecting, even demanding, the creature to function for us as God, who is our true and final end. It seems, in fact, that just about any attractive creature might do: for some it is the food on the table, for others it is sex, or wealth, or another human being, or family, or job, or home, or nation.

The brothers Wesley write that the creatures are "changed." In a superficial sense, we might be prone to think that it is not so much that the creatures themselves are changed as it is that our relations to those creatures have changed, having become idolatrous and thus poisonous. However, if we take seriously the implications of a relational world, then we recognize that changed relations necessarily entail changed creatures. The nature and quality of our relations are not merely accidental, incidental, or external; instead, our relations flow into the very constituting of ourselves and of all beings. If we are out of proper and healthy relations with our fellow creatures, human or nonhuman, we in-fluence them—we "flow into" them—for the worse. They are indeed changed, and their power to attract us and others can indeed become baneful.

An obvious example occurs in our Hollywood-inspired expectations for our intimate relationships such as marriage. All too often, those expectations have been so trumped up, so inflated by "happily ever after" endings that no relationship could ever meet the imagined standard. And when our loved one cannot deliver on our expectations, we eventually become embittered and disappointed, and all too often we go looking for another human icon at which to kneel, once more, in romanticized and idealized "love" expectations. What a cycle of mutual disappointment our human relations can create! Idolatry inevitably creates hopes and desires that

7. See especially the reading of Aquinas offered by G. Simon Harak, S.J., in his *Virtuous Passions: The Formation of Christian Character* (Mahwah, N.J.: Paulist Press, 1993).

cannot be fulfilled—and thus creates the addictive desire to find the more beautiful, the better thrill, the stronger attraction.

This is not meant as a negation of the potential beauty, joy, and fulfillment to be shared and received in our relations to other creatures, but only as a deeply needed warning to our culture of consumerism fed by media advertising that creates false needs and unrealistic expectations, going all out to sell its bogus satisfactions. Our idolatrous drive is, after all, rooted in our legitimate and blessed need for creaturely relations of all kinds to sustain our lives physically, emotionally, and spiritually. Martin Buber was correct to challenge Kierkegaard's self-imposed quest to live as an "individual," supposedly cut off from all creaturely loves and relations—most specifically, of course, symbolized in his break with his fiancée Regina Olsen. In response to Kierkegaard's lonely isolationism, Buber wisely wrote that "creation is not a hurdle on the road to God, it is the road itself. We are created along with one another and directed to a life with one another. Creatures are placed in my way so that I, their fellow-creature, by means of them and with them find the way to God."[8]

On the other hand, as attractive as Buber's sentiment is and as important and influential as it has been in much of Christian thought over the past half-century, it is likely that Buber did not take seriously enough the human heart's proclivity for idolatry. For Kierkegaard, it appears that his sundering of relations with his fiancée was, at least at one level, an act that embodied his rejection of the easy marriage of God and culture in nineteenth-century Danish society. Just as Martin Luther had taken Katharina as his wife in defiance of Roman Catholicism's extolling of celibacy, so three centuries later Kierkegaard, himself of course a Lutheran, wrote, "Put the other way round, one could say . . . in defiance of the whole nineteenth century I cannot marry."[9]

Buber was correct to point out that Kierkegaard had also written in his journal in 1843 that famously mysterious confession, "Had I had faith I would have stayed with Regina."[10] The critical issue that confronts us in our meditations upon idolatry, however, is simply

8. Martin Buber, *Between Man and Man*, translated by Ronald Gregor Smith (New York: Macmillan, 1972), 52.
9. Ibid., 53.
10. Ibid., 57.

this: Do any of us have the sort of "faith" that Kierkegaard describes himself as having lacked? This is not a question of God not having "enough room" in the divine heart to accommodate our creaturely loves; it is, rather, a question of our not having the proper faith so as to love the creature appropriately, a question of our recurring tendency to attempt to elevate the creature to a divine role and status—and so to poison our patterns of relation to the creature. Our fascinated fixation upon the creature leads so readily to frustrating, unfulfilling, and destructive relations! We think inevitably of Augustine's justly famous line in the opening paragraph of his *Confessions*: "You have made us for yourself and our hearts find no rest until they rest in you."[11]

> Cursed for the sake of wretched man,
> They now engross him whole,
> With pleasing force on earth detain,
> And sensualize his soul.

To be "engrossed . . . whole" by a fellow creature is, once more, simply idolatry. Again, we are reminded of Augustine's careful and conscientious *Confessions* regarding the allurements of bodily existence in a bodily world: (over)eating; tickling the ear with the sounds of music; the eyes' delighting in "beautiful shapes of different sorts and bright and attractive colours"; even the sense of smell is given brief consideration.[12] In fact, it is difficult not to conclude that Augustine is hypersensitive in these material matters. While granting the valid point underlying Augustine's, and Wesley's, fastidiousness regarding our sensory and sensual experiences, it is difficult not to conclude that Plato's ghost has haunted not only them but countless other Christians throughout history. There is a fine line to be walked in a properly Christian estimation of the world and its goods and pleasures. As I touched on earlier, though, it is somewhat ironic to suggest this need for walking a fine line to Christians of North America—we who have all too readily conformed to the materialism and economism of the modern West. Even so, we must avoid a gnostic denigration of the body

11. Augustine, *Confessions*, 21.
12. Ibid., 234-41.

or dismissal of the good and legitimate pleasures inherent in living responsibly, lovingly, and appreciatively in God's creation. "For everything created by God is good, and nothing is to be rejected, provided it is received with thanksgiving; for it is sanctified by God's word and by prayer" (1 Tim. 4:4-5).

There is, then, undoubtedly a proper "biblical sensuality," accentuated not only by the biblical affirmations of creation's goodness but also by Scripture's instructions regarding the incarnation of the Word and the bodily resurrection of Jesus. Bodily existence and its attendant pleasures—and, to be sure, its pains as well—are deemed the good creation of God. On the other hand, as Calvin has rightly warned, human beings have repeatedly proved their particular proclivity for becoming thoroughly "sensualized" by idolatry.[13] We tend easily to immerse ourselves simply in the creaturely realm and its attractions that all too easily and soon become addictions, when all along we are created to be immersed in the life and love of God. Again, Augustine's classic *Confessions* seem to loom just beneath the surface of Wesley's table grace:

> I have learned to love you late, Beauty at once so ancient and so new! . . . You were within me, and I was in the world outside myself. I searched for you outside myself and, disfigured as I was, I fell upon the lovely things of your creation. You were with me, but I was not with you. The beautiful things of this world kept me far from you and yet, if they had not been in you, they would have had no being at all. You called me; you cried aloud to me; you broke my barrier of deafness. You shone upon me; your radiance enveloped me; you put my blindness to flight.[14]

For Augustine, who repeatedly refers to his spiritual defects as "wounds" and "sickness" in need of divine healing, the calling and shining and healing of God has been graciously bestowed upon us in the medicine of the Word "made flesh and come to dwell among us."[15] It is at this same point—the christological point—that Wesley begins in his "mourning prayer" a note of hope.

---

13. See Calvin's *Institutes of the Christian Religion*, especially chapters 3 through 6.
14. Augustine, *Confessions*, 231-32.
15. Ibid., 251.

CHRIST OUR PHYSICIAN

Grov'ling on earth we still must lie
Till Christ the curse repeal,
Till Christ, descending from on high,
Infected nature heal.

"Groveling on earth" is an all-too-apt description of what so easily becomes of us. Though we are created by God from the dust of the earth to stand in dignity as God's image, God's reflection in the world, we instead become so absorbed in the goods and pleasures of creation that we become utterly forgetful of our vocation. How often have we seen ourselves and others reduced by the addictive power of sin to groveling in filth, to looking for a new fix, a new thrill, a new pleasure that will satisfy our spiritual and emotional thirsts? Those addictive, habit-forming relations can be pursued in so many directions: codependent relationships with friends and loved ones; eating disorders; drug or alcohol dependencies; sexual perversions in the swirling black hole of pornography—the daunting, haunting list never ends. No wonder Augustine confessed, "You see how my heart trembles and strains in the midst of all these perils and others of a like kind. It is not as though I do not suffer wounds, but I feel rather that you heal them over and over again."[16]

The one who offers us healing, of course, is Christ; we are debilitatingly engrossed in our destructive cycles of behavior "till Christ, descending from on high, infected nature heal." Much has rightly been made of Wesley's "therapeutic" understanding of salvation—that God in Christ has come to bring a true healing, an actual restoration and renewal, of our sin-diseased lives.[17] Wesley insisted that salvation is "not barely [i.e., merely] . . . deliverance from hell, or going to heaven, but a present deliverance from sin, a restoration of the soul to its primitive health, its original purity; a recovery of the divine nature; the renewal of our souls after the image of God."[18] For Wesley, following particularly in the stream of the early Greek Fathers, salvation is truly a *salving*, the healing

16. Ibid., 248.
17. See especially Maddox, *Responsible Grace*, 112-13, 121-22.
18. *A Farther Appeal to Men of Reason and Religion*, Part I, §I.3, *Works* 11:106.

balm of Christ's own presence and participation in the human and creaturely realm.[19]

It is a central theme of this book that Christ graciously offers this healing not simply to us human beings, but also to "infected nature." If nature is this complex of relations among creatures who in their living together no longer lead one another to God, then Christ is the second Adam, or "the last Adam" (1 Cor. 15:45), who has come to restore and redeem this poisoned relational web. How is Christ accomplishing this restoration, this healing? Let us pursue the question.

> Come then, our heavenly Adam, come,
> Thy healing influence give,
> Hallow our food, reverse our doom,
> And bid us eat, and live.

Is there any question but that this lovely invitation is the heart of the Wesleys' prayer? Here they draw upon Paul's image of Christ as the "last Adam," an image that second-century pastor and theologian Irenaeus had woven so beautifully into his theory of recapitulation. Irenaeus taught that the second Adam has come to reverse, undo, and heal the effects of sin as wrought within creation by the first Adam. Inspired particularly by Paul's Adam-Christ parallelism in Romans 5 and 1 Corinthians 15, Irenaeus wrote,

> So the Lord now manifestly came to his own, and, borne by his own created order which he himself bears, he by his obedience on the tree renewed [and reversed] what was done by disobedience in [connection with] a tree. . . . He therefore completely renewed all things, . . . that as our race went down to death by a man who was conquered we might ascend again to life by a man who overcame; and as death won the palm of victory over

19. It should be said, however, that it is possible to overstate the "Eastern" roots of this understanding of salvation as the Divine Salve applied to our wounds through Jesus Christ; certainly the "therapeutic" imagery in Augustine's *Confessions* is pervasive. See also Ellen Charry's *By the Renewing of Your Minds: The Pastoral Function of Christian Doctrine* (New York: Oxford University Press, 1997). Charry argues well that the great Christian theologians, both East and West, have understood doctrine's foremost function as being to remake believers into persons of excellence as they are drawn into participation in the life of God.

> us by a man, so we might by a man receive the palm of victory over death.[20]

The heavenly Adam is invited to come and give his "healing influence," and surely it is important to remember that to "influence," etymologically speaking, is to "flow into." Christ, the new human—the embodiment of humanity's renewal—is called upon in Wesley's prayer to flow into us in such a way that our proper relations are healed. The prayer longs for renewed relations to God, to one another at the table and at all tables around the world, and of course to all other creatures, including the very creatures awaiting our consumption. Further, there is a tantalizing eucharistic hint in the plea that this eschatological Adam "bid us eat, and live." As we sit at table with this one whom we confess to be the truly human, we eat with the One who comes to heal and restore creation in all of its manifold relations. Perhaps we learn to eat rightly at all tables by first learning to eat at the Lord's Table (1 Cor. 11:17-34).

CHRIST THE NEW ADAM

How does the heavenly Adam accomplish this redemption? How does he "reverse our doom"? The Adam-Christ parallel with which Wesley is here working provides us with a fascinating direction. We begin with the words of one of the Psalms:

> When I look at your heavens, the work of your fingers,
> the moon and the stars that you have established;
> what are human beings that you are mindful of them,
> mortals that you care for them?
> Yet you have made them a little lower than God,
> and crowned them with glory and honor.
> You have given them dominion over the works of your hands;
> you have put all things under their feet,
> all sheep and oxen,
> and also the beasts of the field,

20. Irenaeus, *Adversus Haerses*, translated and edited by Cyril C. Richardson in *The Library of Christian Classics, Volume I: Early Christian Fathers* (Philadelphia: Westminster, 1953), 389, 390, 391.

the birds of the air, and the fish of the sea,
whatever passes along the paths of the sea. (Ps. 8:3-8)

In this psalm we encounter a hymnic commentary on the opening chapter of Genesis, with human beings marvelously called upon to function as the Creator's representatives, to *re-present* God in creation and especially to the rest of the creatures, whether of land, sky, or sea. Human beings, created a little lower than *elohim* (variously translated, in this case, by "angels," "divine beings," or "God"), are called upon to *image* God in the world. In Psalm 8, then, we are offered a somewhat idyllic portrait of the human creatures living in proper relations to the rest of creation. We may be troubled, and appropriately so, by the subjugation implied in the phrase "all things under their feet"; I propose that we begin to read it in a different way. If we are careful to recognize the fragility of the ecological web in which we and all things exist, we will know that we must tread lightly on the earth beneath us. To the extent that creation is indeed "under our feet"—and of course very little of it actually is, either literally or metaphorically—to that extent it behooves us to "go barefoot," to actually *be in touch* with the ground and grass beneath us, to live in creation as though we are striding unshod in a garden, perhaps "in the cool of the day." In any case, there is no question as to the role and responsibility entrusted to human beings in this psalm as it sings over the creation story of Genesis 1.

Given the clear reference in Psalm 8 to all human beings, male and female alike created in God's image, it is striking that when the psalm is cited in the New Testament writings it is not applied to all human beings but to one: Jesus. In 1 Corinthians 15, where Paul consciously employs the Adam-Christ contrast, we read of a redemptive process even now in the works:

> But in fact Christ has been raised from the dead, the first fruits of those who have died. For since death came through a human being, the resurrection of the dead has also come through a human being; for as all die in Adam, so all will be made alive in Christ. . . . For [Christ] must reign until [God] has put all [God's] enemies under [Christ's] feet . . . For "God has put all things in subjection under his feet." But when it says, "All things are put in subjection," it is plain that this does not include the one

> who put all things in subjection under him. When all things are subjected to him, then the Son himself will also be subjected to the one who put all things in subjection under him, so that God may be all in all. (vv. 20-28)

It appears that Paul interprets Psalm 8 to be fulfilled, or "filled full" with new meaning, by Jesus Christ. It is under Christ's feet that all of creation is subjected or, more precisely, is being subjected. For Paul, Jesus Christ is the "true Adam" who perfectly images God (2 Cor. 4:6) and in whom all of creation is being restored to its proper relations. Perhaps here we may also begin to understand "subjection" in a new way, a christological way. For just as "all things" shall be "subjected to" Christ, so shall Christ "be subjected to" God. Whatever else a trinitarian reading of this text might yield, certainly it deconstructs hierarchicalism. "Subjection" in the Abba-Jesus relationship is not domination or abuse of power. It is not as though God ends up "on top," with Christ below God, and everything else below Christ. Rather, God ends up being "all in all," a tantalizing if difficult phrase that suggests infusion rather than subjugation. Perhaps the phrase implies that God shall be present to all creatures in such a way that all creatures shall be fully cognizant of the Presence. Surely this holds implications for the way we tread on "all things" under our own feet. Beyond that, who can say what it is for God to be "all in all"? Perhaps all we can add is that it is this mysterious Pauline phrase that the Wesleys probably had in mind when they penned the final line of this table grace: *and all we taste be God.*

God may not be all we taste, and certainly God is not yet "all in all." Nonetheless, the apostle is confident that the day is coming through Jesus Christ when in fact God and creation will be so related, so united, so reconciled, that God will actually be "all in all." In other words, God is not yet all that God shall be! In the time between the resurrection of Christ and that indescribable union of God and creation, we live in the processes of nature and history that Paul describes as the time when God is "put[ting] all things in subjection under [Christ's] feet." All of creation has a forward-straining impetus rooted in God's raising of Jesus from the dead; therefore, we do not find our clues about the meaning of creation, nor about our destiny as God's image-bearers, by looking backward to the "old age" of a fallen Adam. Rather, we seek those clues by peering forward to the "age to come" that is even now in the process of coming through the New Adam, God's pioneer of the future.

We encounter a similar use of Psalm 8 in Hebrews 2:5-9:

> Now God did not subject *the coming world, about which we are speaking*, to angels. But someone has testified somewhere,
> "What are human beings that you are mindful of them,
> or mortals, that you care for them?
> You have made them for a little while lower than the angels;
> you have crowned them with glory and honor,
> subjecting all things under their feet."
> Now in subjecting all things to them, God left nothing outside their control. As it is, we do not yet see everything in subjection to them, but *we do see Jesus*, who for a little while was made lower than the angels, now crowned with glory and honor because of the suffering of death, so that by the grace of God he might taste death for everyone.

What a fascinating reading of Psalm 8! Our unknown biblical writer first assures us that he (or she!) is writing about "the coming world," the age to come that we know in fact to be already coming (Heb. 6:5) precisely because "we do see Jesus"! In other words, God has created all human beings to be image-bearers and care-takers of creation, but when it comes to the new creation ("the coming world") Jesus is God's "Adam," God's truly human, the earthling in whom the world receives its re-creation.

There is a tantalizing but sobering implication in the text's claim that "God left nothing outside their control." Such freedom and responsibility is given to us human creatures! But there is also the note of harsh realism: "We do not yet see everything in subjection to them." The world is not under our control, and in fact the more we try to exercise control (as "control freaks") in our addictive, idolatrous state—in our heavy-handed, technologized drive to consume—the more the world appears to be veering out of control and toward ecological destruction. Suddenly, we recall that the pretext for all of our reflections here is a prayer before eating, offered by mourners convinced of their sin! It is a prayer that opens in confession, "Father, our helplessness we own, and trembling taste our food."

But we do see Jesus. For the author of Hebrews, then, Jesus is the true Adam who is now "crowned with glory and honour," just as Psalm 8 describes the human destiny. However, Jesus is so "crowned" precisely "because of the suffering of death, so that by the grace of God he might taste death for everyone." In other words, Jesus embodies the truly human not by heavy-handed control but by the surrender of "control" in the suffering and vulnerability of death. This Adam restores and renews creation through the utterly unexpected and inglorious path of voluntary suffering and death, thereby participating in the death of all (2:9). We might even say that the New Adam participates in the eventual death of the universe itself (Heb. 1:10-12), a theme we shall explore in chapter 9. No wonder, then, that the author continues by arguing that it "was fitting that God . . . should make the pioneer of [our] salvation perfect through sufferings" (2:10). This Adam is tested, tried, and stretched; and through that process of testing is made "complete" or "fully functional" as our Pioneer. In his captivating commentary on Hebrews, *Letter to Pilgrims*, Robert Jewett writes,

> What [the author of Hebrews] sees in Jesus is the glory of finitude within a world subject to deterioration and death. He was "crowned with glory and honor" in his exaltation not by having gained control of the fallen world in a theocratic sense, but by suffering within that world on behalf of others. In sharing human limitations . . . Jesus overcame the alienation that had made finitude so threatening. . . . [T]he Christ of Hebrews is . . . one who redeems by sharing human suffering, temptation, and death.[21]

This is a remarkable portrait of God's mode of redeeming all of creation, and especially of the human creatures entrusted with the godlike task of caring for it. The "heavenly Adam" gives his "healing influence," his inflowing of divine life and love, by becoming an earthly human in our midst, God's Word-become-Earthling sharing in the limitations and struggles, as well as the joys and

21. Robert Jewett, *Letter to Pilgrims: A Commentary on the Epistle to the Hebrews* (New York: Pilgrim, 1981), 44-45.

satisfactions, of creaturely life. The words of the controversial medieval theologian Peter Abelard (1079–1142) seem pertinent: God's Son "has taken upon himself our nature and persevered therein in teaching us by word and example even unto death," and thereby "has more fully bound us to himself by love, with the result that our hearts should be enkindled by such a gift of divine grace."[22] This is not a magical transformation of the world with the mere flip of a wand; it is, instead, the painstaking and longsuffering process of transformation that comes about by God the Word becoming *flesh*—keeping in mind, to be sure, that the Hebrew term for "flesh" connotes not only human beings but all living creatures—and "persevering" in "our [and thus in *all*] nature" in a ministry that was defined by participation with, and in, the lives of others. As we sit at the table, we pray for the "healing inflowing" of this Incarnate Word to bring a salving to our relations to all our fellow creatures, and to our relation to the Maker of us all.

The Sanctifying of All Life

The bondage of corruption break;
For this our spirits groan;
Thy only will we fain would seek,
O save us from our own!

The operative language of this stanza—"bondage of corruption" and "groan"—obviously alludes to Romans 8, a text we will draw upon deeply in the chapters to follow. The most important point for us presently is that in this stanza Wesley transposes what Paul envisioned to be a *future fulfillment* of all creation into a *present possibility*. For Paul, "the whole creation has been groaning" as it "waits in eager expectation for the [children] of God to be revealed," and for its liberation "from bondage to decay . . . into the glorious freedom of the children of God"; indeed, "we ourselves, who have the firstfruits of the Spirit, groan inwardly as we wait eagerly for our adoption as [children]" (Rom. 8:22, 19, 21, 23 NIV).

22. Peter Abelard, *Commentary on Romans* in Eugene R. Fairweather, ed., *Anselm to Ockham*, Vol. X of *The Library of Christian Classics* (Philadelphia: Westminster, 1961), 283.

Wesley, however, teaches us to pray that our bondage—the bondage to idolatrous, destructive relations as we have explored them in this chapter—might be broken now, even as we sit at the table. What Paul envisions as a longed-for eschatological denouement, Wesley envisions as realizable, at least in principle, in this very moment. Indeed, this is the essential meaning of entire sanctification: that we may love God and all others *perfectly in this life, in this very moment of life.* Corruption's bondage can be broken now, in this moment, as we gather at the table—a table that has become the Lord's table! The heavenly Adam has, after all, been invited to come join us, to "hallow our food, reverse our doom, and bid us eat, and live."

It becomes all the more apt to suggest that the above lines provide an incisive description of entire sanctification when we consider the final two stanzas, since it is these two that Wesley cites in his *Plain Account of Christian Perfection*. One stanza at a time:

> Turn the full stream of nature's tide;
> Let all our actions tend
> To thee their source; thy love the guide,
> Thy glory be the end.

What does it mean to "turn the full stream of nature's tide"? Because nature has been infected with human idolatry, we are alienated from God and fellow creatures. "Nature's tide" all too often flows away from its Maker and Molder, and so also from its Mender, its Healer. Wesley prays that through the incarnation of the "Heavenly Adam" and his full participation in the creaturely realm of our relational web, we by partaking in his life might be cured. Again, we note that Wesley's prayer implies that indeed the poisonous stream—so dramatically embodied in our consumerism, our materialism, our rapacious industrialization, and our user-mentality and practices—can be turned! The question before us, of course, is very simple: Do we desire such a turning, such a re-turning to love for God and all neighbors? Do we want to be healed?

Wesley's grace before the meal teaches us that the second Adam has come, and by his "healing influence" or in-flowing our very lives in all their particular actions and influences may be redirected. We may be guided by divine love toward the *telos* of divine glory—and we are reminded by Elizabeth Johnson of Irenaeus's evocative description of divine glory as "the human being fully alive!"[23] To employ Wesley's lovely phrase, this is the human being "renewed in love": love for God, for neighbor, for stranger, for enemy, *for all*. If the source of our lives is God who is love, and if God's love is our guide, then surely God's glory can be nothing else but love! And if indeed we should be made new in this love freely given through Christ, Wesley teaches us finally to pray:

> Earth then a scale to heaven shall be;
> Sense shall point out the road;
> The creatures all shall lead to Thee;
> And all we taste be God.

This is simply incredible. Obviously, this final stanza provides a redemptive reply to the doom and trembling of the opening stanzas of the prayer, where "no more to Thee the creatures lead." By now, after such a lengthy and theologically intricate prayer, our food is cold: but better cold food that leads us to God than hot meals that are poison to us because of the dis-integrating power of idolatry and gluttony! In this finale Wesley envisions the sort of relations to God and fellow creatures that properly characterizes a life of Christian perfection. Earth and all its creatures, while remaining what they truly are as particular, unique, material creatures, become at the same time ladders and pointers toward the Creator and Goal of all things. "Sense," by which the Wesleys appear to mean the whole range of human sensory experience, is now deemed trustworthy not on epistemological grounds but on soteriological grounds. Because God has entered into the web of creaturely relations as the Word-become-human, so now "sense" can "point out the road" of trafficking between Creator and creation. God's condescension in Christ has put us on a right scent.

Is it really possible to live in this way? Is it possible to live consistently in blessed relations with God and all neighbors, human and otherwise? Wesley certainly thought so, and in fact insisted that the very purpose of the Methodist movement was "to spread

23. Johnson has effectively used Irenaeus's maxim as a norm for feminist critique of patriarchal practices in Christianity. See, for example, *She Who Is: The Mystery of God in Feminist Theological Discourse* (New York: Crossroad, 1992), 14.

scriptural holiness over the land"[24]—a holiness which is nothing other than "the pure love of God and man; . . . love governing the heart and life, running through all our tempers, words, and actions."[25] In such a life of interrelations, we are called to live in such a way that in all our connections and interactions we are led, and also lead other creatures—including, indeed, "the land" itself as we "spread scriptural holiness"!—to the encompassing mystery of God who is love. Thus Wesley insisted on the social nature of grace when he wrote in his *Plain Account*, "Although all the graces of God depend on his mere bounty, yet is he pleased generally to attach them to the prayers, the instructions, and the holiness of those with whom we are. By strong, though invisible attractions, he draws some souls through their intercourse with others."[26] This wondrous picture of creation's possibilities lies at the heart of a Wesleyan reading of the world. It is a truly optimistic vision of God's Christic grace at work in the world as the "healing influence," and at work in the Church as "strong, though invisible attractions." And at so simple a setting as the table!—whether the Lord's Table, or the table of a common meal shared together.

So may it be that "all we taste be God"—not by denying or denigrating the concrete particularity and specificity of the creature (human or otherwise) who confronts us, but by receiving that creature's in-fluence for what it is: the presence of a *fellow* creature, gifted to us by God for us to love, through whom God draws near to us and through whom we may draw near to God.

24. "Minutes of Several Conversations," Q. 3, *Works* (Jackson) 8:299.
25. *Plain Account of Christian Perfection*, §19, Q. 8, *Works* (Jackson) 11:397.
26. Ibid., §25, Q. 38, *Works* (Jackson) 11:435.

Part III
Mending

CHAPTER 7

"TO (PRE)SERVE THE PRESENT AGE"

Eschatology in a Wesleyan Way

Thou dost create the Earth anew,
Its Maker and Preserver too,
By thine Almighty Arm sustain;
Nature perceives Thy secret Force,
And still holds on her even Course,
And owns Thy Providential Reign.

Charles Wesley, *Hymns of Petition and Thanksgiving for the Promise of the Father*, #28

There is an intriguing little passage on eschatology in John Wesley's *A Plain Account of Christian Perfection*. In this passage Wesley appears to have only slight sympathy and even less patience for people who obsess about the end of the world. I harbor no illusions that the ends to which I shall employ the passage in question would have all been lurking in Wesley's mind. Nonetheless, what follows in this chapter flows naturally, I think, from reading the world in a Wesleyan way.

On the face of it, eschatology is not a prominent theme in *A Plain Account*; the slim volume's immediate and obvious concern is to espouse the possibility of the entire sanctification of our hearts and lives *in this life*. In his strictures against "enthusiasm," however, Wesley occasionally deals with eschatological issues. It is instructive for our purposes to remember that Wesley often decried "enthusiasm" as the product of an illegitimate expectation of achieving certain religious ends in our lives without pursuing the requisite means.[1] Eschatology has to do precisely with the expectation of a certain end—an end which is often thought to be achievable only by God. Might Wesley's judgment regarding religious enthusiasm in general be fruitfully applied to eschatological enthusiasm in particular? Might we, following Wesley's lead, argue that the ends of eschatology require of *us* the pursuit of particular means?

The following is the passage in which Wesley hints at some kind of relation between eschatological fervor and "enthusiasm":

> About the same time [1762], five or six honest enthusiasts foretold the world was to end on the 28th of February. I immediately withstood them, by every possible means, both in public and private. I preached expressly upon the subject. . . . I warned the society, again and again, and spoke severally to as many as I could; and I saw the fruit of my labour. They made exceeding few converts. . . . Nevertheless, they made abundance of noise . . . and greatly increased both the number and courage of those who opposed Christian perfection.[2]

While Wesley does not explicitly specify the grounds on which he opposed these "honest enthusiasts," it is not difficult to piece together the reason for his adamant denial of the value of their prediction. We know that the February 1763 date had been set by a London Methodist named George Bell, whose religious enthusiasm had boiled to the point of his testifying to a sinless and errorless perfection.[3] By the logic of Bell's perfectionistic claims, anyone swayed by the power of his zeal would be constrained to believe his prediction. The fact that Bell also proclaimed himself "in no danger of living after the flesh and had no deeds of the body to mortify"[4] demonstrates that he apparently believed that he—and anyone else living in the perfection of the Spirit—was *already* existing entirely in a thoroughly unambiguous eschatological state. The world we experience is one of difficulty, pain, struggle, temptation,

1. See, for example, "Minutes of Several Conversations," Q. 34, *Works* (Jackson) 8:316; and *Plain Account of Christian Perfection*, §25, Q. 33, *Works* (Jackson) 11:429.
2. *Plain Account of Christian Perfection*, §22, *Works* (Jackson) 11:408.
3. See W. Stephen Gunter, *The Limits of 'Love Divine': John Wesley's Response to Antinomianism and Enthusiasm* (Nashville: Kingswood Books, 1989), 217-22.
4. Cited in ibid., 217.

ambiguity, and—most important for our purposes in these final chapters—agency and responsibility. It was this world that Bell deluded himself into believing he was *beyond*. Bell believed, or at least testified, that he had received through the Spirit's power a complete deliverance from the conditions of existence in this world; small wonder, then, that he would expect soon a corresponding universal end to the world as we know it—and as he, supposedly, knew it no more.

Undoubtedly one reason Wesley resisted such eschatological enthusiasm was the pastoral concern for people who would undergo shattered hopes, or even a shipwrecked faith, after a failed prediction. Near the end of the passage in *Plain Account*, though, we detect a theological clue that provides the thread of argument for this chapter: these enthusiasts, Wesley writes, stimulated opposition to "Christian perfection." Of course, the specific way in which Bell and his followers generated such opposition is that they testified that Christian perfection had given them a perfected rationality (incapability of error) and a thoroughgoing freedom from temptation's powers (incapability of sinning). To put it simply, these enthusiasts had convinced themselves that God had freed them from creaturely existence altogether.

I believe that Wesley's understanding of Christian perfection provides the key to his determined resistance to eschatological speculations. After all, how could Wesley be so sure that they were *wrong*?[5] Further, why bother to include the account of his opposition in a book dedicated entirely to explicating this doctrine of perfection? The obvious, stock reply would be that he wanted to distinguish very clearly between his teaching about Christian perfection and the scandalous embarrassment of enthusiasts standing on a hillside overlooking London on the eve of the end of the world, awaiting Jesus' return. I believe, though, that we can probe this question further. I submit that there is a correlation between Wesley's teaching on Christian perfection and his disavowal of eschatological enthusiasm, even though this correlation existed at a level of Wesley's thinking that he himself never entirely unearthed. Let us, then, do a little digging!

5. There were, on the other hand, a considerable number of Londoners who were more inclined than was Wesley to believe in the veracity of Bell's prediction. See ibid., 218-19.

In a 1788 letter to one of his Methodist preachers that reflects his typical reticence to engage in eschatological scenarios, Wesley wrote:

> I said nothing, less or more, in Bradford church, concerning the end of the world, neither concerning my own opinion, but what follows: That Bengelius [Johann Albrecht Bengel] had given it as his opinion, not that the world would then end, but that the millennial reign of Christ would begin in the year 1836. I have no opinion at all upon the head: I can determine nothing at all about it. These calculations are far above, out of my sight. I have only one thing to do, "to save my soul, and those that hear me."[6]

Here we detect Wesley's usual impatience with matters that move past the particulars of God's saving labors in the world. In fact, his dismissal of Bengel's date-setting—offered with the "too much protesting" of a mind supposedly incapable of following the detailed calculations—has a tone not unlike his response to an article he read regarding the unlikelihood of life on other planets. He wrote in his journal, "I know the earth is [inhabited]. Of the rest I know nothing."[7] Wesley tended to dismiss such speculation as unimportant, particularly as it veered toward sensationalism. It was *soteriology*—"to save my soul, and those that hear me"—that most moved him.

Of course, our contemporary apocalypticists would also say that their motivation is the salvation of "souls." The key difference, therefore, might not be so much soteriology per se but instead the *nature* of soteriology. What *is* salvation, and how does God bring it about?

One thing is certain: Wesley's reservations about end-of-the-world scenarios and predictions are strikingly different from our apocalypticists, who range from the still occasional traveling evangelist with detailed charts to the far more prominent (and wealthy!) Lindseys and LaHayes, whose widely popular books trade on the curiosity and fear inspired by their end time depictions. Such eschatological sensationalism encourages its fans to reserve a place in a future age. Wesley teaches a different approach, one concerned

6. Letter to Christopher Hopper (3 June 1788), *Letters* (Telford) 8:63; cf. *Works* (Jackson) 12:319.

7. *Journal* (17 September 1759), *Works* 21:230.

that eschatological preoccupations may readily becloud the nature of God's salvation of human beings, and of the world, *in this life*. We might suggest that Wesley's approach encourages us to *serve* the present age, indeed to *pre*serve it, rather than to flee it or to hope for its soon demise.

Interestingly, right around the time that Bengel had predicted for the beginning of Christ's millennial reign (1836), apocalyptic fervor was reaching fever pitch in the United States. William Miller, a farmer raised in Baptist circles and an avid Bible student, had become convinced that he had unlocked the mysteries of the books of Daniel and Revelation. His complex calculations helped him to arrive at the year 1843 for Christ's return. One young Methodist woman, Ellen Harmon of Portland, Maine, heard Miller preach about Christ's scheduled coming and became convicted of her need to seek entire sanctification in anticipation of the end of the world. Indeed, she testified subsequently of God's sanctifying grace in explicit connection with her apocalyptic anxieties.

Harmon—who would later marry James White and become Ellen G. White, a central founding figure in the Seventh-day Adventist Church—began to speak to fellow Methodist class meeting members of her experience of entire sanctification, connecting her narrative intimately with Millerite predictions about Christ's second coming. I believe it is entirely fitting with Wesleyan sensitivities that the presiding elder of her class meeting strongly suggested that she desist—not in testifying to entire sanctification, but in stirring up apocalyptic imaginations. He asked her "if it would not be more pleasant to live a long life of holiness here, and do others good, than to have Jesus come and destroy poor sinners." The young prophetess-in-the-making replied that with Christ's coming "sin would have an end, and we should enjoy sanctification forever."[8] Thus undeterred, Ellen Harmon weathered three failed predictions by Miller—the last of which, October 22, 1844, is still remembered by Adventist Christians today as "The Great Disappointment."

The question before us in this chapter is, essentially, can and should Wesleyans share in the "great disappointment" that Christ

8. Cited in Ann Taves, *Fits, Trances, & Visions: Experiencing Religion and Explaining Experience from Wesley to James* (Princeton, N.J.: Princeton University Press, 1999), 156.

has not returned? Fundamentally, my reply is *no*. The aim of what follows in this chapter is to offer a theological rationale for this reply, and for Wesley's strongly stated reservations about the predictions of "five or six honest enthusiasts," and for the Methodist elder's attempt to quiet young Ellen Harmon's apocalypticism. Again, I believe this rationale arises directly from a Wesleyan reading of the world.

PERFECTING GRACE IN THIS LIFE, THIS WORLD

The obvious place to begin is with the recognition that eschatology is, in fact, at the very heart of Wesley's doctrine of entire sanctification. In the words of Theodore Runyon, "This doctrine is distinctive from notions of sanctification in other Christian traditions in that it expects the finite equivalent of eschatological fulfillment (i.e., entire sanctification) as something which can happen in history rather than beyond it."[9] By differing with most of his contemporaries who taught that Christian perfection occurs only at the point of death, or very near to it, and by insisting that divine grace may perfect us in love in this life, Wesley proclaimed an eschatological hope that could be more than simply a hope; it could become a gracious reality in the here and now. In short, because Wesley's doctrine of entire sanctification insists on the possibility of a perfection of love for God and neighbor, his was a *realizable* eschatology.

Wesley's insistence upon the possibility of entire sanctification in this life testifies not only to the transforming power of God's loving grace, but also to the possibility of this present world becoming a place where divine love is truly experienced and actualized. It may be surmised that Wesley's reticence to use the language of being in a "state" of perfection—because such language appeared to rest in a past experience—might pertain in an inverted form to

9. Theodore Runyon, "Sanctification and Liberation: A Re-examination in the Light of the Methodist Tradition," a manuscript essay presented in 1977 at the Oxford Institute of Methodist Theological Studies. See also his "Wesley and the Theologies of Liberation," his editorial essay opening the volume of plenary lectures from this Institute, *Sanctification and Liberation: Liberation Theologies in Light of the Wesleyan Tradition* (Nashville: Abingdon, 1981).

those who peer past the present moment to anticipate a future "state" of eschatological perfection. The crucial nature of the "now" moment before God and neighbor—"that we need not stay another moment . . . that 'now,' the very 'now' is the accepted time . . . now is the day of this 'full salvation'"[10]—can be obscured either by the fixation upon past moments or the anticipation of future ones. In either case, one is dwelling within moments other than the "now" of sanctifying grace and human response. If "now" holds the real possibility of entire sanctification, then "now" is potentially a moment of eschatological fulfillment.

Wesley took a certain delight in quoting Augustine's words, "He who made us without ourselves will not save us without ourselves."[11] He did so partly because this notion appears to run counter to so much of the rest of Augustine's unilateral soteriology, which at its most extreme was an unmitigated predestinationism. But Wesley delighted in these words also because he so thoroughly agreed with them. If Augustine and Wesley were correct in saying that God "will not save us without ourselves"—without our cooperation, our responses to grace—we might ask whether it is correct even to say that God "made us without ourselves." How *has* God "made us," each of us? Certainly not in a unilateral act of creation, but in and through the act of procreation. Indeed, everything that God creates includes and involves the cocreating contributions of countless other creatures. In every moment of God's continuing act of creating, countless others lend their energies and their materials. Process theologians argue that if we take our experience of each present moment as our guide to understanding the nature of creation, the conviction will take shape within us that God's labor of making a world ever and always begins *in the midst* of the creaturely buzz and bustle of every new moment—and that it has always been that way.[12] While Wesley would not go so far as this—

10. *Plain Account of Christian Perfection*, §14, *Works* (Jackson) 11:383.

11. See, for example, Sermon 63, "The General Spread of the Gospel," §12, *Works* 2:490; and Sermon 85, "On Working Out Our Own Salvation," §III.7, *Works* 3:208.

12. For example, Cobb writes in *God and the World*, "We can meaningfully think of God as creator only when we combine the understanding of God's power as persuasion with the recognition implied by this understanding of power that God in every moment works with and upon the world that is given to him in that moment" (p. 91). When as a young seminary student I read those words, I wondered, "Given to him in that moment?—by whom?" Much older now, I understand that the world essentially gives itself to God in every moment, according to the process view. This issue, of course, is the heart of chapter 3 of this book.

for, as we have seen already in chapter 3, he believed that there was a distinct moment in the past when God created the universe *ex nihilo*—he certainly did assume that now, in the present time, God works only in partnership *with* the (human) creature, not in spite of or "over the head" of creaturely realities. God "will not save us without ourselves"—without our own divinely empowered, yet truly creaturely, contribution to God's labors.

But does not eschatological expectation, particularly (but not only) as it is peppered with apocalypticism, inevitably veer toward the idea that God will indeed "save us without ourselves"? Obviously in this case the "us" in question is meant in a much broader, cosmic sense—that God will at some point intervene to save a world that can only get worse without that intervention. To the extent that Christian eschatology concerns itself with what God is going to do to bring an end to the world as we know it, specifically in the coming again of our Lord Jesus Christ, then it seems that, in the end, Christians *do* believe that God will "save us without ourselves." Further, to the extent that many traditional eschatological scenarios either imply or encourage a certain hopelessness about history, do they not to that extent mitigate against Wesley's doctrine of Christian perfection as a realizable eschatology in this world?

The postmillennialism that was popular among many Christians in the late nineteenth and early twentieth centuries placed great emphasis upon human cooperation with God in history toward the accomplishing of God's purposes, toward an eschatological "end." After the virtually countless horrors of the past century, however, few Christians are officially or intentionally postmillennial anymore, and such a reading of history has fallen out of fashion. Perhaps more to the point, however, is that even in the postmillennial end time scenario, optimistic as it is, Christ's eventual coming presumably brings about the *end of history*. But what if the real "end" of history, God's most fundamental *telos* or purpose for our world, is the gracious (re)creation of human beings to become, *in this life*, creatures made, molded, and mended by divine love? What if God's "end" for the world is that love might flourish—that we might become lovers of God and all of our neighbors? Might this provide a more adequate Wesleyan reading of eschatology?

Indeed, it is precisely this kind of vision that surfaces in Wesley's sermon entitled "The General Spread of the Gospel." After surveying the world of his time, and admitting that, humanly speaking, the prospects for winning the world to Christian faith were not encouraging, Wesley remained undaunted. He insisted that "the loving knowledge of God, producing uniform, uninterrupted holiness and happiness, shall cover the earth; shall fill the soul of every man."[13] Note carefully the unmistakably eschatological tone of Wesley's language—and yet, Wesley continues, this will not be accomplished by God acting irresistibly. If God were to effect salvation in unilateral fashion, by the sheer power of divine fiat,

> then man would be man no longer; his inmost nature would be changed. He would no longer be a moral agent, any more than the sun or the wind, as he would no longer be endued with liberty, a power of choosing or self-determination. . . . .How can all men be made holy and happy while they continue men? . . . As God is one, so the work of God is uniform in all ages. May we not then conceive how he *will* work on the souls of men in times to come by considering how he *does* work *now?* And how he *has* wrought in times past?[14]

Interestingly, Wesley counsels us not to expect a radical change in the manner and mode of God's creating and redeeming activity in the world. The pattern of divine activity that Wesley detects in human experience, "God's general manner of working," is that of gracious assistance, not of force. It is an enlightening and strengthening of human understanding and affections, not their deletion or destruction. This grace-empowered synergism provided Wesley with a model not only for divine-human interaction, but for the entirety of the God-world relation. After all, "as God is One, so the work of God is uniform in all ages"—and assuming that Wesley was fundamentally correct in this theological conviction, we need only to expand considerably on his relatively limited awareness of just how numerous, wide, and vast all those ages actually are. It is clear that for Wesley the essential point is that God's character does not change, and so God's manner of laboring in the world does not

13. Sermon 63, "The General Spread of the Gospel," §8, *Works* 2:488.
14. Ibid., §9, *Works* 2:488-89.

change. "Now in the same manner as God has converted so many to himself without destroying their liberty, he can undoubtedly convert whole nations, or the whole world; and it is as easy to him to convert a world, as one individual soul."[15]

Writing out of this optimism of grace, Wesley predicted the triumphal spread of the gospel from one nation and people to another as God gradually "renews the face of the earth" until the vision of the Revelator is fulfilled and "the Lord God omnipotent reigneth!" After the technologically enhanced horrors of world wars and mass genocides of the past century, we are likely to smile dismissively at Wesley's naive optimism—and we probably should. Even so, is there any good reason to reject his interpretation of God's mode of working in the world as persuasive and empowering *presence* (i.e., prevenient grace) in contrast to a unilateral, heavy-handed, apocalyptic inbreaking of history? Which manner of working best suits God's end for the world—*in order that love might flourish*—as proposed in this book?

Wesley's insistence on human response to, and cooperation with, divine grace raises profound questions regarding our understanding of the role and importance of human activity in the direction(s) that our world takes. It stands in direct contrast to notions of absolute sovereignty, whether understood on the individual or the cosmic level, that view God as someday unilaterally fulfilling the divine intentions for creation. Of course, it is apocalypticism that most ardently insists upon the notion of divine foreclosure of the world. It is also apocalypticism that provided the eschatological milieu for Christianity in its birth pangs, provides much of the traditional Christian doctrine of the end times, and shapes the common expectations of many Christians filling the pews.

Thus the question is worth asking again: How does belief in the return of Christ, particularly as framed in terms of an apocalyptic conclusion to human history, fit with Wesley's understanding of divine-human interaction as a crucial dynamic in the world's course? Can we not, indeed ought we not, interpret the idea of synergism in categories that are larger, more encompassing, and more cosmic than simply those of the individual's relationship to God? Indeed, is it consistent or coherent to insist upon synergism at the

15. Ibid., §12, *Works* 2:490.

level of the individual human and yet hold to an eschatological hope of unilateral divine intrusion at the cosmic-historical level?

WOLFHART PANNENBERG AND APOCALYPTICISM

Probably no contemporary theologian has used the apocalypticism of Christianity's roots more comprehensively or creatively than has Wolfhart Pannenberg (b. 1928). With his characteristic emphasis upon the category of the future, Pannenberg argues that God's reality and true deity will become evident only in the divinely ordained end of all things. Nonetheless, Pannenberg argues, God has been proleptically revealed to be the God of history in and through the resurrection of Jesus; the resurrection of the dead, after all, is the fulfillment of the Jewish apocalyptic hope and Jesus' resurrection functions as a signal and promise of the final, universal resurrection. Pannenberg argues that Jewish apocalyptic hopes were anchored in the symbol and hope of the resurrection of the dead as the *sine qua non* of final judgment, the end of the world, and God's self-vindication as *truly God*.[16]

Pannenberg insists that to understand any event is to understand it within its own contexts of tradition, expectation, or meaning. This has important implications for what he has to say about Jesus' resurrection and its significance. If one interprets Jesus' resurrection from within the prevailing worldview of apocalypticism in first-century Palestinian Judaism, then "resurrection from the dead" implies the end of the world, the final judgment, and the full revelation of God. No wonder the early Christians expected Jesus' imminent return! The day of the Lord was already inbreaking. The fact that their expectation went unfulfilled, and is yet unfulfilled two millennia later, should not be lost on us. Thus, Pannenberg's claim that "with the resurrection of Jesus, the end of history has already occurred,"[17] while virtually a cliché among the "theologians of hope," suffers from oversimplification and a failure

16. See his early, ground-breaking work in Wolfhart Pannenberg, et al., *Revelation as History* (New York: Macmillan, 1968).
17. Pannenberg, *Jesus—God and Man* (Philadelphia: Westminster, 1968), 142.

to understand the ongoing, interwoven processes of nature and history as the complex site of God's covenantal laboring with humanity and all of creation. In response to Pannenberg, Paul van Buren wrote,

> Perhaps we must say that in the resurrection of Jesus something about the end has been shown us; but to say it "has already occurred" is to sweep all following history, including the history in which we now live, into the bin of insignificance. That is a high price to pay for protecting the importance of the history of Jesus as revelation. Surely it can be done in some other way.[18]

Further, the thread of argument in this chapter is that Pannenberg's apocalyptic reading of the world comes into conflict with the Wesleyan eschatology of a perfect love for God and neighbor that is realizable in this life. This Wesleyan "spin" on the world, I believe, has much more in common with a prophetic understanding of history than it does with the apocalyptic. This is a difference explored by biblical scholar D. S. Russell:

> In the prophetic writings . . . the triumph of God is seen within this present world-order; but in the apocalyptic writings the emphasis comes to be laid not so much on his judgment within time and on the plane of history, as on his judgment in a setting beyond time and above history. Instead of acting through human agencies, God is seen here to act directly, intervening personally in the affairs of the world.[19]

Jewish apocalypticism, then, tended toward a denial of the world and of the real significance of human activity, indeed of human co-creativity with God, within history. It anticipated the full revelation of God in terms of a vengeful, sword-bearing messiah who would eliminate Israel's oppressors and establish justice and peace throughout the earth. More than anything else, the apocalyptic mood is a theodicy: it attempts to justify God's goodness in a world of injustice and radical suffering, particularly when suffered by God's faithful ones, by insisting that very soon—*any day*

18. Paul van Buren, *A Theology of the Jewish-Christian Reality, Part I: Discerning the Way* (San Francisco: Harper & Row, 1980), 43.
19. D. S. Russell, *The Method and Message of Jewish Apocalyptic* (Philadelphia: Westminster, 1964), 95.

now—the present order will be overthrown and perfect justice, love, and peace will be ushered in by the irresistible power of God.[20]

Do the character and ministry of Jesus make any difference, shed any light, on such apocalyptic wishes? This one whom Christians confess to be the Messiah, God's Anointed One, did not (and I believe does not and shall not) fit the description of the world-conquering, apocalyptic lord. Catherine Keller writes regarding the apocalyptic expectation of a second coming in glory, "The vulnerability of the first appears shoddy in the glaring light of the second: Jesus turned his cheek one too many times—never again!"[21] Christian theological tradition has too often not seen the profound implications of its own central claim that it was in a suffering servant, a humble Jewish peasant, that God has visited and is redeeming creation. Christians, particularly at the popular level, have often castigated the Jews of Jesus' time for not perceiving his messiahship ("they were looking for a political messiah"), all the while making the same mistake in their own apocalyptic anticipations.

Could it not be argued that the very nature of God's incarnation in Christ dispels such yearnings for the end of the world? As the one who the Church has confessed to be "truly God and truly human," Christ is our paradigm for understanding how God reveals the divine character in all of history and how God labors in covenantal partnership with creation. If God has indeed made known the divine character and intentions in Jesus, then we can say with confidence that God chooses to come to us, to labor toward God's own ends for creation, in and through the sort of human cooperation that Jesus embodied and exemplifies. *Jesus' life and ministry unveil the nature of God's workings in the world.* I suspect that apocalypticism, born as it often is in social contexts of extreme suffering and injustice and thus also of hopelessness, is a religious expression of the desire to be rid of human responsibility for how the world turns (out). Is it possible that the revelation we receive in Christ, rather than validating this apocalyptic desire—as

20. For a masterful treatment of this idea, see Stephen D. O'Leary, *Arguing the Apocalypse: A Theory of Millennial Rhetoric* (New York: Oxford University Press, 1994).

21. Catherine Keller, *Apocalypse Now and Then: A Feminist Guide to the End of the World* (Boston: Beacon Press, 1996), 92.

Pannenberg has tended to argue—actually poses a judgment upon, even a negation of, apocalypticism?

The Wesleyan proclamation of perfect love for God and neighbor in this life provides an optimism about the possibilities of grace in human existence, societies, history, and nature that belies any apocalyptic despair. The fact that, for Wesley, Jesus is the great model and exemplar of such love—and thus the embodiment of human perfection *in this life*—supports the idea that God's revelation in Christ, a revelation both about God and about our ideal selves, is a direct challenge to apocalyptic scenarios that write off history. The synergism of grace underlying Wesley's doctrine of Christian perfection points to the validity and importance of history, of the human responsibility *to* God and *for* creation.

Creation and Eschatology

Eschatological anticipations of a divinely ordained closure to the rich and complex processes of nature and history seem to exist in tension with, if not in contradiction to, the teaching on creation offered in Genesis. If the universe is God's "other," called into existence and sustained by God, and if creation's otherness from God finds its highest expression in beings of intelligence and moral agency (such as we are, at least at our best), then such considerations cannot be alien to God's original intention in creating. The question of why God has created the world is one of the enduring mysteries of theological reflection. Regardless of the view one takes, it will be difficult to sustain if one also assumes that God shall, at some future point, undo or foreclose on this labor of making that which is truly other than (and therefore sometimes even opposed to) God's own self. What would have been the point in creation to begin with? The Argentine Methodist theologian Jose Míguez Bonino has framed the dilemma well:

> Is God a substitute subject for [human beings] in historical action, or is he the where-from and the where-to, the pro-vocation, the power, and the guarantee of an action that remains fully human and responsible? If [God] is a substitute subject—however much

> we may try to explain it away—history is a meaningless game and [our] humanity a curious detour.[22]

Again, is it not the case that most eschatological scenarios do indeed crown God as the "substitute subject" par excellence, whose foreclosure on the processes of nature and history, and on human activity and responsibility within the world, finally renders those processes null and void? What then becomes of God's venture to create? In consideration of such queries, I submit that a thoroughly Wesleyan eschatology does not posit an "end," as in a temporal closure point, for creation; rather, Wesleyan eschatology bears witness to God's "end," as in an inner *telos* grounded in God's character: God's "end" for us is that we human beings, those creatures fashioned to image God and thus to be God's representatives in the world, would join our Maker in covenantal relationship and cooperation toward the redemption and mending of creation. God's (re)creative activity is an ongoing labor of love. While we human creatures generally have not done an effective job of contributing to the wellness or *shalom* of God's world, there is no reason to assume that God is yet ready to give up on this difficult work of calling us toward covenantal freedom and responsibility. Christians might be able to take to heart the Jewish concept of *tikkun*—that God invites and awaits the efforts of human beings to effect a mending or healing of God's tragically fractured world.[23]

It is noteworthy that Genesis tells a powerful story of God's desire to sustain creation, even in all its brokenness, in order that there might be *tikkun*. According to the narrative, God did nearly give up on the project of laboring with the creatures made in the divine image. "The LORD saw that the wickedness of humankind was great in the earth. . . . And the LORD was sorry that he had made humankind on the earth, and it grieved him to his heart"

22. Jose Míguez Bonino, "Wesley's Doctrine of Sanctification from a Liberationist Perspective," in Runyon, ed., *Sanctification and Liberation*, 62. Bracketed changes in the text are mine.

23. Interestingly, Jewish theologian Eugene B. Borowitz has put a finger on the contribution that Wesley's theology could make to Jewish-Christian dialogue regarding the human calling and responsibility to labor toward *shalom*. He writes, "Wesley's emphasis on the deeds that sanctifying grace should produce has something of the emphasis on 'deed' that Judaism makes primary. In any discussion of Christian and Jewish ethics John Wesley's thought might be a useful, near-middle ground with which to begin." *Contemporary Christologies: A Jewish Response* (Mahwah, N.J.: Paulist Press, 1980), 118.

(6:5, 6). Even with a grieving heart, the Maker of heaven and earth began anew with Noah and his kin. Indeed, in the aftermath of the Flood God covenanted with Noah and all his descendants "and with every living creature . . . every animal of the earth with you," that "never again shall all flesh be cut off by the waters of a flood, and never again shall there be a flood to destroy the earth" (9:10-11). How remarkable that the first covenant described in Holy Writ involves not only human beings, with the promise to sustain their lives, but also includes all creatures of our planet! There is an underlying ethic of creation-care that ascends to the surface of those floodwaters! Admittedly, there is a popular tradition of interpretation arguing that God only promised never to destroy the world with a flood (cf. 2 Peter 3:5-7). But the text's intent undoubtedly is to underscore our Creator's intention to sustain creation in covenantal faithfulness. God establishes this covenant precisely in the face of, and even as an answer to, human sin and failure. "I will never again curse the ground because of humankind, for the inclination of the human heart is evil from youth; nor will I ever again destroy every living creature as I have done" (8:21).

The Genesis doctrine of creation, particularly as it is actually *re*-creation that is described in the Flood narrative, is a profound affirmation of God's creative intentions. In light of the recurring popularity of apocalyptic hopes for the world's end, it is instructive to consider how often the Psalms proclaim God's faithfulness to maintain the world in the face of the threats of chaos to destroy it. We have read already in Psalm 104 that God "set the earth on its foundations, so that it shall never be shaken" (v. 5). This biblical theology of creation goes hand in hand with Wesley's optimism of grace, which insists, as we have seen, that it is possible in this life (and hence, in this world) to love God and neighbor with all of our being. If such love is a gracious possibility for anyone, then it is in principle possible for all. Thus, human beings and societies, graced and empowered by God's prevenient presence, can yet move (at least in principle) toward the divine vision of *shalom*. *Tikkun*, the mending of God's broken world, is not impossible! This perspective has obvious implications for developing a Christian, and particularly a Wesleyan, commitment to social and economic justice as well as to the ecological well-being of our planet. Good stewardship of God's world, entrusted to the creatures called upon to image or reflect God, is stewardship for the long haul! One might ask once more, then, whether the purposes of God's venture in creating get shortchanged by eschatological scenarios in which human partnership with God, in this present world, is brought to closure.

Even if our Maker and Molder truly is invested in the venture and risk of freedom exercised by the creature, there is no guarantee that this great labor of God will end successfully. Our mending is not guaranteed, not simply a matter of course. While the prevenient grace of God's presence in the world is faithful and true (Ps. 146:6-9), the nature of this grace is persuasive rather than coercive. Of course, the great majority of eschatological scenarios that Christians historically have entertained are coercive in nature. But if indeed divine grace is persuasive, then the underside is that we may yet enact our own apocalypse. The words of Nazarene theologian H. Ray Dunning are sobering: "Since grace is persuasive . . . rather than coercive, [there] unfortunately is no absolute guarantee against the blood-chilling possibility that the human race will finally destroy itself, as the present threat of nuclear war attests."[24]

Eschatology and Contemporary Cosmology

Apocalyptic doomsaying need not be restricted to the real possibility of self-annihilation of the human race, and even of all living things, whether by nuclear holocaust or environmental degradation. Even if, by the grace of God, we should find a way to avoid total nuclear warfare or the strangling death of ecocide, we can be fairly confident that the world as we know it will not go on forever. Eschatology has made a new place for itself in the thinking of some of the theologians currently working in the pioneering dialogue between theological reflection and scientific theory. Particularly when one reflects upon the course of the universe from within a Big Bang paradigm, in which it appears that "the universe is walking

24. H. Ray Dunning, *Grace, Faith and Holiness: A Wesleyan Systematic Theology* (Kansas City: Beacon Hill, 1988), 296. See also Gordon Kaufman, *Theology for a Nuclear Age* (Philadelphia: Westminster / John Knox Press, 1985).

a one-way street from hot to cold" and "our cosmic house is moving from centralized heating to decentralized freezing"[25] as our universe flows inexorably toward entropy, there is an inevitable conclusion to the world as we know it. Indeed, even before such a heat death, it is inevitable that our sun will one day burn out in a great explosion of cosmic fire that will incinerate several planets in our solar system, including our beautiful Earth. Thus, even if some of our earthling descendants are able to escape this death of our solar system by colonizing some distant orb, eventually the universe will expand away all its heat and become cold, black death.[26]

We will explore this rather bleak scenario much more extensively in chapter 9, but at this point we should appreciate the fact that contemporary cosmology offers us a secular version of the end time vision of the book of Hebrews, compiled of a string of quotations from the Psalms and the Prophets:

> "In the beginning, O Lord, you laid the foundations of the earth,
> and the heavens are the work of your hands.
> They will perish, but you remain;
> they will all wear out like a garment.
> You will roll them up like a robe;
> like a garment they will be changed.
> But you remain the same,
> and your years will never end." (Heb. 1:10-12 NIV)

This text and others like it join with the secular eschatology of Big Bang cosmology to remind us that the world as we presently

25. Ted Peters, "Cosmos as Creation," in Peters, ed., *Cosmos as Creation*, 51.

26. There have been a couple of notable attempts by relatively secular physicists to envision a more hopeful future for us human beings and our descendants, in spite of what appears to be the inevitable heat death of the universe. See Frank J. Tipler, *The Physics of Immortality: Modern Cosmology, God, and the Resurrection of the Dead* (New York: Anchor Books, 1994) and Freeman J. Dyson, *Infinite in All Directions* (New York: Harper & Row, 1988). While neither of these authors has received a particularly warm reception among theologians, their ideas are engaged seriously by several theologians in Carol Rausch Albright and Joel Haugen, eds., *Beginning with the End: God, Science, and Wolfhart Pannenberg* (Chicago: Open Court, 1997). For a more wide-ranging collection of essays by Christian theologians addressing eschatological doctrine in concert with contemporary cosmological theories, see John Polkinghorne and Michael Welker, eds., *The End of the World and the Ends of God: Science and Theology on Eschatology* (Harrisburg, Pa.: Trinity Press International, 2000).

know it is finite. The critical question for us in this chapter is whether or not such a conclusion to the universe will also mark the conclusion of God's *telos* of covenantal relation. Will the extinction of our vast universe into cold darkness entail an ending of the God-creation synergism of grace that characterizes a Wesleyan reading of the world? Of course, a partial reply is that the New Testament echoes Isaiah's prophecy of a "new heaven and a new earth" in which righteousness dwells (2 Pet. 3:13; Rev. 21:1-5). Christian eschatology presents the promise of a new reality from the God who makes all things new—a reality not dependent on or threatened by the apparently inevitable dissipation of this present order.

We have already seen in chapter 1 that Ted Peters, one of those contemporary theologians working to interpret Christian doctrine within the context of contemporary cosmology, suggests that we need to interpret creation as God's ongoing act, a continuing process yet to be completed. Its completion is, for Peters, what eschatology is all about. Yet, because Peters essentially is an American interpreter and follower of Pannenberg's thought, with Pannenberg he understands that completion to be essentially a "done deal." "God," he writes, "is constantly in the process of creating the world in light of its forthcoming end."[27] In this chapter we have explored the possibility of an "end" that is decidedly *open-ended*. If a Wesleyan reading of eschatology includes the idea that God's end in creating is that responsible relations with creatures might be sustained—in order, finally, *that love might flourish*—then whatever "new heaven and earth" God might create would presumably also include the adventurous risk of creaturely agency.

Most traditional eschatology is uncomfortable with the expectation of a new creation that continues to proceed along the cusp of creaturely agency. Eschatology traditionally dreams of closure, on the idea of God finally saying "Enough!" to the project of creaturely otherness and freedom. Paul van Buren, struggling to understand Paul's eschatological vision of God finally becoming "all in all" (1 Cor. 15:28), suggests that it "seems unlikely, having made the commitment and self-limiting move entailed in having begun this creation that [God's] final goal were to be rid of it; but

27. Peters, "Cosmos as Creation," 104.

who knows? Perhaps for God, too, enough can be enough."[28] *But can God forget rainbows?*

In the vision of the book of Revelation, the new heaven and new earth are no longer plagued by the sea (21:1), that recurring symbol of swirling chaos that ever threatens the stability of God's creation. The Revelator seems to be suggesting an entirely secure re-creation in which all contingency, threat, and danger shall be utterly removed. It is difficult to picture how such a scenario would also have any room for the possibilities of covenantal relationship to God and to others, the sort of relation which presumably requires true creaturely agency. On the other hand, it is difficult to imagine the God who is Love, the God who gifts the creatures with "responsible grace,"[29] ever denying or negating that gift that makes possible the human capacity for authentic love. This argument seems all the more compelling to anyone willing to weigh the possibility that Wesley was right to follow the early Greek Fathers in postulating that redeemed human beings would grow eternally in their capacities for love toward God and fellow creatures. Would such growth be possible apart from true creaturely agency? And would such agency open the door to the possibility of a "perfect world" going wrong?

Perhaps the best Wesleyan solution to this conundrum is found in the theme of eschatological love as addressed in 1 John, a document of paramount importance to Wesley. "Love has been perfected among us in this," wrote the beloved apostle, "that we may have boldness on the day of judgment. . . . There is no fear in love, but perfect love casts out fear; for fear has to do with punishment, and whoever fears has not reached perfection in love. We love because he first loved us" (4:17-19). Such love is possible only in the atmosphere of true agency, of freedom in relation to God and to others. Moreover, such love is also the deepest meaning and fulfillment, or end, of human agency. Such a consideration sheds light on the concluding sentence of Wesley's sermon "The New Creation": "And, to crown all, there will be a deep, an intimate, an uninterrupted union with God; a constant communion with the Father and his Son Jesus Christ, through the Spirit; a continual

28. Van Buren, *Discerning the Way*, 200.

29. It should be obvious that Randy Maddox's masterful study of John Wesley's theology, *Responsible Grace*, is a critical influence in this work.

enjoyment of the Three-One God, and of all the creatures in him!"[30] The final end of human beings, then, is to live freely in joyful communion with the divine community that is God, and to share in that very communion with "all the creatures in [God]." "And all we taste be God," indeed!—and yet our tasting of God in this Wesleyan vision does not entail a loss of our creaturely relations. All creatures remain what they are—truly creatures—and thus they too, all in their own distinctive ways, shall contribute to the joy of all the other creatures in divine glory.

Perhaps the eschatological experience of God's new heaven and earth—presumably laced with inexplicable and unimaginably joyful relations of love with the Maker and Mender of all things, and of all things in their Maker and Mender—will truly liberate us to love in ways unknown to us now, and thus paradoxically to make us more truly free than we can ever experience in the present life. For in the glory that is to be revealed, we shall be truly free to love, truly liberated to serve one another in love. Paul, after all, wrote two millennia ago that such love is the mark of the eschatological community of the Spirit, the sign of the age to come, and the deepest meaning of *freedom in Christ* (Gal. 5:1, 13).

In the final chapter of this volume we shall bring these speculations into conversation with eschatological possibilities explored by process theologians in the past couple of decades. However, let us conclude this chapter by offering the following implications of reading eschatology in a Wesleyan way.

First, the Wesleyan proclamation is that it is possible by divine empowering to love God and neighbor perfectly in this present life and thus in this present world. This, particularly when joined with the Genesis affirmation of our world as good and this life as God's designated arena of covenantal faithfulness, ought to energize and embolden Wesleyan Christians to be laboring toward the divine transformation of this present age toward universal love as God's intended end for creation. We shall explore this point in greater detail in the following chapter.

Second, even the eventual termination of the world as we know it need not dampen our hope in God's transforming love. Because Scripture holds out hope to us for a "new heaven and a new earth,"

30. Sermon 64, "The New Creation," §18, *Works* 2:510.

the Wesleyan tradition's commitment to the notion of gracious synergism within the context of divinely willed "otherness" is not necessarily dependent upon the survival of the present universe. We shall have more to say on this point in chapter 9.

Third, whatever eschatological fulfillment of creation that Wesleyans might envision is coherent and consistent with the first two points only if it upholds an eschatological *perfection in love,* which seems inevitably to imply an everlastingly continuing situation of creaturely agency and responsibility. Simply put, the God who is Love would never say "Enough!"

CHAPTER 8

"TO TURN THE STREAM OF NATURE'S TIDE"

Ecology in a Wesleyan Way

Turn the full stream of nature's tide;
Let all our actions tend
To thee their source; thy love the guide,
Thy glory be the end.

John and Charles Wesley, "Grace before Meat"[1]

I have suggested often in this book that God's intended end for the world is that love might flourish. For love even to exist, let alone to flourish, it is necessary that the world be truly an "other" for God, that is, that creaturely agency and responsibility thrive. The argument in the previous chapter was that traditional ways of thinking about eschatology tend to undercut this necessity for creaturely agency and responsibility. Perhaps the doctrine of end times should no longer to be thought of as dealing primarily with the sudden cessation of the world as we know it, but rather with the slow and painstaking transformation of the world through the energies and activities of divine love mediated through human love and deed.

If the world truly is to be transformed by divine love laboring in and through us, then it is obvious that the world requires a viable future. In this reading of eschatology, we are not encouraged to wait for a divine deliverance *from* the world, but rather to labor

1. Hymn #104, lines 25-28, *Works* 7:211. This hymn was titled "Grace before Meat" in *Hymns and Sacred Poems* (1739).

patiently and faithfully as creatures made in God's image to care *for* the world we inhabit with all the other earthlings. As far as we presently know, among God's creatures it is uniquely we humans who are beckoned toward the possibilities of a transformed world—a world that might truly be deemed good by being redeemed well.

The past few centuries of industry, technology, population explosion and resource depletion do not inspire much hope for a viable future for this planet. All indications are that we have precious little time to make the necessary changes in our modern habits of resource consumption and demand. Some experts, in fact, are convinced that it is already too late to turn the tide of our depletion and destruction of the environment. Of course, it is not likely that human beings will destroy all life on the planet, even if we succeed someday in entirely erasing ourselves. If that should happen, there is no reason to assume that God would not continue to labor creatively and lovingly to lead what is left of the world in the paths of the highest possible good, given the new situation. Further, it is far from impossible that God has created—or, better stated, is in the long process of creating—beings of intelligence, agency, and responsibility on many of the millions of planets of our Milky Way galaxy alone, to say nothing of the millions of other galaxies in the observable universe. To put it simply, human beings are not all there is to God's creation of life!

Nonetheless, I am a human writing for other humans. Theology, as far as we know at this point, is a strictly human art. Our biblically informed traditions do teach us that we have been created to "image" or reflect God, to represent God on this orb. According to Genesis, this implies a responsibility for caretaking, for tending to God's green, blue, and brown earth. Even if it were to turn out that the tide of destruction is past turning, this would change neither our calling nor our responsibility before our Maker. The question at the heart of this chapter is whether John Wesley's theology has anything new or unique to contribute to the pressing contemporary need for a theological ethic of caring for the environment. I believe that it does, that there are four fundamental themes in the Wesleyan theological tradition that, especially when combined, may offer a contribution to the important theological work that has already been done.[2] These four are the doctrines of *prevenient grace, God as holy love, entire sanctification in this life,* and *the witness of the Holy Spirit.* We shall consider each of these in order, giving particular attention to the fourth, the doctrine of "the witness of the Spirit," or assurance, especially within its scriptural context in Romans 8.

PREVENIENT GRACE

While Wesley was not the first religious thinker to employ either the phrase "prevenient grace" or the idea to which the phrase refers, he certainly offered a unique and critical development of the idea of prevenient grace in response to the dominant Reformed theology of his era. In opposition to the Calvinist idea of God's unconditioned election of particular individuals foreordained from the foundation of the world, Wesley identified himself as a follower of James Arminius (1560–1609), a rebellious son of the Dutch Reformed Church. Arminius, and Wesley after him, argued for the idea of a universal grace offered to all people. This grace is, in effect, nothing other than God's own empowering Spirit enlivening all people to a sufficient extent that all may make a response to God that is truly their own. In what has become an often-cited passage, Wesley wrote:

> No man living is entirely destitute of what is vulgarly called "natural conscience." But this is not natural; it is more properly termed "preventing [or prevenient] grace." Every man has a greater or less measure of this, which waiteth not for the call of man. . . . Everyone has some measure of that light, some faint glimmering ray, which sooner or later, more or less, enlightens

2. Some of the more helpful books on ecotheology include Elizabeth Achtemeier, *Nature, God and Pulpit* (Grand Rapids: Eerdmans, 1992); Robert Booth Fowler, *The Greening of Protestant Thought* (Chapel Hill: University of North Carolina Press, 1995); David G. Hallman, ed., *Ecotheology: Voices from South and North* (Maryknoll, N.Y.: Orbis Books, 1994); John F. Haught, *The Promise of Nature: Ecology and Cosmic Purpose* (Mahwah, N.J.: Paulist Press, 1993); Sallie McFague, *Super, Natural Christians: How We Should Love Nature* (Minneapolis: Fortress, 1997); Mary Elizabeth Moore, *Ministering with the Earth* (St. Louis: Chalice, 1998); and James A. Nash, *Loving Nature: Ecological Integrity and Christian Responsibility* (Nashville: Abingdon, 1991).

> every man that cometh into the world. . . . So that no man sins because he has not grace, but because he does not use the grace which he hath.[3]

As I have indicated already in chapters 4 and 5, this doctrine of prevenient grace can be understood to be a facet of a larger theological category that I have designated *creative grace*. God lovingly sustains and "draws near" not only to human beings, but to all creatures and all creation. Wesley never employed this particular phrase "creative grace," but it names well an explicit theme he explored especially in several sermons relatively late in his life. We have already encountered Wesley's strong language about the God who "holds [all creatures] in being . . . by his intimate presence," indeed, "who pervades and actuates the whole created frame, and is, in a true sense, the soul of the universe"![4]

Wesley offers us a surprisingly immanent and intimate God whose everlasting love and sustaining presence encompass the entirety of creation. In reality, it could be no other way; if for Wesley all human beings are graced, it is equally true that all human beings are creatures who share inextricably in the complex webs of creaturely existence as a whole. Thus, there can be no sharp arbitrary line drawn between God's loving, sustaining presence offered graciously to humans and God's presence offered graciously to all of creation, since it is the one gracious Holy Spirit "who pervades and actuates the whole created frame." Thus, while we may create theological categories for prevenient grace and creative grace, there is finally one grace, for there is but one God, one Spirit.

It is particularly instructive in this connection to compare Wesley's notion of prevenient grace to the corresponding doctrine in Reformed theology, common grace. The comparison demonstrates that for Wesley creation has inherent, redeemable value, while for Calvin it has only instrumental value. For Calvin, common grace is a divine gift to all human beings that essentially helps to keep sin in check; because of common grace, human cultures, political systems, and artistic endeavors, for example, are all possible in spite of the violent and destructive tendencies of fallen

3. Sermon 85, "On Working Out Our Own Salvation," §III.4, *Works* 3:207.
4. Sermon 23, "Sermon on the Mount, III," §I.11, *Works* 1:516-17.

humanity. But common grace has no saving possibility, since those who are saved are the elect from all eternity. Hence, common grace only preserves the world, finally, for the sake of an elected elite. For Wesley, on the other hand, prevenient grace is the loving, persuasive presence of God lavished upon all people, and indeed upon all creation. Thus all creatures, human and nonhuman, and indeed creation as a whole, are loved *in themselves* and *for their own sakes.* Nothing is of simply instrumental value, since every creature is graciously sustained and loved by God for itself. Further, every creature is a "glass" or mirror of the Creator, and no creature should be perceived or used by us as though it is "separate from God."[5]

God as Holy Love

Not unrelated to his doctrine of prevenient grace, Wesley's recurring insistence that God's nature is essentially that of *holy love,* that is, a love unlike any other, is also an important contribution to an eco-theological ethic. For Wesley, the fundamental fact about God is that "God is love" (1 John 4:8, 16), which spurred his confidence that God loves all people, everywhere, at all times—a confidence he could not find in the Reformed doctrine of predestination. If it is the very nature of God to be love, self-offering and other-receiving love, then there is no one and no thing excluded. As we touched on earlier in chapter 2, probably the most dramatic example of this principle is Wesley's reply to those who insisted on a literal reading of the biblical statement, "Jacob have I loved, but Esau have I hated" (Mal. 1:2-3; Rom. 9:13 KJV). "Now," wrote Wesley, "what can possibly be a more flat contradiction than this, not only to the whole scope and tenor of Scripture, but also to all those particular texts which expressly declare, 'God is love'?"[6]

We should give Wesley due credit, particularly as a late eighteenth-century man, for his happy willingness to extend the concept of divine love to all creatures, thus challenging the conventional notion that the animals are here only for the ingenious use of human

5. Ibid.
6. Sermon 110, "Free Grace," §20, *Works* 3:552.

beings. Wesley understood that "the Lord's mercies are over all of his works"—and as we have seen, Wesley invariably placed his accent upon the *all*. Because for Wesley it is the very character of God to be love, the mercy or compassion of God cannot be extended to some in exclusion of others. God *is* love, and thus God *loves all*. Just as Wesley felt constrained to reject a Reformed interpretation of salvation as the predestining decree of God for a certain "elect" group of human beings, so now we may argue by analogy that God's saving love does not stop with human beings as though they were some kind of "elect" species over against excluded nonhuman creatures.

We find, then, that the very theo-logic of divine love presses us beyond our anthropocentric borders; perhaps Wesley most clearly recognized this in the sermon on Romans 8, "The General Deliverance," which will figure significantly in this and the following chapter. Wesley opened this sermon with these words: "Nothing is more sure than that, as 'the Lord is loving to *every man*,' so 'his mercy is over *all his works*'—all that *have sense*, all that are *capable of pleasure or pain*, of happiness or misery."[7] Wesley then quotes copiously from Psalms 104 and 147 to demonstrate the rich, nurturing care that God lavishes upon not only the human creatures, but upon cattle, wild asses, and "every beast of the field"; indeed, God "openeth his hand and filleth all things living with plenteousness."[8]

Small wonder, then, that Wesley was willing to consider animal pain as a legitimate, indeed an important, theological problem. Such considerations were certainly ahead of his time, for the most part, and even now a good deal of contemporary theological reflection on the problem of evil proceeds with little attention given to the suffering of nonhuman earthlings. Wesley, though, insisted on reading Romans 8 for its "plain meaning": "While 'the whole creation groaneth together' (whether men attend or not) their groans are not dispersed in idle air, but enter into the ears of him that made them."[9] If their groans are heard and taken into account by God, then surely also the promises of deliverance are intended for all the creatures as well. "Nothing can be more express," insisted

7. Sermon 60, "The General Deliverance," §1, *Works* 2:437. Once more we find Wesley citing Psalm 145:9 as a favored proof text regarding God's universal love.
8. Ibid.
9. Ibid., §III.1, *Works* 2:445.

Wesley. "Away with vulgar prejudices, and let the plain word of God take place."[10] For each and every creature of God—according to its capacities as that particular creature—there shall be deliverance from bondage into "the liberty of the children of God," wherein all tears shall be wiped from their eyes, and there shall be no more pain or sorrow or crying. Wesley explicitly denied that these are eschatological promises addressed only to human beings, "for there is no restriction in the text."[11]

Such an understanding of God's lavish love did not lead Wesley to what is today known as deep ecology, where all living things are deemed to be of equal value and importance. While God "the Father of all has a tender regard for even his lowest creatures . . . yet I dare not affirm that he has an *equal regard* for them and for the children of men."[12] It is interesting, in fact, that Wesley deemed it necessary even to mention the notion of "equal regard." It is not surprising that Wesley insisted on a higher regard for human beings, but it is gratifying that he nonetheless also insisted on God's "tender regard" for all living things.

In a sermon emphasizing God's boundless compassion for all creatures, it is natural that Wesley would raise a question regarding the difference between creatures that are human and those that are not. Though a child of the Enlightenment, Wesley rejected one of the hallmark distinctions of the era:

> What then makes the barrier between men and brutes? The line which they cannot pass? It was not reason. Set aside that ambiguous term: exchange it for the plain word, understanding, and who can deny that brutes have this? We may as well deny that they have sight or hearing. But it is this: man is capable of God; the inferior creatures are not. We have no ground to believe that they are in any degree capable of knowing, loving, or obeying God.[13]

The critical point here is that Wesley finds nothing inherently distinctive about human beings; rather, it is the *relation toward God* for which the human creature is made, the *telos* toward which we are called, that marks our unique place in God's creation. Thus, for

10. Ibid., §III.2, *Works* 2:446.
11. Ibid.
12. Ibid., §III.5, *Works* 2:447.
13. Ibid., §I.5, *Works* 2:441.

Wesley the image of God is essentially the relational possibility of "knowing, loving, [and] obeying God." While differences in brain complexity and size are undoubtedly necessary to such relational capacity, Wesley wisely avoids making physiology or biology the distinctive mark of the human. It is, rather, to be "capable of God," to be a creature of self-transcendence, ever opening up toward richer possibilities of love for God and for what God creates. While Enlightenment deists fixated upon human reason as the essence of the image of God, "Wesley," Runyon writes, "sees the image more relationally, not so much as something humans possess as the way they relate to God and live out that relation in the world."[14] Wesley draws on Scripture and tradition to claim that human beings are "the channel of conveyance between [their] Creator and the whole brute creation,"[15] and from this we extrapolate the unique role of human beings as the image of God in God's world-in-the-making. Human beings are the vanguard of God's ongoing labors to create a world of which it might be said, "It is very good."

It is certainly worth noting that, even granting God's creation of human beings in the divine image, Wesley haltingly speculated on what kinds of possibilities might await nonhuman creatures in the "general deliverance" yet to come:

> May I be permitted to mention here a conjecture concerning the brute creation? What if it should then please the all-wise, the all-gracious Creator, to raise them higher in the scale of beings? What if it should please him, when he makes us "equal to angels" (Luke 20:36), to make them what we are now? Creatures capable of God? Capable of knowing, and loving, and enjoying the Author of their being? If it should be so, ought our eye be evil because he is good?[16]

Thus we find, fascinatingly enough, that Wesley was unwilling to make "the barrier between humans and brutes" a firmly uncrossable one. By even weighing such a possibility before us, Wesley challenges us to think differently about the creatures with whom we share this world; we are struck by the fact that we

14. Runyon, *New Creation*, 13.
15. Sermon 60, "The General Deliverance," III.3, *Works* 2:446.
16. Ibid., §III.6, *Works* 2:448.

humans exist in unique relation to God not because of inherent superiority to other creatures, but because of God's good and gracious desire to create and sustain us in this capacity. But who knows what God's glorious future might hold, either for us or for our fellow earthlings? Shall even they become "capable of God"?

At this point in his sermon, Wesley anticipated a new objection: "But of what use will those creatures be in that future state?" Wesley's reply is classic: "I answer this by another question—'What use are they of now?' . . . Consider this; consider how little we know of even the present designs of God; and then you will not wonder that we know still less of what [God] designs to do in the new heavens and the new earth."[17] Undoubtedly, evolutionary theory gives us a heightened and much more historically and geographically nuanced appreciation for the diversity of species in our world, such that we would not think of a creature's "utility" in the way that Wesley and his world did. Nonetheless, given precisely the historical context in which Wesley lived, it is remarkable that he was quite unwilling to allow the world's nonhuman denizens to be reduced simply to the category of human usefulness. He resisted a purely instrumental valuing of other creatures, as though their only purpose is to serve *our* purposes. There is, instead, a mystery about the rich diversity and sheer numbers of creatures in the world that Wesley's sermon teaches us to celebrate simply as *God's creation*. We know little of "even the present designs of God," and how much might our ignorance be magnified if we attempt to consider the future designs of God! Think of the implications: there is nothing inherent in human beings that distinguishes them from other creatures; it is only the will and calling of the Creator that make for this difference. Thus, the difference is not absolute and all creatures are pliable toward an as-yet-undefined future; what would it mean, for example, that human beings shall become "like the angels"? For Christian faith this future is, nonetheless, defined proleptically and with great hope in the ministry of Jesus Christ. We can make the point yet once more: in such an understanding of creation, we human beings *and all other creatures* are defined primarily not by the past, but by a future, a destiny, a beckoning from the God of hope.

17. Ibid., §III.7.

Wesley, then, directs us to think more deeply on the mysteries of creation, in all its rich diversity and inherent inscrutability—*and* in its relation to God quite apart from human interests! When Wesley reminds us of "how little we know of even the present designs of God," let alone the future designs, he provides us with an eighteenth-century echo of the divine sermon-in-a-whirlwind of Job 38–41:

> "Has the rain a father,
> or who has begotten the drops of dew?
> From whose womb did the ice come forth,
> and who has given birth to the hoarfrost of heaven? . . .
> Who has the wisdom to number the clouds?
> Or who can tilt the waterskins of the heavens . . . ?
> Do you know when the mountain goats give birth?
> Do you observe the calving of the deer?
> (Job 38:28-29, 37; 39:1)

Such a barrage of questions from the ancient wisdom of Job reminds us that the Wesleyan tradition has generally taken as its fundamental theological principle not simply that God is love, but that God is holy love.[18] The adjective *holy* reminds us that God's love is utterly unique, thoroughly mysterious in its unsearchable depths, and thus very unlike human loves or conceptions of love. Human loves, after all, inevitably draw the line somewhere, and all too often the lines are drawn very near to ourselves. But in the words of a gospel song, God's "love has no limit," and thus it is constant and universal, embracing all creation. God's love therefore cannot be managed or manipulated by human beings for merely human ends. *Pure, unbounded love Thou art*!

Wesley anticipated a further objection to his speculations about creation's deliverance: the question might be raised, "But what end does it answer to dwell upon this subject which we so imperfectly understand?" To this query he offers two replies: first, to get a taste, or even simply a glimpse, of the wondrous love and "mercy of God which is 'over all his works' . . . may exceedingly confirm our

18. See, for example, Wiley, *Christian Theology* 1:324, 365-87; Dunning, *Grace, Faith and Holiness*, 192-204; or Oden, *The Living God*, 98-125.

belief that much more he is 'loving to every man'" (Ps. 145:9), and thus give us each a deep assurance of God's matchless love for each of us; second, to consider the future possibilities of glorious freedom for all the creatures may "furnish us with a full answer to a plausible objection against the justice of God in suffering numberless creatures that never had sinned to be so severely punished."[19] In other words, the problem of evil cannot be solved by an appeal to future glory if that appeal cannot or does not include the sufferings of *all* creatures.

We may not be able to affirm literally, as apparently Wesley did, the resurrection of "suffering numberless creatures" in the world to come. It is nonetheless significant that Wesley considered such a scenario to be worth hoping for! If for Wesley it was finally only in the age to come that the problem of evil could and would be sufficiently addressed, the problem would *not* be sufficiently addressed if the suffering of nonhuman creatures was ignored. The point here is not whether or not our favorite pets will be "in heaven," though it would not be surprising to learn that Wesley had a favorite horse or two in mind as he penned this sermon. (We should keep in mind, by the way, that Wesley is not really speaking of a "heaven above" *per se*, but of a world to come—a future!—that looms before us and toward which creation yearns as its divinely intended end.) The main point, though, is more pedestrian: Wesley at least considered the pain of animals to be of sufficient import that it demanded theological attention. Thus this general deliverance, "this subject which we so imperfectly understand," provides Wesley with an eschatological solution to the problem of the unjust suffering of sentient life.

This is a world of pain. Of course, it is much more than that: there is joy, pleasure, love, culture, visual and musical arts, unexpected deeds of great goodness and empathy—the listing of such blessings is virtually endless. The pleasures of animals tend to be less complex, and perhaps their pains as well. But is there any question that, given millions of years of evolutionary struggle for survival undertaken by a mass of creatures only God could count, the weight of animal misery, terror, and pain is beyond calculation? It is not so surprising that a considerable number of Christians

19. Sermon 60, "The General Deliverance," §III.9, *Works* 2:449.

reject the evolutionary story of the world for precisely this reason. After all, the story of evolution makes suffering and death to be part and parcel of God's creation, rather than aberrations due to human sin.

This problem should not be taken lightly. It certainly is a contributing factor to the development in our century of process theology. As we have seen earlier, process thinkers suggest that God is always at work with the world, as it is, calling it forward but unable unilaterally to create a utopia. The world, at least for most process theologians, has its own energies and integrity that God did not ultimately create and cannot ultimately control. Thus the processes of evolution are the evidence of God's patient and painstaking labors in the world, and God cannot help but that in such a world there is struggle, carnage, and death.

I have already attempted, most particularly in chapter 3, to demonstrate some possible convergences between Wesley's theological vision and that of process theologians, but I am very far from suggesting that Wesley would approve of their solution to the problem of evil. I am only suggesting that Wesley and the process tradition are correct to insist that addressing the problem of animal pain is a necessary element in a truly adequate theodicy.

ENTIRE SANCTIFICATION

Wesley's faith in the transforming power of God's love led him to embrace the doctrine for which he is probably best known: that of *entire sanctification*. Essentially, Wesley defined the entirely sanctified life as one in which "the two greatest commandments" of the Torah—love for God with all of one's being, and love for one's neighbor as oneself—are actually fulfilled. Such a life of love is possible because God is love, and love pours itself out to us; hence, as we become open and receptive to this transforming love given to us through Jesus Christ, we are empowered to love as God loves and to walk as Christ walked, *according to our capacities*. God always works with what and where we are, in order to lead us to what we might become in Christ: fully loving, fully open, fully giving and receiving of love. While there is always room for further growth in love, perhaps even into eternity,[20] Wesley was also deeply confident about the power of God's transforming love in this world, and in this life, to make us lovers of God and neighbors. Surely such a doctrine as this also can and should contribute effectively to an environmental ethic.

Wesley very often referred to entire sanctification as our being restored to the image of God. We noted earlier in this chapter that in his "The General Deliverance," the doctrine of humanity in the image of God is explicitly *not* interpreted in such a way as to create an inherent distinction between human beings and other creatures. There is, for Wesley, a "great gulf" between human and nonhuman earthlings, but it is not our ability to reason or any other characteristic residing within the human *per se*; rather, the operative difference is that human beings are "capable of God" and other creatures are not. We may, however, legitimately push Wesley a little on this point. Since he was unwilling to identify reason as being some distinctive gift that separated humanity from other creatures—noting instead that other creatures certainly do exercise some "understanding"—it seems reasonable to question Wesley's unqualified language about nonhuman creatures as not "in any degree capable of knowing, loving, or obeying God." It would fit more readily with the theological vision of the creation psalms, and with his own theology, to say that all creatures are "capable of knowing, loving, or obeying God" *according to their capacities.* Particularly since Wesley was willing to speculate about the possibility of nonhuman creatures becoming "capable of God" in the indescribable eschatological future, it would seem appropriate to assume a measure of continuity between their present capacities, incipient as those capacities might be, and their future possibilities for "knowing, and loving, and enjoying the Author of their being."[21]

This much is certain: for Wesley, to be entirely sanctified is to live in a quality of relationship to God and neighbor characterized by love, and to live in such love is to be restored to the image of God. For God is love and has created human beings especially to reflect and image this love; indeed, the same writer who told us that "God

20. See, for example, Wesley's certainty on the issue in *Plain Account of Christian Perfection*, §25, Q. 29, *Works* (Jackson) 11:426.

21. Sermon 60, "The General Deliverance," §III.6, *Works* 2:448.

is love" (1 John 4:8, 16) also wrote, "We know love by this, that [Christ] laid down his life for us—and we ought to lay down our lives for one another" (3:16).

It is also noteworthy that Wesley's happy identification of entire sanctification with the restoration to God's image provides a creational context for the doctrine of sanctification; it is first, and primarily, in Genesis 1 that we discover the biblical teaching that human beings are created in God's image. Most important for our purposes, by thinking of entire sanctification as a restoration to God's image, we most decidedly are not thinking of it as somehow a means of escaping the world. Rather, God's sanctifying grace in our lives draws us back into *proper* and *restored* relations to our fellow creatures in the complex web of creation so profoundly celebrated in the Bible's opening chapter. Entire sanctification does not tear us out of creation; instead, it roots us more deeply in it.

Because sanctification is our restoration to the image of God, and because God is in very nature holy love, Wesley could and often did talk about it as our *being renewed in love*. God's sanctification of our lives is God's very sharing of the Holy Spirit with us; if on the one hand we humans are "capable of God," then the complementary truth is that God is also capable of us—capable of sharing God's own self, of pouring out the divine Spirit toward and within us. Wesley was partial to the words of Paul, "Now we have received . . . the Spirit who is from God, so that we may know the things freely given to us by God . . . for the Spirit searches all things, even the depths of God" (1 Cor. 2:12, 10 NASB)[22]—and God freely outpours this same Spirit upon us, and indeed "upon all flesh" (Joel 2:28; Acts 2:17). So it is that we frail human creatures, fashioned from the dust of distant stars, are divinely intended to "become partakers of the divine nature" (2 Peter 1:4 NASB), indeed to "be filled up to all the fullness of God" (Eph. 3:19 NASB). Further, in an ecotheology it is crucial to recognize that the Spirit who desires to fill and sanctify us is the same Spirit who creates and enlivens all creatures, and who renews the face of the ground (Ps. 104:29). If it is this creative and recreative Spirit who fills, transforms, and overflows our lives through Jesus Christ, then as we grow in grace, we shall increasingly find it our "second nature"—

---

22. Cf. *Plain Account of Christian Perfection*, §25, Q. 19, *Works* (Jackson) 11:421.

our redeemed and restored nature as the image of God—to care for all of God's creatures and to labor also to renew the face of the ground.

Similarly, if to be so "renewed in love" is to participate in the holy love that is God, then just as God's love is universal in scope and includes "all his works," so also our renewal in love shall ever be moving us more deeply toward a universality of scope that embraces all of God's creatures. Admittedly, Wesley generally followed the biblical pattern of focusing on love for God and neighbor—and even here we have not taken seriously enough that a great many of our neighbors are denizens of the future, people yet to be born, whom we are called upon to love by doing all we can to see to it that they inherit a habitable world. Loving our neighbors of the future demands nothing less. However, if indeed God's "compassion is over *all* that he has made" (Ps. 145:9), as Wesley so liked to repeat, then we may legitimately ask whether the category of "neighbor" should stop with fellow human beings. What of the animals we befriend? What of those "wilder" creatures of God's good world? What of those creatures for whom we see little or no value? Wesley, in fact, offers a strong reply near the end of his sermon:

> One more excellent end may undoubtedly be answered by the preceding considerations. They may encourage us to imitate him whose mercy is over all his works. They may soften our hearts towards the meaner creatures, knowing that the Lord careth for them. It may enlarge our hearts towards those poor creatures to reflect that, as vile as they appear in our eyes, not one of them is forgotten in the sight of our Father which is in heaven. Through all the vanity to which they are now subjected, let us look to what God hath prepared for them.[23]

Thus, finally, for Wesley yet another value in more deeply appreciating God's tender love for all creatures is that, in contemplating such love, we might be moved—our hearts "softened" and "enlarged"—toward a divinely inspired compassion for fellow creatures. Hearts that are "soft" are malleable, movable, moldable—and thus *mendable*. In Wesley's day, such compassion or

23. Sermon 60, "The General Deliverance," §III.10, *Works* 2:449.

empathy was often called "fellow-feeling," and for Wesley this "fellow-feeling" in human life and interaction arose as a response to the operations of God's prevenient grace. Of course, it is this same grace—the convicting and alluring presence of the Holy Spirit—that labors in us toward our sanctification. The implication here is that, through prayer, meditation, and increasing openness to the working of God's Spirit within us, we may actually begin to *feel God's feelings* for all of God's creatures—for all of our fellow earthlings. And if Jesus' famous parable about the compassionate Samaritan is any indication, then feeling compassion is the first and prerequisite step on the road toward healing, mending actions in behalf of the other.

THE WITNESS OF THE SPIRIT

Another distinctive hallmark of John Wesley's theology was his emphasis on the doctrine of assurance, or the witness of the Spirit. Drawing primarily on Romans 8:16—"When we cry, 'Abba! Father!' it is that very Spirit bearing witness with our spirit that we are children of God"—and influenced by Moravian piety, Wesley developed a distinctive motif in his proclamation of the gospel. That motif is that while we are created and called to love God with all our being and to love our neighbors as though they were our very self, we *cannot* love so freely and so deeply—not *until* "we know he loves us. . . . And we cannot know his pardoning love to us till his Spirit witnesses it to our spirit."[24] This means that for Wesley the love of God is to be experienced, in some sense *felt*, deep within our beings. Wesley was not content with a purely intellectual faith, nor even with a simply volitional faith, but with a faith of conscious and experienced relation to God and neighbor.[25]

Another explicit reference to the witness of the Spirit is in Paul's letter to the Galatians, where he describes it as the "Abba! Father!" cry of "the Spirit of [God's] Son [within] our hearts" (4:6), presumably an echo of Jesus' prayer in Gethsemane (Mark 14:36). The synoptic portrayal of Jesus' prayer of desperation in a garden evokes

24. Sermon 10, "The Witness of the Spirit, I," §I.8, *Works* 1:274.

25. See Runyon's excellent discussion in *New Creation*, chapter 5: "Orthopathy and Religious Experience."

the interpretive imagination; it is as though Jesus' prayer of submission signifies the beginning of the reversal of the effects of the first Adam's transgression in a garden. This, in turn, sheds a new light on the larger context of the "Abba! Father!" cry of Romans 8. For if the gardens of Eden and Gethsemane can be read as metaphors for our planet as a whole—first in its rending by sin with the first Adam, and second in the beginnings of its mending with the Second Adam—then their pertinence to Paul's remarkable reflections in Romans 8 becomes evident. A significant part of the appeal of the biblical passage for many contemporary scholars is that it encourages thinking about all of God's creation as the object of God's saving intentions: "the creation itself will be set free from its bondage to decay and will obtain the freedom of the glory of the children of God" (v. 21).

The precise nature of this deliverance that Paul envisions is not at all clear, but as Wesley stubbornly insisted in "The General Deliverance," this passage disallows the kind of anthropocentric and individualistic notions of salvation that have so often held sway in Christian preaching. In the words of Daniel Migliore, "Under the present conditions of life, humanity and nature are caught in a web of mutual alienation and abuse. . . . According to the biblical witness, we human beings exist in a solidarity of life and death with the whole groaning and expectant creation."[26] It was this solidarity with all of God's creatures that Wesley, remarkably enough, seems to have captured in his sermon. In order to appreciate how this sense of solidarity might be properly associated with the doctrine of the witness of the Spirit, it is necessary to probe Paul's understanding of creation's yearnings and coming redemption a little further.

It is not difficult to sense Paul's deeply Hebraic roots in this hope for the liberation and salving of God's creation. There are numerous texts in the Hebrew Bible that teach a close, indeed inseparable spiritual (not to mention physical) relation between human beings and their physical environment. For example, in Isaiah we read,

> The earth dries up and withers,
> the world languishes and withers,

26. Migliore, *Faith Seeking Understanding*, 83.

> the exalted of the earth languish.
> The earth is defiled by its people;
> they have disobeyed the laws,
> violated the statutes
> and broken the everlasting covenant.
> Therefore a curse consumes the earth;
> its people must bear their guilt. (24:4-6 NIV)

In this and similar passages it becomes clear that human disobedience to God brings pollution to the land. This biblical theme undergoes further development in Jewish apocalyptic writing, reflecting an intellectual milieu much closer to Paul's own era. For example, in 4 Ezra 7:11-12 we read, "And when Adam transgressed by statutes, what had been made was judged. And so the entrances of this world were made narrow and sorrowful and toilsome." Similar ideas appear in *Genesis Rabbah*, a collection of rabbinic commentary: "Although things were created in their fulness, when the first man sinned they were corrupted, and they will not come back to their order before Ben Perez (the Messiah) comes" (12:6). In texts such as these, in fact, the polluting power of human sin has assumed cosmic proportions. Further, in Jewish rabbinic thought such suffering and sorrow in the world were the "birth pangs of the Messiah," the evidence that the present age was nearing its end and the age to come was perhaps just around the corner.

Largely through Paul's mediation, of course, this idea that human sin has corrupted an otherwise and originally perfect world became standard fare in Christian thought and proclamation. It continues to be a widely held assumption in many Christian circles, but of course is one of those ideas that would appear to require radical reinterpretation in the face of evolutionary history. If the world has painstakingly evolved over unimaginably immense eons of time, from the simplest of life-forms to the complex variety of living things in our world today, then it cannot also be true that at one time the world was a "perfect place" of no suffering or death. Whatever might be entailed in the Christian affirmation that God's creation is good, it cannot mean that there once was a pristine, painless perfection from which the world has fallen due to human disobedience.

Of course, this does not imply at all that there is no real and vital connection between human beings' spiritual condition and the welfare of our world. If anything, an evolutionary understanding of the world and of the human role in it would accentuate the tight connection between our relation to the Creator and our relation to fellow creatures and creation as a whole. Even without the assumption of a primordial original sin in a pristine Garden of Eden, it is not difficult to perceive how human selfishness, greed, and violence—especially in tandem with industrial and technological developments of the past several centuries—have done perhaps irreparable damage to our planetary home. No wonder, then, that Paul's image of creation as groaning like a woman in the pains of childbirth has figured prominently in contemporary attempts at ecological theology. No one pretends that Paul had our ecological crisis or concerns in mind when he wrote about the groaning creation, but it is inevitable and proper that such concerns should enter our minds when we read Romans 8.

Paul is not at all clear about whose will it was that "creation was subjected to futility" (8:20). Given what he writes in Romans 5 it is not illogical to assume that this creaturely frustration is due to Adam's transgression, but it is easy for us, again, to read this in the light of our ecological crisis. Creation is indeed subjected to futility, but Paul teaches us nonetheless to hope for a future for all of creation, a future of glorious freedom. Again, it is the dominant traditional reading to assume that it is because of human sin that creation has become subject to frustration. However, the alternative notion that God, in the very act of creating a finite world of interdependent creatures and limited resources such as ours, has subjected the creation to suffering and struggle *with an eye toward its future glory* is not out of the question. As C. K. Barrett has written,

> It is reasonable to ask whether it was simply by being created that the created universe was in this way made subject to vanity or whether subjection was the result of a culpable fall, through which creation lost its pristine freedom and entered into bondage which it had brought upon itself. No clear answer can be read out of the text; the next sentence is compatible with both alternatives.[27]

27. C. K. Barrett, *The Epistle to the Romans*, revised ed. (Peabody, Mass.: Hendrickson Publishers, 1987), 155-56.

That "next sentence" to which Barrett refers is critical, for it refers to the future "hope" for which creation groans and toward which it strains. It is all about *hope!* The whole point is that creation is here not seen as a paradise lost in the dim mists of an idyllic past, but rather as a world not yet finished—a world whose fulfillment lies up ahead in a future of glorious freedom. From this point of view, creation's struggles are indications precisely of its unfinished character, suggesting to us a world whose truest and richest meanings yet await divine realization. "Christian hope," writes Migliore, "encompasses the entire creation. The fulfillment for which we yearn cannot be found apart from the renewal and transformation of the heaven and the earth to which we are bound in life and in death."[28]

No wonder, then, that Paul proceeds to include Christian believers in this groaning of the world. It is possible to assume that Paul's meaning was that even "we ourselves . . . groan inwardly," *despite* the fact that we "have the first fruits of the Spirit" (8:23). In other words, our having received the initial taste of the world to come in the outpouring of the Spirit does not tear us out of creation's fabric: the world groans, and we who enjoy the first fruits of the eschatological outpouring of God's Spirit are nonetheless yet creatures who cry and suffer in that groaning, old cosmos. There is another reading of this text, however. It is quite possible that Paul is stating that it is precisely *because* Christians have tasted of the world to come in the present reality of the Spirit that we now find ourselves groaning with the rest of God's creation—sharing, indeed, more fully in its pains, sorrows, and frustrations even as we strain forward along *with* creation toward God's deliverance *of* creation. In this latter reading, it is precisely because we anticipate a renewed and redeemed creation that we should, and can, more truly suffer with all creaturely suffering. Because the Spirit is present and active in our lives, we are not content with "the world as we know it"; instead, the same Spirit who in Genesis 1 brooded and blew over the face of the chaotic, watery deep, stirring up new possibilities for a world-in-the-making, is the Spirit who continues to stir things up, to challenge the status quo, to create a deep sense of unrest in the hearts and hopes of those who follow the Second

---

28. Migliore, *Faith Seeking Understanding*, 239.

Adam. It is because Christians are people of hope, whose entire lives are oriented toward the always-coming rule of God in Jesus Christ foretasted in the Spirit, that they would groan in solidarity with the present groaning creation. "[Paul] thus creates room for love and service not just in the community but also to tormented creation," writes Ernst Kasemann. "Those who groan with creation . . . are truly potential and called instruments of the Spirit."[29]

Either way, it is clear that for Paul our redemption is not a redemption *from* the material creation, but instead a redemption *in*, *for*, and *in company with* this world created and sustained by God. Paul writes here not only of some kind of liberation for God's creation, but also of the nature of the redemption for which Christian believers, having received a taste of the world to come in the gift of the Spirit, groan longingly: it is "the redemption of our bodies" (Rom. 8:23)! There is here no dualistically tinged longing to slough off the material body as a wispy soul wafts its way into heaven; rather, there is a salvation hope—a hope for *salving*, for *healing*—of material bodies in a material, bodily world.

Further, what Paul claims for human hopes of life beyond death is in Romans 8 extended to creation itself: those hopes for freedom, for glory, for redemption are, for Christian faith, utterly contingent upon the resurrection of Jesus from the dead. The "life-giving spirit," which "the last Adam became" (1 Cor. 15:45) in the resurrection, is the life-giving and liberating Spirit for the groaning creation—God in Christ, then, both *provides* and *embodies* the world's future.

It cannot be a coincidence that Paul proceeds to employ this term *stenagmos*, generally translated "groaning," in his description of the Spirit's activity. Paul uses this term only three times in all of his extant writings, and all three are in this passage in Romans 8. The creation groans, we who have the Spirit groan, and even the Spirit groans within us in intercession as we offer our faltering prayers. What a fascinating possibility in Paul's language here: not only do we who are Christ's groan in solidarity with the groaning-in-childbirth creation, but the Spirit too groans within us in a profoundly divine solidarity with creation's deep yearnings for a redemption beyond imagining. James Dunn observes, "Having the Spirit does

29. Ernst Kasemann, *Commentary on Romans* (Grand Rapids: Eerdmans, 1980), 239.

not distance believers from creation but increases the solidarity of believers with creation,"[30] precisely because God's own Spirit dwells within, and in deep solidarity with, our wounded world. Indeed, Wesley in his *Explanatory Notes* made the connections in the Pauline text, writing, "Nay, not only the universe, not only the children of God, but the Spirit of God also Himself, as it were, groaneth, while He *helpeth our infirmities*, or weaknesses."[31]

The universe and its creatures groan as they strain and yearn for ultimate fulfillment of their being in relation to their Creator and to one another. God, whose compassionate love extends to all creatures and the whole of creation, groans with the world as "the fellow-sufferer who understands," in Whitehead's famous phrase. And believers in Jesus the Anointed of the Spirit, who through him have received the Spirit and are thereby being renewed and transformed in their very natures, are drawn up by the Spirit into God's own groanings. To be filled with God's Spirit is, then, to begin to see the world through God's eye of compassion and to feel the creatures' pains in the fellow-feelings of God.

We must say in this connection, too, that the infirmities and weaknesses in which "the Spirit helps us" (Rom. 8:26) are not only a human problem. If indeed creation shall be delivered from its frustrations, futilities and pains, it can ultimately be so only if it is *helped* and *healed* by its Creator. Physicists and cosmologists, we should remember, generally are not overly optimistic about the universe's ultimate future given what we can piece together about its beginning and its present energy, density, and trajectory. It appears increasingly likely that the universe will eventually freeze in universal entropy, a bleak destiny to be faced more squarely in the following chapter. Nonetheless, even given this chilling scenario and "hoping against hope" (Rom. 4:18) in the God of re-creation, Christian faith rooted in the resurrection of Christ and the outpoured Spirit as the foretaste of God's future teaches us to live in hope for a future we are thoroughly unable to envision. And who knows how God might bring about such a world-to-come? In John Haught's words,

30. James D. G. Dunn, "Spirit Speech: Reflections on Romans 8:12-27," in *Romans and the People of God*, edited by Sven Soderlund and N. T. Wright (Grand Rapids: Eerdmans, 1999), 88.

31. *NT Notes*, Romans 8:26.

> The fifteen billion years of cosmic evolution now appear, in the perspective of faith, to have always been seeded with promise. From its very beginning this extravagantly experimental universe has been bursting forth with potential for surprising future outcomes. . . . Thus, if it is now evident that the ambiguous cosmic past held such enormous promise as the eventual emergence of life and mind, can we claim confidently that the *present* state of the cosmic story is not also pregnant with potential for blossoming into still more abundant new creation? . . . [I]n the panorama of cosmic evolution disclosed by science, faith is still permitted, perhaps even encouraged, to think of the cosmos as being called into yet newer ways of being.[32]

Is it possible for us yet to hope that the Spirit who "helps us in our weakness" (Rom. 8:26), even as she groans with a world "groaning in labor pains until now," shall lead the whole of creation into an unimaginable future? We shall explore the vistas this question opens to us in chapter 9; for now, let us keep our feet on this soil and our eyes on its earthling creatures. Whatever may be the ultimate fate of the universe, we have hope and responsibility for this world, this planet, and its life-sustaining atmosphere. Clearly, our planet is groaning under the weight of our abuse of its goods, our rapacious consumption of its resources, our practices of extinction. How fitting, then, that the Spirit who bears witness to our spirits that we are God's children can and does speak in the inarticulate language of creation itself—in its *groanings*. How appropriate that this Spirit should be symbolized in Scripture as wind, flame, water, dove! Wesley preached that the creatures' groans enter their Maker's ears, even if no human being should hear or care; but if the Spirit of the Maker should indwell us, will we not hear creation's cries and respond in accord with that Spirit?

Obviously this Pauline passage should play a central role in the development of a Christian interpretation of this wondrous universe we inhabit. It instructs us to look, hope, and labor for a redemption for all of creation, not only for humans and certainly not only for a select group of humans. It teaches us to value ourselves and our world precisely in their stark physicality—pains

32. John Haught, *God after Darwin: A Theology of Evolution* (Boulder: Westview Press, 2000), 115, 118.

and struggles and all—and to anticipate a bodily redemption for God's creation. It hints at a deep, suffering divine presence groaning and interceding in and for the world's own straining toward deliverance. And in all of these points we are encouraged to think of creation not so much in terms of a lost paradisaical past but of a future yet to be realized—and thus of a world-yet-in-the-making, a world that can only be truly understood as God's creation as it is seen to be dynamically yearning and moving toward its divinely envisioned future. Such considerations as these should, from now on, be at home in Wesleyan conversations regarding the doctrine of the witness of the Holy Spirit.

THE IMPERTINENCE, AND PERTINENCE, OF WESLEY'S "GENERAL DELIVERANCE"

If we do indeed take seriously the story of the universe as told by evolutionary theory, then we shall also have to rethink, and reject, some of Wesley's ideas about creation. For example, in the sermon under consideration Wesley posits that "the original state of the brute creation . . . was paradisiacal, perfectly happy" and that Adam (no explicit mention of Eve!) "had such strength of understanding as no man ever since had . . . perfect in its kind; capable of apprehending all things clearly . . . without any mixture of error" and a will hindered by no "bias of any sort, but all his passions and affections . . . guided by the dictates of his unerring understanding."[33] As Wesley waxes eloquent about Adam's perfections, it becomes increasingly incomprehensible that such a perfect creature could ever have erred or sinned at all!

If we were to inquire about the "cash value" of such descriptions of Adam and Eden, it would appear that Wesley was concerned to protect God from any accusation of having made the world less than perfect. After all, Wesley was convinced that God's compassion extends to every one of God's creatures, human or not, and it is difficult to reconcile such a conviction with "the present state of things"; if God "wills even the meanest of them to be happy according to their degree, how comes it to pass that such a complication of evils oppresses, yea, overwhelms them?"[34]

33. Sermon 60, "The General Deliverance," §I.1, 2, *Works* 2:438, 439.
34. Ibid., §2, *Works* 2:438.

One can readily raise an objection to this traditional scenario of a perfect paradise by questioning how its perfection could be so delicately balanced (and apparently so radically unstable) that human disobedience could throw things so totally out of whack. From his heaven-on-earth descriptions of Eden, Wesley moves quickly to the despoiling effects of Adam's fall. Those effects, opines Wesley, have deeply defaced "the brute creation":

> what savage fierceness, what unrelenting cruelty, are invariably observed in thousands of creatures. . . . Is it only the lion, the tiger, the wolf . . . the shark . . . or the eagle . . . that tears the flesh, sucks the blood, and crushes the bones of their helpless fellow-creatures? Nay, the harmless fly, the laborious ant, the painted butterfly, are treated in the same merciless manner even by the innocent songsters of the grove![35]

Is it not possible to affirm the goodness of creation without assuming the utterly pristine perfection of traditional visions of Eden? After all, such speculations about creation's original idyllic perfections far outstrip the actual language of Genesis. In the two opening chapters of this book, I have already argued against a literal reading of the creation narratives. But even when we read them seriously as theological narrative we encounter none of the ideal perfections that have often been traditionally assumed. To employ against Wesley a phrase from his own sermon, "This is exceeding pretty; but it is absolutely false."[36] To be sure, Wesley's scenario of forfeited perfection is typically more at home in Western-Latin interpretations of Christianity inspired particularly by Augustine; more than a few theologians have pointed out that Irenaeus, on the other hand, interpreted our first parents not as pinnacles of perfection inscrutably fallen but as naïve and childlike, created to grow and mature through the experiences of suffering and moral decision.[37] To be sure, a theology based on evolutionary assumptions cannot simply and uncritically adopt Irenaeus, any more than it can Wesley and the host of Western theologians before

35. Ibid., §II.3, 2:443.

36. Ibid., §III.5, 2:447.

37. See especially John Hick's treatment of Irenaeus as the basis for an evolutionary theodicy in his landmark work *Evil and the God of Love*, rev. ed. (San Francisco: Harper & Row, 1978).

him back to Augustine. Nonetheless, Irenaeus's developmental scenario undoubtedly is more conducive, and thus more readily adapted, to an evolutionary framework.

If we assume an evolutionary history of God's creation, we will forfeit the theodical value of placing the world's suffering and death solely and squarely upon human shoulders. (As I have already suggested, the idea that God would create a world that could be so easily and thoroughly ruined by a single act of disobedience raises questions anyway, either about God's power or God's goodness or both.) But we can still recognize the human power for "overkill" and the significant extent to which we humans are indeed responsible for "creation's groanings." Scripture as well as experience can instruct us on the human complicity in the suffering of fellow creatures and the pollution of the land upon which we and many other creatures depend. In fact, Wesley goes to considerable lengths to make this very point. Human "violence and cruelty," coupled with human technology (what Wesley refers to as "art"), have increased the creatures' cries a thousandfold.

> And what a dreadful difference is there between what they suffer from their fellow brutes and what they suffer from the tyrant, man! The lion, the tiger, or the shark, give them pain from mere necessity, in order to prolong their own life; and put them out of their pain at once. But the human shark, without any such necessity, torments them of his free choice; and perhaps continues their lingering pain till after months or years death signs their release.[38]

Yes, in our relatively brief tenure upon planet Earth, we human beings have done much to create unnecessary suffering and death for numberless creatures and species, not to mention the violence and bloodshed we have committed against one another. In an evolutionary history this human aggressiveness can be understood as a necessary element in the creaturely struggle to survive, and of course we continue to inherit those survival instincts. That is our past. That is creation's past. One of the questions that poses itself is, *Are we entirely bound by, and to, that past?* Is it not possible that the real momentum of creation is not so much an anchoring in the past, but an invitation, an opening up of new possibilities, from God's envisioned future?

---

38. Sermon 60, "The General Deliverance," §II.6, *Works* 2:445.

Another question that poses itself is, *Given the evolutionary scenario of death, dead ends, and creaturely pain and frustration, can we still call God's creation* good? Wesley assumed the traditional scenario: creation began as "good" but became corrupted and polluted by human sin. Thus Wesley could conclude his imaginations about Eden by preaching, "How true then is that word, 'God saw everything that he had made: and behold it was very good.' But how far is this from being the case now!"[39] But in order to offer this reading of Genesis, and of creation, Wesley had to ignore the New Testament judgment that "everything created by God is good, and nothing is to be rejected, provided it is received with thanksgiving" (1 Tim. 4:4). In other words, it is a biblical and Christian conviction that the goodness of God's creation is to be affirmed, even acknowledging the presence of destructive effects of sin.

But can a *groaning* creation also be considered a *good* creation? Perhaps we must acknowledge that the goodness of God's creation is a project yet-in-the-making, and thus in a sense the naming of an eschatological hope. Simply stated, it is a *divine hope for the world's future*! "The God of hope" yet longs for a world in which love might flourish! The goodness of creation is a *telos* toward which God our Maker, Molder, and Mender is laboring, and for which creation "has been groaning in labor pains until now." Further, human beings are not simply to join in the groaning and wait passively for deliverance; we groan, yes, but we can also act, as Wesley himself was to point out in this same sermon. Even a cursory reading of Genesis 1, that strongest biblical claim for creation's goodness, reminds us that human beings are created in God's image precisely in order to re-present or image God in the world. Hence, the goodness of creation is "a charge to keep," a calling to be fulfilled; we are charged with considerable responsibility to co-labor with God *toward the goodness of creation.*

The goodness of creation is in this case something of an open question; creation's goodness (at least as far as our planet is concerned) hangs in the balance of human accountability as a project on which, as it were, the jury is still out. If it is indeed the case that "everything created by God is good, and nothing is to be rejected," and that "God . . . richly provides us with everything for our

39. Ibid., §I.6, 2:441-42.

enjoyment" (1 Tim. 4:4, 6:17), a critical question arises regarding *who* the "us" is, *whose* enjoyment is "our enjoyment." God's creation cannot be felt to be "good" by a starving child or a tortured animal. We disciples of Jesus Christ are called upon by God "to do good, to be rich in good works, generous, and ready to share" (1 Tim. 6:18)—which is surely a call to live in this world toward creation's goodness for as many of God's creatures as we are able. If sanctification is about the hallowing of all of life, then the divine labor of sanctification is not limited to the human heart and life but is cosmic in scope. Paul's ruminations in Romans 8, perhaps especially as read and proclaimed by Wesley, inspire us to perceive the Spirit's sanctifying work in all of creation.

So it is that, as we have seen, near the conclusion of his sermon Wesley writes that "one more excellent end" in reflecting upon Romans 8 is that it may encourage us to imitate God, whose mercies extend to all of creation.[40] I believe that this is the *most* "excellent end" of Wesley's proposed ends served by his, and our, reflections upon a general deliverance of creation. For here Wesley hints at a "practical eschatology"—a vision and hope for the world in which we are called to participate and for which we are challenged to strive. Hence, we are beckoned by a hope for the future to act in behalf of that hope. We are beckoned, in Wesley's words, to "habituate ourselves to look forward."[41] Not, however, only to *look*—but to *act*, to imitate the Creator whose compassion flows to every last creature.

This final consideration helps us to reiterate the overall tack of this chapter. All of creation is in-the-making; all creatures receive life from the hoped-for future that God in Christ both gives and embodies. But human beings appear to play a particularly crucial role in this being-toward-the-future. We are the creatures who truly and consciously anticipate what is to come, who can act with possible futures in mind, whose self-conscious momentum—even when we sometimes feel chained to our pasts—is always forward. It appears that the future toward which we are moving is not a static or foreclosed given, but has more of the character of a vision to be enacted, a lure to be striven for, a possibility itching to be

40. Ibid., §III.10, 2:449.
41. Ibid.

realized. The specific future called for in "The General Deliverance" is one in which human beings act in mercy and compassion toward their fellow creatures, a future in which we "soften our hearts towards the meaner creatures."[42] This is not a matter of romanticizing nature as though to pretend that all creatures are cute as bunnies, but it is to live toward the conviction that "the Lord careth for them. It may enlarge our hearts towards those poor creatures to reflect that, as vile as they appear in our eyes, not one of them is forgotten in the sight of our Father which is in heaven."[43]

Wesley's eschatological vision for the redemption of all creation, if read with a discerning eye, is captivating and challenging. It must be reinterpreted in the light of our better informed understanding of the immense and painstaking history of our planet and indeed of our universe, but his hope for all of God's creatures can nevertheless enlarge our hearts and our minds to think radically hopeful possibilities for this groaning creation, to groan in solidarity along with it by the power of the Spirit, and to throw our energies into living toward creation's deliverance from bondage and toward its goodness. To do so is to live in the reality of a world to come that is, we hope and trust, always already *coming*. We confess with 1 John that "what we will be has not yet been revealed," and yet our confidence in behalf of all creation is toward a future that glimmers in the light of Christ. In this interpretation of the creatures human and nonhuman, our truest identity is hidden in the destiny for which, and toward which, God is hoping to create all things.

42. Ibid.
43. Ibid.

CHAPTER 9

"AND NEW-CREATE A WORLD OF GRACE"

Shall the World Reflect God's Love?

Spirit Immense, Eternal Mind,
Thou on the Souls of lost Mankind
Dost with benignest Influence move,
Pleased to restore the ruined Race,
And new-create a World of Grace
In all the Image of Thy Love.

Charles Wesley, *Hymns of Petition and Thanksgiving for the Promise of the Father*, #28

Our universe is a world on the go. It appears to have begun somewhere between fifteen and twenty billion years ago in an unimaginably hot explosion of impossibly dense quantum protomatter and has been continually expanding and arranging itself in surprising and wondrous ways ever since. It appears that we human beings and other living creatures are presently thriving on our beautiful blue-green orb during a relatively narrow window in the universe's life of star generations, during a virtual sliver of time in the universe's long but always dynamic duration. Precarious change is of the essence in this strange world we inhabit.

For centuries Christians have sung,

Glory be to the Father, and to the Son and to the Holy Ghost.
As it was in the beginning, is now and ever shall be:
World without end, Amen, Amen.

But it is not now how it was in the beginning, and it seems highly unlikely that it shall remain forever as it is now. Things change, and a world without end is certainly not the sort of world that most astronomers, physicists, and cosmologists currently project. Instead, given the continuing if qualified dominance of a big bang scenario for our universe's origin, most cosmological conjectures follow one of two routes: if the rate of the universe's expansion is sufficient to outrun the slow but relentless drag of gravity, our world will eventually dissipate, writes physicist Paul Davies, into vast reaches of "cold, dark, expanding, near-empty space, populated at an ever-decreasing density by a few isolated neutrinos and photons, and very little else"; if, on the other hand, the gravitational effects of our universe's matter finally win the cosmic tug-of-war, at some point billions of years from now the universe will begin slowly but inexorably to contract until it "shrivels into less than the size of an atom, whereupon spacetime itself disintegrates."[1] One might suggest that, at least in terms of this model, our world's *destiny* depends upon its *density*. Though there is no unanimity among physicists on this matter, the latest projections tend to favor Davies's first scenario, in which the elements of the universe continue to expand ever outward toward ultimate entropy: cold, dark, and lifeless.

What implications, if any, does this bleak cosmological destiny hold for Christian eschatology? One might even wonder whether the variety of possible fates of the universe, billions upon billions of years ahead, are actually relevant to Christian faith, practice, or reflection. In the past three decades or so, largely under the impulse and leadership of German theologians Jürgen Moltmann and Wolfhart Pannenberg, issues of eschatology have assumed a crucial and central role in Christian theology. This renewed regard for the category of a universal hope has been instrumental in breaking Christian faith out of its captivity to Western individualism and dualism, for a primary thrust of contemporary eschatological reflection has been to recognize the Pauline vision of a renewed and fulfilled *creation*. This in turn has inspired a much-needed critique of the all-too-traditional Christian understanding of redemption, essentially gnostic in nature, that even today tends to envision

1. Davies, *God and the New Physics*, 204, 205.

salvation as the individual soul's postmortem ascent to heaven. Further, Paul's much more inclusive, cosmic, and corporeal view of God's redemption of the world through Christ has become increasingly compelling in our age of ecological crisis.

Such values as these are all to the good. The particular issue I wish to explore in this final chapter, however, is whether or not the predicted demise of the universe, albeit many billions of years away, raises serious challenges to a biblical eschatology that teaches us to hope for a redemption for all of creation.

Theologian and physicist Robert John Russell has argued that this issue is of critical importance to Christian eschatology, and thus to Christian faith. He suggests that the apparent futility and relative brevity of life in the universe have "contributed to disbelief in a God who is 'trustworthy.'" When the long-range projections of cosmologists provide our theological context—and they must "if we are to take creation seriously," argues Russell—then "our ability to construct an adequate theology of creation is challenged to the core as nowhere else."[2] Indeed, even the generally temperate Anglican theologian John Macquarrie went so far as to write that "if it were shown that the universe is indeed headed for an all-enveloping death, then this might seem to constitute a state of affairs so negative that it might be held to falsify Christian faith and abolish Christian hope."[3]

It is arguable, then, that the tension between the eschatological hope for all creation and cosmological predictions about the universe's demise is not trivial. Indeed, if Russell is correct in claiming that such predictions challenge "to the core" our attempts to construct an adequate theology of creation, then the endeavor to rethink eschatology within the context of cosmological prognoses is crucial. This shall be our task in this final chapter. We shall undertake it by exploring the ideas of a handful of process theologians, all Methodists, who have attempted to address issues of eschatology. By now this recourse to process thinkers comes as no surprise, given the obvious debt I owe to this theological tradition that resonates in certain significant ways with a Wesleyan reading

2. Robert John Russell, "Cosmology and Eschatology: The Implications of Tipler's 'Omega-Point' Theory for Pannenberg's Theological Program," in Albright and Haugen, eds., Beginning with the End, 196.

3. John Macquarrie, *Principles of Christian Theology* (London: SCM, 1977), 256.

of the world. I do not believe, however, that we can *end* our eschatological reflections with the process conversation, and we will try to move beyond it, finally, by looking once more to Wesley and his sermon "The General Deliverance."

Schubert Ogden and the Reality of Our Creaturehood

While the notion of "objective immortality" can typically be found in the musings of many process theologians, one of the most concise and best-known declarations of the idea appeared in Schubert Ogden's 1975 article, "The Meaning of Christian Hope."[4] In this piece Ogden characterizes what he calls "the traditional mythology of Christian hope" as "an amalgam of Jewish apocalypticism and Gnosticism" and therefore "nothing specifically Christian." His criterion for deciding what *is* "specifically Christian" is "the specifically Christian understanding of man's relation to God," defined by Ogden as "the boundless love whereby all lives are knit together into one integral and everlasting life."[5] For Ogden, this criterion does not necessarily entail the notion of subjective immortality, that is, of the human being existing after death as a conscious, self-aware intelligence. As an alternative to this notion, he suggests:

> Because what is ultimately real is not merely the world but God's all-inclusive love of the world, there is a ground for hope beyond the limits of a world of death and transience. Although it is the destiny of the world and of everything in it that it should come to be and pass away, the world is nevertheless the good creation of God and the object of his everlasting love. Thus whatever is created is also redeemed, in the sense that it is fully embraced by God's love and there cherished forever for exactly what it is.[6]

---

4. Schubert Ogden, "The Meaning of Christian Hope," *Union Seminary Review* 30 (1975): 153-64. I recognize that Ogden has offered subsequent reflections that nuance what he says in this brief article. I focus on it, not as Ogden's last word, but as emblematic of a dominant sentiment in process thought. The article also played a crucial role in instigating much of the subsequent theological conversation explored in the present chapter.

5. Ibid., 160, 158.

6. Ibid., 159.

Note Ogden's stipulation that it is "the destiny of the world and of everything in it that it should come to be and pass away." He apparently accepts that, as creatures in this world, we all shall someday be no more, at least as subjects of experience. But he does not believe that this fundamentally contradicts the Christian hope that "in spite of the death and transience of all things, their [and our] final destiny is to be embraced everlastingly by God's love for them." The contradiction is avoided, Ogden goes on to suggest, if we do not assume that the divine embrace entails our "subjective survival of death, but our objective immortality or resurrection in God, our being finally accepted and judged by his love, and thus imperishably united with all creation into his own unending life."[7] In other words, all that is essential to Christian hope is the conviction that we creatures shall be everlastingly remembered and cherished by God, and this should be enough for us. Indeed, Ogden suggests that the more traditional hope for subjective immortality is generally rooted in self-assertion and even idolatry, an expression of our stubborn and sinful refusals to accept our creaturely limits.

When Christian hope is understood in Ogden's terms, the eventual demise of our universe also poses it no fundamental challenge. We are creatures in a creaturely world that is in a continual process of coming-to-be and perishing. The only "resurrection" that our universe needs is one that it is always undergoing by being lovingly experienced, and somehow integrated into, the unimaginably rich life of the omniscient God. It is a kind of resurrection *in* God.

We should appreciate the positive value in Ogden's acknowledgment of creaturely transience and finitude, for it connects well with the Hebrew Bible's insistence that all creatures, including humans, are *dust*. Indeed, Scripture's testimony about the finitude of creaturely existence pertains to creation as a whole. As we saw in chapter 7, the opening chapter of Hebrews stitches together several quotations from the Hebrew Bible to testify to the finitude of creation: "In the beginning, Lord, you founded the earth, and the heavens are the work of your hands; they will perish, but you remain; they will all wear out like clothing; like a cloak you will roll them up, and like clothing they will be changed. But you are the

7. Ibid., 160.

same, and your years will never end" (Heb. 1:10-12). Scripture repeatedly states that heaven and earth shall pass away, going the route of all creaturely "flesh," and thus all creation is clearly distinguished from the God whose word shall never pass away. In this regard, a universe that eventually shall "freeze or fry" seems quite consonant with the harsh realism of at least some strands of thought in the Bible.

It is important to recognize, however, that the universe's creatureliness would not *necessitate* its temporal demise any more than the doctrine of *creatio ex nihilo* necessitates a dramatic temporal beginning point. As Russell has insisted, the finite age of the universe as implied in the Big Bang cosmology may contribute "corroborating evidence" for the doctrine of creation, but that the fundamental issue in *ex nihilo* is not that the universe has a temporal beginning point.[8] Indeed, one of the arguments of chapter 3 of this book was that the point of *ex nihilo* is primarily negative; its first purpose is to exclude the notion that there is a nondivine reality that exists by metaphysical necessity rather than by the will of God, a reality that God is constrained to use in the shaping of creation. If one would look for a positive implication of *ex nihilo*, it would be that the universe is utterly contingent and ontologically dependent upon the creative, sustaining power of God. There is nothing in this idea of contingency or dependency that would demand a temporal beginning for the universe; the universe could *in principle* be God's finite creation but nonetheless exist everlastingly by the power of divine love. Likewise, there seems to be no theological reason the universe as a whole should expire, and in fact an implication—indeed, virtually a prediction—of the argument in chapter 7 is that God's continuous creation of world upon world shall have no end.[9] Even so, the main point here is that the cosmologists' predictions that our universe shall gradually expire should not necessarily come as a surprise or disappointment to those of us shaped by biblical traditions.

Ogden does a service, then, to remind us of the creaturely status of the universe and all it contains, including us. The biblical insistence that all creatures are dust or, to employ another biblical

8. See Robert Russell, "Cosmology from Alpha to Omega," *Zygon* 29 (1994): 560.

9. I have also argued along these lines in *Shekhinah/Spirit*, particularly in Part III, "The Spirit of God and the Problem of Eschatology."

metaphor, that "all flesh is grass," implies strongly that it is natural for creatures to degenerate, die, and decay. Admittedly, there is a dominant tradition in Christianity that death is somehow a result of sin; after all, Paul did write that "sin came into the world through one man, and death came through sin" (Rom. 5:12), so it is not unusual to hear Christians still make the assumption that death is an alien invader, an unnatural intrusion into God's original purposes. Of course this notion overlooks the blunt fact that all creatures who have lived on this planet have done so at the expense of other creatures, and there is no good or compelling reason to believe that there was a time when those conditions were different. The death of many creatures is necessary to the ongoing sustenance of those who live. "The young lions" may indeed "roar for their prey, seeking their food from God," as the psalmist writes (104:21), but zebras and gazelles are not necessarily happy with that arrangement. But this is the way of creation, not a strange or unexpected result of sin. As Moltmann asks facetiously in *The Coming of God*, "Did the dinosaurs become extinct because of the sin of the human beings who did not yet exist?"[10] Many fundamentalist creationists reject old-earth and evolutionary models at least partly on the grounds that they make death an inevitable aspect of the processes of life, rather than seeing death as a curse or result of human sin. Instead, we must understand that the tooth and claw of creation are not *evil* but in fact *necessary* to the kind of world we inhabit. Whatever else we might say about cosmic redemption, it cannot imply that somehow death is an unintended or unmitigated evil. We are dust, and to dust shall return.

For the majority of process theologians, following the tendencies of Whitehead and his best-known theological interpreter Charles Hartshorne, the only immortality likely to be available to us is the objective immortality Ogden described in his early essay: our being remembered lovingly, and everlastingly, by God. This may seem to be a tenuous thread of eschatological hope, but it does keep the focus on our living and acting *now*. John Haught, who in his stimulating little book *The Promise of Nature* brings a process perspective to bear on ecological ethics, writes, "We preserve nature,

10. Jürgen Moltmann, *The Coming of God: Christian Eschatology* (Minneapolis: Fortress, 1996), 83.

among other reasons, because part of its promise is to add depth and intensity to God's own experience."[11] For the process tradition, our efforts to save and sustain the creation contribute to God's own ever-enriched appreciation of the world. Perhaps if we followed strictly enough Hartshorne's dictum that we take with utter seriousness the first commandment—to love God with all our heart, soul, mind, and strength—it would be enough that our lives and efforts contribute to God's own experience of the world, and thereby also to God's capacity to call the world toward greater depths of peace and satisfaction.

We may certainly want to affirm the tone of this selfless sentiment; the question is, is it *enough*? To live and to act only for the sake of the love of God sounds noble and self-sacrificial, but finally, what sort of God would we be loving? Is such a God truly one of boundless love, as Ogden insists—a deity who seems to "use" the creatures as modes of experience whereby God is enriched?

Ogden has shown a strong predilection for identifying God as boundless love—in this he is likely echoing Charles Wesley's hymnic line, "Pure, unbounded love Thou art"—and insists that for Christian faith such divine love as this is "decisively re-presented in Jesus Christ."[12] But in the New Testament, especially in Paul's writings, both the death *and* the resurrection of Jesus are appealed to as revealing God's unbounded love (1 John 4:8, 16; cf. Rom. 8:31-35). And the biblical accounts of the resurrected Jesus interacting with his disciples make little sense if he was not a subject (i.e., *subjectively present*) in the interactions. It is hard to understand how one can affirm fully the revelation of God in the person and work of Jesus Christ without accepting the implications of the gospel proclamation that the Christ, who died once for all, now truly *lives*—or, to put it in Paul's words, that "the life [Christ] lives, he lives to God" (Rom. 6:10). And this proclamation is centrally connected in the New Testament to the eschatological promise that those who belong to Christ "will be like him, for we will see him as he is" (1 John 3:2). This certainly seems to imply more than just our "objective immortality" in God's loving memory!

Ogden appropriately quotes from 1 Timothy 6:16 that it is God

11. Haught, *Promise of Nature*, 134.
12. See, for example, Ogden, "Meaning of Christian Hope," 158, 159.

"alone who has immortality and dwells in unapproachable light, whom no one has ever seen or can see." This is a very important contribution to our consideration of eschatology in a cosmological context: the world, including its human inhabitants, is a creaturely, mortal realm. Only God is immortal by nature, and Christian theology should reject all attempts to deny our creaturely finitude. However, in this article Ogden appears to assume that our finitude excludes the possibility that God can and will *gift* the creature with eternal life, will fill the creature with divine life and love, will draw the creature into unspeakable divine reality itself. It is precisely because God is "pure, unbounded Love" that God is also the one who, in Paul's words, "gives life to the dead and calls into existence the things that do not exist" (Rom. 4:17). Proper as it is to cite 1 Timothy 6:16 regarding divine immortality, surely it is not unfair to cite the same letter when its author states that training in godliness "hold[s] promise for both the present life and the life to come" (4:8), or when he clearly identifies "the life that really is life" with "the future" (6:19). Surely God alone possesses immortality, but apparently the God and Father of our Lord Jesus Christ is not above *sharing the divine life*, or gifting the creature with the Creator's own Spirit, in such a way that God does not *possess* but instead *passes on* God's own life to the creaturely, the finite, the mortal.

Against the tendency in Christian tradition to adopt the philosophical assumption of our *native* immortality, Ogden's emphasis helps us remember deeply and in our bones that we truly are frail, transient, vulnerable, and mortal creatures. For this we should be grateful, since it requires of us a humble recognition of creaturely finitude in order to appreciate the wildly unexpected, virtually unimaginable nature of the resurrection for which most Christians (along with Muslims and many Jews) hope—and thus to appreciate that such a hope is a matter of sheer and amazing *grace*.

MARJORIE SUCHOCKI AND THE PROBLEM OF EVIL

In response to Ogden's programmatic essay, Marjorie Suchocki wrote an essay entitled "The Question of Immortality" in which she initiated an extended argument for the necessity of *subjective immortality*.[13] In essence, Suchocki has argued that the issue of theodicy demands an eschatology that includes subjective immortality. In her words, "The victory of God over evil must be greater than that which is experienced in the world, either individually or as a whole—but only a doctrine of God which allows subjective immortality for the world can provide such a vision of redemption."[14]

For Suchocki, then, the perduring issue has been *justice*. It is one thing for privileged, well-educated, and well-fed theologians to say that this life is all there is, and quite another thing to say it to starving children, or to political prisoners tortured to death, or to the more than ten million victims of Nazi labor and death camps. There simply has been too much waste, pain, and carnage in creaturely experience to restrict the overcoming of evil to a privileged experience within God's omniscient experience. Suchocki is correct to inquire about this "boundless love" that Ogden insists is the very nature of God: if God really does love us humans and indeed the whole of creation, then it is proper and necessary to ask about the radical injustices and sufferings of our world. Is God finally able to overcome evil? Suchocki is confident that the answer is yes—and God's overcoming of evil must include our conscious awareness and participation as subjects even after death.

Suchocki has tried to argue for subjective immortality within the confines of process categories, seeking hints even in the writings of Whitehead and Hartshorne. In her article "Charles Hartshorne and Subjective Immortality," Suchocki has suggested that "co-experiencing might work both ways: that God co-experiences our suffering with us, and that we co-experience its transformation in and therefore with God."[15] It is crucial, though, to keep in mind that for process theologians, God's experience and redemption of the world is a present, ongoing reality. There is no notion of some future *eschaton* in which all shall be well; rather, God continuously receives or "prehends" the countless momentary experiences of all

13. Marjorie Suchocki, "The Question of Immortality," *Journal of Religion* 57 (1977): 288-306.
14. Ibid., 298.
15. Marjorie Suchocki, "Charles Hartshorne and Subjective Immortality," *Process Studies* 21 (1992): 119.

creatures into the immense wealth of God's own becoming, weaving those experiences into a kind of eschatological fulfillment *within* God. This is why Ogden could speak of our "resurrection in God," but he, like many (if not most) other process thinkers, sees this as involving not *our* conscious participation or awareness, but rather *God's* awareness and everlasting remembrance of us. The essential point where Suchocki veers from the process mainstream is in her arguing that even our own moment-by-moment experiences of subjectivity are "prehended," or received into, God precisely as *occasions of subjectivity*. In this scenario, "I" (in the virtually countless occasions "I" undergo) continually and repeatedly am received and integrated into the dynamic life-experience of God precisely as the "I" who is the subject of experience. Since God receives the world into the divine experience and becoming, *and* since my own subjective experiences of this world are in fact a part of the world that God receives, then God must receive my experiences precisely as "my own"! The subjective knower must exist in God's own experience precisely as an "I," a knowing subject. Therefore we may legitimately hope for a subjective immortality, and not only an objective immortality as a series of events in God's memory.

Lest the prospects of being integrated into the life of God sound overly trite or decidedly lacking in the element of divine judgment that would be necessary to Suchocki's own concerns for justice, it must be said that she has developed a finely nuanced doctrine of judgment. She writes:

> [J]udgment would be in the form of the fullness of self-knowledge . . . a self-knowledge never possible in the limitations of finite existence: the individual would know as he [or] she was known. This would mean that, as successive occasions affected by one's actions were added to the nature of God, one would feel one's completion through others, be it for good or ill. For the knowledge of oneself in God would include the living feeling of one's effects . . . [and also] would include a knowledge of what he [or] she might have been.[16]

16. Suchocki, "Question of Immortality," 303-4.

There is much in this understanding of divine judgment to commend itself to us: our lives are judged not in terms of an atomistic individualism, but within the entire context of the world and the effects of our lives in it. Accordingly, it is a judgment that can only be completed in "the end of the world." Who we are, what we have believed, how we have lived, cannot be extracted from that all-embracing, universal flow of the world of relations in and from which we exist. To know as we are known, to feel the world as God feels the world, would also be to know and feel what our living has meant and means to God's creation as a whole. (Imagine what such an experience would entail for a Hitler; contrarily, imagine such an experience for Mother Teresa.)

The gospel, of course, assures us that such a judgment occurs under the merciful eye and gracious care of God in Christ, so that we are not simply left on our own and to our own devices, as it were, to experience eschatologically a kind of karmic retribution/reward for our lives. I suspect that in such an experience of cosmic self-knowledge we shall be loved, judged, and purged by the God who loves the world (cf. John 3:16, 19-21). On this point, we might consider the evidence in what Ted Peters, taking a cue from John Hick, has called "para-eschatology"—in this case specifically in the testimonies of people who have undergone so-called "near-death" experiences and have testified to "seeing" their entire lives, and intimately "feeling" all the effects of their lives on the world, for good or for ill.[17] Many such people testify to having undergone that harrowing and winnowing experience in the palpable presence of the light of Love.

The problem that Suchocki must wrestle with, however, is that of "when" and "how often" (for lack of more appropriate adverbs) such a judgment occurs. In her process/subjective immortality scenario, a virtually innumerable multitude of momentary subjective experiences—all of them "I"—have been and continue to be received into the ongoing, vastly complex life of God, there to be judged, purged, and fulfilled in God's satisfaction of all things. Describing this as "the problem of 'the million Marjories,'" she writes: "I am bound by the metaphysics to

17. Peters, "The Physical Body of Immortality," *Center for Theology and the Natural Sciences Bulletin* 15:2 (Spring 1995): 14-15.

posit not that God prehends each finite person and so resurrects the person, but that God prehends each finite occasion, and so resurrects the occasions, some of which are indeed personal. What are we to do with so many of ourselves around?"[18]

Suchocki has offered some noble and typically novel attempts to answer her own question, and while these proposals have not been without value, the fact that the Whiteheadian metaphysic, when combined with a belief in the necessity of subjective immortality, is forced to entertain such a question suggests that either the metaphysic or the belief needs to be revised if not rejected. To quote her out of context, she is "bound by the metaphysics"; I wonder if such binding might be unloosed by returning to the Christian proclamation of the resurrection of Jesus from the dead as the beginning and grounding point for our speculations about subjective immortality. In this light, I offer three criticisms of Suchocki's eschatology.

First, by binding herself to the process metaphysical system, Suchocki seeks solace primarily in the traces of subjective immortality in the writings of Whitehead and Hartshorne. Even as a broadly processive thinker, I find the language and hope of Scripture to be much more compelling, relevant, and persuasive. Suchocki's argument for subjective immortality is in no way tied specifically or particularly to Jesus' resurrection, such that God could be typified as the One "who raised Jesus our Lord from the dead" (Rom. 4:24). Instead, she begins with a Whiteheadian metaphysic grounded in the processive and transient nature of our experience of the world, and injects that metaphysic with the hopeful expectation that its deity shall overcome evil. This victory over evil, she argues, can only be complete if we creatures subjectively experience this victory in God. She movingly writes, "It seems a strange anomaly if, in a thoroughly relational metaphysics, God alone in solitary splendor is the only one to experience the fullness of justice."[19] But of course, given the Whiteheadian metaphysic, she still has the problem of "a million Marjories" (in which case, to be sure, God would *hardly* be "alone in solitary splendor"!)—a problem that is adequately addressed in the specificity of the singular

18. Marjorie Suchocki, "Evil, Eschatology, and God: Response to David Griffin," *Process Studies* 18 (1989): 67.

19. Suchocki, "Hartshorne and Subjective Immortality," 119.

resurrection of Jesus Christ from the dead. While we surely do not comprehend what this act of God entails, shrouded as it is in mystery, we are certain that it somehow involves the entirety of Jesus' socio/psychosomatic being. It is not the mental, spiritual, or subjective experiences alone that are "raised up in glory" by God; it is the whole person.

A second, related criticism is that the subjective immortality that Suchocki espouses, given her process metaphysics, sounds suspiciously gnostic. All the gains that contemporary eschatology has made in its hope for the fulfillment of creation *as creation* seem to disappear in her eschatological scenario. While there is a fulfillment for all occasions as they are prehended by God and thus become integrated and beautified in God, it is difficult to see how that experience *of God's* makes any real difference for this creaturely realm we inhabit in this moment (or in any future moments). In *God, Christ, Church* Suchocki claims that her eschatology requires "subjective immortality for the world within the life of God"; she goes to considerable lengths to align this with Christian belief in the resurrection of the body, and then to extend this hope to "the entirety of the world, in all its manifold forms." However, she proceeds to clarify, "This resurrection is spiritual, not material. . . . [T]he subjectivities that are resurrected in God are no longer definable in terms of material togetherness. Materiality falls away, since the conditions for materiality do not exist in the single reality of God. Resurrection is to a spiritual body."[20] Thus the "hope of the age to come" is nothing shared with us by the nonhuman creaturely elements and experiences. There is no ultimate salvation for this material world—nothing more than what we experience right now. Even if in God the events of this world are weaved lovingly into a divine tapestry of experience, it apparently means relatively little to this transient, creaturely, material world *right now* or at any time later.

Suchocki's line of reasoning is as clear and cogent as her prose, and within the process metaphysic it makes good sense. It seems, too, to soften the problem of the eventual demise of our universe; after all, authentic creaturely fulfillment occurs everlastingly in God rather than in the observable or foreseeable universe, so it

20. Suchocki, *God, Christ, Church*, 205, 206.

really does not matter, ultimately, what occurs in this world of ours. To put it bluntly, however, her eschatology is simply *too spiritual* for a healthy doctrine of creation. Granted, the apostle Paul does use the phrase *soma pneumatica*, or "spiritual body" (1 Cor. 15:44). It is clear both in the context of that passage and in the Gospel descriptions of the resurrected Jesus, though, that there is a real, identifiable continuity between the earthly body and the resurrection body. Materiality does not simply "fall away," as though it is of no use or interest either to us or to the God who redeems us in Christ.

The upshot is that we must insist on a more robust interpretation of resurrection than what Suchocki offers, even if it causes metaphysical fits. Russell is correct: "The historicity of the Resurrection keeps Christianity from a Gnostic, world-denying tendency and opens the door to nature's relation to eschatology."[21] The Christian creeds have had sound instincts to confess that Jesus has been raised in all respects "appertaining to the perfection of man's nature,"[22] a confession that has been properly interpreted to include the body.

This leads to a third criticism. Suchocki intends her eschatology to provide a theodicy not simply for human beings, but for all creatures in their struggles and sufferings. But it is *precisely as bodies* that all of us creatures exist in this material world, and Suchocki's emphasis on spiritual resurrection and subjective experience, while not necessarily excluding all other creatures, nonetheless drops hints of anthropocentric elitism. It certainly fosters a spiritual/material dualism that does not honor well the flesh, blood, bone, rock, plant, and water of our world—to say nothing of the elements of other worlds. This, again, solves the problem of our universe's final expiration by finally subtly devaluing materiality and retreating to a resurrection that occurs "within" God. After Christian theologians in the past few decades have labored so diligently to enlarge our eschatological vision and hope to include the material, nonhuman world, it is disappointing to read

21. Russell, "Cosmology from Alpha to Omega," 572.

22. The third Anglican Article, concerning the resurrection of Christ, as cited by Thomas C. Oden, *Doctrinal Standards in the Wesleyan Tradition* (Grand Rapids: Francis Asbury Press, 1988), 113. Oden's study traces the language of this and other Anglican Articles through the various branches of the Wesleyan tradition.

that "the resurrection is spiritual, not material" or that "materiality falls away." We ought not surrender this ground so quickly!

In Ogden's essay we find a theological model in which we do not presume to expect the Creator, even as boundless love, to *gift* the creature with the transforming, divinizing Spirit, or to *lift* the creature, precisely as an experiencing subject, into God's eternity. In Suchocki we find a theological model in which God can *sift* the creature, as it were, and save it "spiritually" while "materiality falls away." This *rift* between the spiritual and the material means that, for Suchocki, creation's multifarious bodies are not destined for "the freedom of the glory of the children of God" (Rom. 8:21). Neither model is consonant with the Christian confession that the Word became flesh and thereby entered into the creaturely realm as a fellow human creature to redeem and restore creation, nor with the Christian confession that this same Jesus of Nazareth was raised from death in such a way that his body was transformed and "taken up in glory."

JOHN WESLEY AND GOD'S UNBOUNDED LOVE

Both Ogden and Suchocki are United Methodists and possess more than a passing knowledge of John Wesley; Suchocki in particular has speculated on the possible connections between Wesley's thought and the apparent attractions of process theology for theologians in the Wesleyan tradition.[23] It is a legitimate transition, then, to turn in this final section of this final chapter, as we have so often, to the founder of Methodism.

For most of his career as an evangelist and pastoral theologian, Wesley assumed the traditional dualistic and privatistic eschatology that concerned itself with the soul's fate at death. It is thus all the more fascinating that, near the end of his life, his preaching on eschatological themes took a distinctive turn toward the biblical hope of a renewed creation.[24] Some of the sermons we have explored in this book reflect Wesley's interesting shift, but

23. See Suchocki's "Coming Home: Wesley, Whitehead, and Women," *The Drew Gateway*, 57 (1987), 49-65.

24. For a particularly instructive treatment, see Maddox, *Responsible Grace*, 252-53.

undoubtedly the most dramatic example is the sermon that occupied much of our attention in chapter 8: his 1781 sermon "The General Deliverance," based on the apostle Paul's vision of cosmic liberation in Romans 8.

If Wesley is correct in his reading of Paul—that God truly does love all the creatures in their variety and particularity—then perhaps it is not surprising that, like Suchocki two centuries later, Wesley saw the problem of evil as a central issue for eschatology. We have already noted Wesley's relatively unusual concern with the problem of animal suffering as an aspect of theodicy. He was adamant: "Away with vulgar prejudices, and let the plain word of God take place. . . . While 'the whole creation groaneth together' (whether men attend or not) their groans are not dispersed in idle air, but enter into the ears of him that made them."[25] God not only hears the cries of the creatures, Wesley preached, but shall indeed answer their cry in the future glory of the new creation.

Wesley did not explicitly mention resurrection as the divine act whereby these creatures shall be delivered, but it is strongly implied. In one place in "The General Deliverance" he refers to Jesus' words about the resurrection of the dead, spoken in response to Sadducees, in which Jesus describes God as "God not of the dead, but of the living; for to him all of them are alive" (Luke 20:38). For Wesley, the "all of them [who] are alive" would include not just human beings but all creatures. Hence, he speculates:

> May I be permitted to mention here a conjecture concerning the brute creation? What if it should then please the all-wise, the all-gracious Creator, to raise them higher in the scale of beings? What if it should please him, when he makes us "equal to angels" (Luke 20:36), to make them what we are now? Creatures capable of God? Capable of knowing, and loving, and enjoying the Author of their being? If it should be so, ought our eye to be evil because [God] is good?[26]

Wesley was willing to anticipate, then, that the groaning of all creatures of God's vast creation shall be answered by their Maker

25. Sermon 60, "The General Deliverance," §II.2, 1, *Works* 2:445.
26. Ibid., §III.6, 2:448.

and Mender in the resurrection. Wesley certainly did not concern himself with the particulars of such an act of God, but it is a staggering notion, given our more extensive knowledge about the age of the earth and the virtually numberless creatures who have lived in its complex systems over the past many millions of years. Frankly, it makes "the problem of 'a million Marjories'" seem small by comparison! And if we want to hold fast our insistence that the resurrection of the world's creatures really does involve materiality and some kind of continuity with the bodies we are now, another problem is clearer to us than it would have been to Wesley: our bodies, both in this present moment and then over the vast aeons of bustling life on this planet, are so thoroughly enmeshed and interconnected with the rest of the earth, its creatures, and its atmosphere that it would be entirely impossible to delineate where one body ends and another begins. Once again, the realism of the Hebrew Bible is instructive: we are all recycled and recycling *dust*.

What, then, can it mean to speak of the resurrection of the body, particularly as we extend such a hope well beyond humans to include all creatures? Such a question stretches our feeble imaginations to their limits. Granted, Wesley points us in a helpful direction by trying to address the problem of creaturely suffering, and by grounding his reflections in the Christian hope of the resurrection of the body. But we need more help than Wesley can offer in order to press the implications of this hope.

John A. T. Robinson in the early 1950s published a series of essays on eschatology called *In the End, God*. One of those essays, "The Resurrection of the Body," is most helpful in tackling the question with which Wesley leaves us: Given the nature and dynamics of the living systems of planet Earth over the past many millions of years, *what in the world* would the resurrection of all creatures entail? Robinson helps with this question by directing our thinking toward the implications of the Greek word *soma* (body). In his words,

> The *soma* (or body) . . . is the whole psycho-physical unity of man as created for God. It is the nearest word in Greek for "personality" . . . [but] it is not personality as it has been defined abstractly in the Western philosophical tradition, especially since Descartes. It is not the "self" prior to and apart from its relationships. *Soma* is the whole [person] constituted by the network of

> physical and mental relationships in which [the person] is bound up with other persons and things.[27]

Whereas Suchocki was content to speak movingly about the network of mental or spiritual relationships that perdure while "materiality falls away," Robinson's analysis of *soma*—even when it is Paul's "spiritual body"—will not allow such an ethereal interpretation. But neither will his analysis allow an individualistic, narrow, typically Western interpretation of the body. Robinson continues later, "The body . . . is, on this view, the symbol not of individuality but of solidarity. It is that which binds each individual, divinely unique as [he or she] is, in inescapable relatedness with the whole of nature and history and the cosmic order."[28]

Lutheran theologian Philip Hefner has authored a similarly insightful piece on the nature of resurrection in the wake of Ogden's watershed article on objective immortality. Each of us, wrote Hefner,

> [is] the enfleshed reality of many other persons, living and dead. . . . and I am dependent on the network of relationships with persons and nature for my selfhood. What will my resurrection after death be? It cannot be a resurrection of "me" without this ecological network, else it will not be the real "me."[29]

This is a crucial point, and it is well stated. If the resurrection of "me" includes this vast, virtually unending ecological network, then there is no boundary line to be drawn on what constitutes this "me." *We are stardust!*—and the stars, themselves, of course, were formed from gases and materials that ultimately derived from the Big Bang of unimaginable energy billions of years ago. But let us shift the emphasis to the much more recent event of Jesus the Christ, whom Christians confess to be God's Word truly become flesh—flesh of our flesh, and therefore flesh of the entire cosmos. If, in Hefner's phrase, the "real me" cannot be resurrected without its ecological network, then this is also true of Jesus; he could not be resurrected as a subject apart from his ecological network!

27. John A. T. Robinson, *In the End, God* (New York: Harper & Row, 1968), 96-97.
28. Ibid., 98.
29. Philip Hefner, "New Tongues, Strange Tongues, Confused Tongues: A Word in Favor of Lee Snook," *Dialog* 15 (1976): 305.

Conversely, the destiny of the cosmos is inseparable from the destiny of Jesus Christ, who even now "lives to God" (Rom. 6:10). To put it in trinitarian terms: God the Father has raised Jesus the Son by the power of the Spirit; thus, in the Spirit's life-giving power all of creation, which indeed has provided the social and ecological web for this first-century Jew, is raised with Jesus (and thus raised through Jesus) into the presence of the God—the divine reality in whom even now all things "live and move and have [their] being" (Acts 17:28).

MIGHT, THEN, OUR UNIVERSE BE RESURRECTED? "AND WITH WHAT BODY SHALL IT COME?"

This Christian conviction regarding the resurrection of Jesus and the triune richness of God's life enveloping and deifying the creaturely realm—in the Spirit, through the Son, to the Father, "that God may be all in all" (1 Cor. 15:28)—has powerful rhetorical effect for many people. But what do such declarations actually mean? On the basis of such declarations, what do or would Christians actually expect of the future? And do these expectations bear any relationship to our cosmologists' projections about the coming demise of the universe?

These are difficult questions, reminding us of the inherently ambiguous, uncertain, and speculative nature of eschatological reflection. All of theology, of course, deals with the penumbra of mystery necessarily associated with the divine; we recall that Ogden's quotation from 1Timothy includes the claim that God "dwells in unapproachable light, whom no one has ever seen or can see" (6:16). Our blindness regarding the mystery and purposes of God, though, seems to deepen exponentially when we attempt to peer into the future and ultimate end(s) of God's cosmos. We confess with Paul that "now we see in a mirror, dimly" and "know only in part," even as we hope with him to "see face to face," to "know fully, even as [we] have been fully known" in the eschatological fulfillment of all things (1 Cor. 13:12).

But if we who are Christians do see even dimly now, and know even in part, then surely what we who are Christians see and know is grounded in the person, words, works, and destiny of Jesus the Christ. This is the heart of Christian hope for the future of the world! If we think and live in the convictions that "in Christ God was reconciling the world to himself" (2 Cor. 5:19) and that God raised Jesus our Lord from the dead, then surely we can offer our theologically educated guesses regarding the ultimate destiny of the universe we inhabit.

The Apostles' Creed teaches us to confess that Jesus "was crucified, dead, and buried." In dying, of course, Jesus our fellow human traveled the route that we all do and must travel. It appears, too, to be the route that our present aeon is traveling. If death is in fact a natural aspect of what it means to be a creature, then perhaps we can allow for the possibility, not to mention the likelihood, that this vast creature we call the universe shall also expire. Frankly, it will be a marvelous work of divine grace if we humans somehow manage to avoid destroying our planet's living systems in the next century or two; in the light of that consideration, it would be wonderful if the day should come when our descendants actually have to confront the challenge of a planet-smashing asteriod, or the eventual expiration of our sun, let alone the apparent finality of an entire universe in its death throes. While the question of the eventual demise of the universe is not at all a pointless one, it is not really so important as more pressing issues of nuclear or germ warfare, suicidal abuse of our environment and of one another, overpopulation, misuse of our planet's resources, ad nauseum. Of course, the real possibility that human beings may not survive the next century would not render moot the theological problem of the universe's eventual demise in cold darkness, since many other earthly creatures would likely survive us and evolve in the future millions of years. Further, it seems not at all unlikely that there are extraterrestrial living beings in God's vast creation who would also be victims of creation's demise.

Nonetheless, let us return to this simple affirmation of Christian faith that Jesus was crucified, dead, and buried. Just as we observe Good Friday's sober insistence on the real death of our Lord—recalling his words, "Into your hands I commend my life-breath"—so we are called upon to be willing to surrender into the hands and care of God the whole of creation. Perhaps, like all other creatures, the universe itself must die in order for new life to come forth. Perhaps the words of the Johannine Christ, "Unless a grain of wheat falls into the earth and dies, it remains just a single grain; but if it dies, it bears much fruit" (John 12:24), reflect the cosmic mode of divine activity in all times and places.

The Apostles' Creed also teaches us to confess the wondrous mys-tery that Jesus was raised from the dead by God. Christian theologians generally are careful to distinguish Jesus' resurrection from a resuscitation back to the ordinary conditions of space-time as we experience them every day. Nevertheless, the biblical witness insists that the resurrected Christ *truly is this same Jesus* who lived, breathed, and died within the complex living systems of our planet and its universe. There is, then, a continuity of identity, and even in some sense of body, along with the radical discontinuity of a resurrected body that can appear and disappear, but that can be touched nonetheless. This is a body that is not readily recognizable, yet bears Calvary's wounds. Certainly there is metaphor here. Admittedly there is story straining to its limits to narrate the unimaginable. But for all that we confess that Jesus, as a transformed human body, "will never die again" because "the life he lives, he lives to God" (Rom. 6:9, 10). Further, we believe that the life he lives betokens a promise for "all things" (1 Cor. 15:27-28). We may find ourselves constrained to speak of the resurrected Christ as having been "raised" into a different dimension than the ones we presently know, or perhaps it is sufficient to call it a "new creation." What is *not* sufficient, I am convinced, is to say with process thinkers who do believe in subjective immortality, such as Suchocki and Cobb, that it shall be a "spiritual resurrection" where "materiality falls away," or that it shall be a "resurrection of the soul."[30]

In this vein, the Anglican physicist-theologian John Polkinghorne has claimed that the problem of resurrecting a universe is in principle no different from that of resurrecting a single individual human, such as Jesus.[31] The stronger, more distinctively

30. John B. Cobb Jr., "The Resurrection of the Soul," *Harvard Theological Review* 80 (1987): 213-27.

31. See, for example, John Polkinghorne, *The Faith of a Physicist: Reflections of a Bottom-Up Thinker* (Minneapolis: Fortress Press, 1996), 163.

Christian claim is that in the resurrection of Jesus the transformation of creation into something new has begun. But if all of the creation shall in some way be raised in him, then—to adapt the cynical question of some in the early Corinthian church—with what body shall it come (1 Cor. 15:35)? Augustine may have speculated that "the actual physical elements which composed the first body will be retrieved for the new one,"[32] and many others such as Wesley may have believed the same, but we now recognize the ludicrous futility of such an idea. Nonetheless, this does open up a virtually unimaginable possibility: If our bodies are in fact dynamic interactive systems within larger, ever more comprehensive systems, then perhaps we must follow John Robinson's tendency to interpret Romans 8:23 as offering a hope for "the redemption of our body" (NASB; Paul employs the Greek singular *soma*) as some kind of singular reality of deeply interconnected subsystems, rather than for the redemption of our individual bodies. Robinson writes, "The body represents solidarity; and the denial of its redemption and restoration immediately upon death stands for the great truth that no one can be fully saved apart from his brother, or indeed apart from the whole of creation."[33] If Robinson is correct, then the logical consequence is that *none* of the present aeon can be "fully saved" until *all* of the present aeon has spent itself and died. Then, in an act of God that we can certainly understand no better than we understand Jesus' resurrection from the dead, this present aeon shall be "taken up into glory" (1 Tim. 3:16) in Christ. It goes without saying that we cannot conceptualize what such a resurrection would entail.

Finally, the Apostles' Creed teaches us to confess that Christ "shall come to judge the quick and the dead." We should admit that for many Christians worldwide, the questions with which we have struggled in this chapter would seem foreign and perhaps inappropriate. After all, if Jesus is coming again, not only as conservative evangelical and fundamentalist Christians believe but also as liturgically formed Christians confess virtually every Sunday, then worries about the long-term prospects of the universe may seem misplaced. I suspect that the majority of Christian

32. Cited by Peters, "Physical Body of Immortality," 16.
33. Robinson, *In the End, God*, 108.

believers would assume that the eschatological fulfillment in Christ will occur well before the billions of years left in our universe's projected career are up. Even if we balk at simplistic interpretations of Christ's coming, such interpretations surely ought to press us to state what it is that we truly do expect and hope for. I have already argued in chapter 7 that a Wesleyan reading of eschatology should teach us to exercise great reserve regarding end-of-the-world scenarios, that indeed the Christly character and covenantal labors of God—that love might flourish—call us to discipleship for the long haul. Perhaps the most we shall want to say is what Moltmann and Pannenberg have taught us: that the hope of Christ's coming is our confession that God's future—a future we believe to be already embodied and defined in the ministry, crucifixion, and resurrection of Jesus the Nazarene—is always already on its way toward us. Indeed, God's future should be embodied already, to a noticeable extent, in the life, fellowship, and worship of the Church, Christ's body.

It may be worth our considering, however, that since the one who is coming is the One resurrected from the dead, perhaps his coming to us can occur only in the death and subsequent resurrection of this present aeon. Who can say what this might entail? It is not impossible that this universe must "die and be buried" like a seed. Perhaps it must indeed undergo its own vast demise, and be "buried" in its ground—which is nothing other and nothing less than God—in order for it to be resurrected into the life of the resurrected Christ, Healer of the world.

As we saw in the previous chapter, in his speculations regarding what he called "the general deliverance" of all creation Wesley admits that his guesses might be thought idle and pointless. He imagines an objector asking, "But what end does it answer to dwell upon this subject which we so imperfectly understand?"[34] His reply is significant, I believe, in that it has important implications for our speculations in this chapter. Wesley suggests that imagining the redemption of all of God's creation and creatures has three benefits: first, it gives us a taste for just how all-encompassing God's love is, thereby offering the assurance that if God offers the divine embrace even to all the "brute" creatures, then surely God's

34. Wesley, Sermon 60, "The General Deliverance," §III.8, *Works* 2:448.

redemptive love includes all human beings as well, without exception; second, it offers a nonanthropocentric theodicy that addresses the suffering of "numberless creatures that never had sinned" but have nevertheless been "severely punished" by cruel, heartless, or greedy human beings; and third, it "may encourage us to imitate him whose mercy is over all his works . . . , may soften our hearts towards the meaner creatures, [and] . . . may enlarge our hearts towards those poor creatures to reflect that, as vile as they appear in our eyes, not one of them is forgotten in the sight of our Father which is in heaven."[35]

The point of which Wesley reminds us here is that we must continually be asking ourselves about the "cash value" of our eschatological beliefs and statements. This is most essentially why I cannot endorse the notion of objective immortality offered by many process thinkers: the doctrine of God that it implies is that God is either unable or unwilling to gift the creature with divine life, and this I find unacceptable given the Christian conviction that God is the self-giving love revealed in the ministry, cross, and resurrection of Christ. It is also why I cannot endorse the notion of subjective immortality as a resurrection of the soul: the doctrine of creation implied is that materiality is somehow of transient value, ultimately to be cast off. Such a view of bodies and materiality does not "pay off" well in our present bodily existence in our material universe. But in affirming that God shall raise us from death, *and* shall raise us bodily—*and* therefore shall raise the body that is our universe—the cash value is that, right now, in this frail and vulnerable material world, wonderful in its origin and marvelous in its evolution, all creatures are loved and cherished *as bodies* and *in a bodily way* by the Creator we are bold to call our Father through Jesus Christ in the presence and power of the Spirit.

It is a "hope against hope," to be sure. But Christian faith does instruct us to anticipate that the promise we have received in the life, death, and resurrection of Jesus of Nazareth shall be fulfilled, somehow, in the mysteriously redemptive labors of God in this world. In the meantime, we are called to live carefully and lovingly as participants in God's creation and recreation, to act in this world in accordance with the hope of a bodily redemption far beyond our

35. Ibid., §III.9-10, *Works* 2:449.

imaginations. In the light of that hope, we can conclude our study in reading the world in a Wesleyan way in no better way than by citing the concluding sentence of Wesley's sermon "The New Creation":

> And to crown all, there will be a deep, an intimate, an uninterrupted union with God; a constant communion with the Father and his Son Jesus Christ, through the Spirit; a continual enjoyment of the Three-One God, and of all the creatures in him![36]

36. Sermon 64, "The New Creation," §18, *Works* 2:510.

REFERENCE BIBLIOGRAPHY

Abram, David. *The Spell of the Sensuous: Perception and Language in a More-Than-Human World.* New York: Pantheon, 1996.

Albright, Carol Rausch and Joel Haugen, editors. *Beginning with the End: God, Science, and Wolfhart Pannenberg.* Chicago: Open Court, 1997.

Armstrong, Karen. *In the Beginning: A New Interpretation of Genesis.* New York: Alfred Knopf, 1996.

Augustine. *Confessions.* Translated and introduced by R. S. Pine-Coffin. London: Penguin Books, 1961.

Bailey, Lloyd. *Genesis, Creation, and Creationism.* Mahwah, N.J.: Paulist Press, 1993.

Barbour, Ian. *Ethics in an Age of Technology.* San Francisco: Harper & Row, 1993.

Buber, Martin. *Between Man and Man.* New York: Macmillan, 1972.

Cobb, John B. Jr. *God and the World.* Philadelphia: Westminster, 1969.

———. *Grace and Responsibility: A Wesleyan for Theology Today.* Nashville: Abingdon, 1995.

Davies, Paul. *God and the New Physics.* New York: Simon & Schuster, 1983.

Dunning, H. Ray. *Grace, Faith and Holiness: A Wesleyan Systematic Theology.* Kansas City: Beacon Hill, 1988.

Harak, Simon. *Virtuous Passions: The Formation of Christian Character.* Mahwah, N.J.: Paulist Press, 1993.

Haught, John. *God After Darwin: A Theology of Evolution.* Boulder, CO: Westview Press, 2000.

Haught, John F. *The Promise of Nature: Ecology and Cosmic Purpose.* Mahwah, N.J.: Paulist Press, 1993.

Hawking, Stephen. *A Brief History of Time: From the Big Bang to Black Holes.* New York: Bantam Books, 1988.

Hick, John. *Evil and the God of Love,* rev. ed. San Francisco: Harper & Row, 1978.

Keller, Catherine. *Apocalypse Now and Then: A Feminist Guide to the End of the World.* Boston: Beacon Press, 1996.

Keller, Catherine. *Face of the Deep.* New York and London: Routledge, 2002.

Langford, Thomas A. *Practical Divinity: Theology in the Wesleyan Tradition.* Nashville: Abingdon, 1983.

Levenson, Jon D. *Creation and the Persistence of Evil: The Jewish Drama of Divine Omnipotence*. San Francisco: HarperSanFrancisco, 1988.

Lodahl, Michael. *Shekhinah/Spirit: Divine Presence in Jewish and Christian Religion*. Mahwah, N.J.: Paulist Press, 1992.

McFague, Sallie. *The Body of God: An Ecological Theology*. Minneapolis: Fortress, 1993.

Maddox, Randy. *Responsible Grace: John Wesley's Practical Theology*. Nashville: Kingswood Books, 1994.

Migliore, Daniel. *Faith Seeking Understanding: An Introduction to Christian Theology*. Grand Rapids: Eerdmans, 1991.

Moltmann, Jürgen. *The Coming of God: Christian Eschatology*. Minneapolis: Fortress, 1996.

Nash, James A. *Loving Nature: Ecological Integrity and Christian Responsibility*. Nashville: Abingdon, 1991.

Oden, Thomas C. *Systematic Theology: The Living God*. San Francisco: Harper & Row, 1987.

Pannenberg, Wolfhart. *Toward a Theology of Nature: Essays on Science and Faith*. Edited by Ted Peters. Louisville: Westminster/John Knox, 1993.

Peters, Ted. *God—the World's Future: Systematic Theology for a Postmodern Era*. Minneapolis: Fortress, 1992.

Peters, Ted., editor. *Cosmos as Creation: Theology and Science in Consonance*. Nashville: Abingdon, 1989.

Polkinghorne, John. *The Faith of a Physicist: Reflections of a Bottom-Up Thinker*. Minneapolis: Fortress, 1996.

Runyon, Theodore. *The New Creation: John Wesley's Theology Today*. Nashville: Abingdon, 1998.

Stone, Bryan P. and Thomas Jay Oord, editors. *Thy Nature and Thy Name is Love: Wesleyan and Process Theologies in Dialogue*. Nashville: Kingswood Books, 2001.

Suchocki, Marjorie. "Coming Home: Wesley, Whitehead and Women." *Drew Gateway* 57.3 (Fall 1987): 31-43; reprinted in Stone and Oord, *Thy Nature and Thy Name is Love*.

————. *God–Christ–Church: A Practical Guide to Process Theology*. New York: Crossroad, 1984.

————. *In God's Presence: Theological Reflections on Prayer*. St. Louis: Chalice, 1996.

Taves, Ann. *Fits, Trances & Visions: Experiencing Religion and Explaining Experience from Wesley to James*. Princeton, N.J.: Princeton University Press, 1999.

Wiley, H. Orton. *Christian Theology*. Kansas City: Beacon Hill, 1940.

Worthing, Mark William. *God, Creation, and Contemporary Physics*. Minneapolis: Fortress Press, 1996.

NAME INDEX

SCRIPTURE INDEX

SUBJECT INDEX

615-643-1242 ·St
Broad St

Printed in the United States
R744000001B/R7440PG22345LVSX00003B/19}